School Of Prophets

THEODORE S. ALUOCH

CHRONICLE

CTHIM School of the Prophets is an intensive equipping program designed to evoke a venerated yearning for more of God. This training will challenge your devotion, enliven your pursuit, and launch you deeper into elated and lofty places in God. This book is for those called into the prophetic ministry. It is also for those interested in the prophetic and hungry for more! This training will help you grow in your prophetic calling through simple but effective applications.

COPYRIGHT © 2024 BY THEODORE S. ALUOCH
ALL RIGHTS RESERVED

No portion of this book may be printed or recopied without the express written consent of the authors.
FOR INFORMATION CONTACT:
Theodore S. Aluoch
Call to Holiness International Ministry Inc
(614) 783-9712
www.cthim.org
E-mail: Theodore @cthim.org

Printed in the United States by Book Baby

Printed by:
Self-Publishing, Book Printing & Distribution Company | Book baby
Printed in the United States of America
ISBN: 979-8-35094-416-7

Contents

1.	Introduction	7
2.	Insight	8
3.	Ministry Gifts	12
4	What is the school of prophets?	38
5.	Image Formation	42
6.	Definition of A prophet	57
7.	The Calling of a Prophet	66
8.	Office Of a Prophet Vs. the Gift of Prophecy?	78
9.	Common Fallacies Prophecy:	93
10.	The Old Testament Prophet (Classification of the prophets)	98
11.	The Prophets of the New Testament	102
13.	Prophets Office Vs Ministering in the Prophetic	112
14.	Types of Prophets in the bible	121
15.	Going through your gethsemane	124
16.	The Relationship with the Holy Spirit	130
17.	Trichotomy Of Man.	142
18.	Perfecting the hearing, circumcising the ears and eyes	156
19.	Intimacy first	168
20.	Walking in the spirit	171
21.	The Two Offices Of ministry	176
22.	Spiritual Disciplines	181
23.	Assisting The Sheep in Hearing the Voice of The Lord	191
24.	Circumcised Ears	216
25.	How To Minister Prophetically	220
26.	Financial Support for ministry	228
27.	What does the Bible say about ordination?	234
28.	Appendix A	246
29.	Inaugural fast	248
30.	About The Author	263

vi

1. Introduction

If you desire more understanding on the prophetic ministry, its dimensions and its aim, then CTHIM School of Prophets is for you. Learn how to practice the presence of God, speak divine words, subdue environments, and dominate extant.

This Manual is excellent for teaching, training, and developing God's people who covet the gift of prophecy or those called into the office of a prophet.

Whether the gift, ministry, or office, you will be equipped, informed, and empowered to ascend into lofty habitations of consecration with Jesus. Your prophetic essence will flow out of intimacy with God unhindered by sub-astral limitations. Your true nature will dominate your experience and your expression will become divine.

2.
INSIGHT

This course provides a thorough overview of the prophetic office, ministry and functions based on scriptures. The contents of this course are grounded on scriptures and based upon biblical substructure. God often speaks in diverse ways, but everything spoken by God will always have scriptural coherence and point us back to the bible.

PURPOSE

We have five purposes for this training course.

- To help you understand God's mind, intention and vision for your prophetic vocation and ministry within the biblical context.

- To help you understand your gifting, calling, and the character formation process requisite for effective operation.

- To assist you in developing a blueprint or operational template to implement your ministry.

- To activate your gifting, arouse your calling, and provide a safe environment to practice your abilities.

- In the end, you will be commissioned to go forth in power and authority of the Holy Spirit to fulfill your calling.

RETROSPECTION & APPRISAL

We have all been to important training Seminars and returned home with manuals, books, and notes. We add them to our library of spurned publications. We let them amass dust and taper off with all the other books.

We earnestly want to implement what we have been taught, but we always return to doing things in the same manner.

"If you always do what you always did, you'll always get what you always got" - Henry Ford.

The premise is if you want something different out of your life, you must put something different into it. This is where coaching or mentoring would help.

COACHING

A coach motivates you through questions, encouragement, and counsel to apply what you have learned. He or she brings much-needed accountability into your vocation.

A coach is committed to helping you succeed. He develops a relationship with you such that he can influence, motivate, and teach you. This relationship may last for months or years, depending on the needs of your ministry or calling.

The coach makes himself or herself available to you for counsel, observations, direction, encouragement, skill training, and motivation.

He may do this in person, via cell phone, Zoom, or e-mail.

MENTORING

A mentor has an extensive view in mind. He is concerned with developing the whole man, spirit, soul, and body. While the coach may focus on only one or two aspects, the mentor will emphasize character development and relationships. Mentoring is less formal because it is more based on the relationship between the mentor and his subject than is true with the coach.

In ministry, we need both coaches and mentors. Long-term and short-term, depending on goals and vision.

We need competent, experienced, and skillful people who can train you on how to master skills. We also need mentors who are accomplished, stout, and able to oversee others through character formation.

Would you be interested in a coaching or mentoring relationship with CTHIM School of the Prophets at the end of this training?

YES ☐

NO ☐

Name: _____

Email: _____

Cell: _____

School Of Prophets

THEODORE S. ALUOCH

3. Ministry Gifts

In Ephesians 4:11-12, we see that some believers are ministers to the whole body of Christ. Of these, some are called to be Apostles, some Prophets, some Evangelists, and some Pastors and Teachers. These are called the Ministerial Gifts of the Spirit.

Why are the Ministry Gifts given to the Church?

The ministerial gifts are given to the church to prepare the believers to do the work of ministry for which God in Ephesians 4:12 has called them.

According to that Scripture, who has been called to do the work of ministry?

The nature of the ministerial gifts is revelatory and authoritative. Revelation is a matter of knowing what God knows (Genesis 18:17; John 15:15).

Authority is Divine order, doing things the way God does them.

The concept of the five-fold ministry is based on Ephesians 4:11-12 which reads, "And he gave the apostles, the prophets, the evangelists, the shepherds and teachers, to equip the saints for the work of ministry, for building up the body of Christ."

The five-fold ministry has usually been defined as the church leadership ministry that consists of: (1) Apostles, (2) Prophets, (3) Evangelists, (4) Pastors (Shepherds), and (5) Teachers.

The leadership gifts are given to bring the saints to maturity so that they (the saints) can do the work of the ministry, resulting in the edification (or building up) of the body of Christ. This process is designated as discipleship.

Each of the five gifts uniquely serves the Church.

- The apostolic gift establishes the foundations and plants new churches in various places.
- The prophetic gift calls the church to do God's will.
- The evangelistic gift brings new members into the church by winning them to Christ.
- The pastoral gift oversees the local church and disciples the body.
- The teaching gift instructs the church, leaders, and members.

Every spiritual gift has two parts:

- The anointing
- The skills

The anointing of a gift is the inward divine transfusion wrapped up in desire and inclination to operate in that gift. The skills of a gift are the things we must learn, practice, and perfect outwardly to operate successfully in that gift.

Many who struggle in their ministries have the skill or knowledge but need more anointing power. Some have the anointing power but are void in skills needed to successfully operate in their gifts.

If we fail to develop our prophetic skills or fail to cultivate a sacred atmosphere conducive to habitation, we will frustrate the Holy Spirit and those we are sent to minister to.

The breaking of the vessel is a basic foundational experience that every servant of the Lord must go through. God must break your soul before you can effectively serve Him.

You will face two possibilities in working for the Lord.

Your soul has not yet yielded to the spirit fully, and therefore your spirit has not awakened. The Holy Spirit in you is suppressed and cannot be released through you. Therefore, there is no emanation. When your soul is clearly unpaired from the inside, your spirit will be wrapped up with counter-influences from your mind, will, or emotions. The result is a mixture and impurities. This will produce a mixed discharge. The soul will frustrate your service if your emanation is not comprehensively divine. It is the Spirit that gives life.

2 Corinthians 3:6 "Who also hath made us able ministers of the New Testament; not of the letter, but of the spirit: for the letter killeth, but the spirit giveth life."

A prophet must be brought to the end of himself or herself. He or she must realize the vanity of feelings and carnality. They will have to admit sooner or later that only the spirit can give life. Even our best thoughts and feelings cannot give life.

It is a matter of transmission of spirit life from our spirit, resulting in others encountering this life through us.

1 Corinthians 6:17: "But he that is joined unto the Lord is one spirit."

If others can touch our spirit, they're touching God's Spirit at the same time.

Our Spirit transports God's spirit to men. When God's Spirit moves, he must move through the human spirit. This is like electricity; it travels through electrical wires. Your spirit is the wire that bears the current of God. God's Spirit needs the human spirit as a medium to bear His Spirit; through the human spirit, the holy spirit is conveyed and carried to man.

What Does the Fivefold Ministry Do?

Ephesians 4:11-16

The Fivefold Ministry should do the following things:

- Equip the believers for works of ministry.
- Build up the Body of Believers in growth and maturity.
- Create unity of faith.
- Increase in knowledge about God, Jesus, and the Kingdom.
- Grow believers to mature in their faith with sound doctrine.
- Develop strong believers who are secure in their faith and mature.

Ephesians 2:20: having been built on the foundation of the apostles and prophets, Jesus Christ Himself being the chief corner stone.

The Prophets and Apostles are gifted to bring revealed knowledge to the church. This revelation is not carnal. What I mean by bringing revealed knowledge to the church is that through the prophets and apostles, God shines his light on the scriptures or illuminates the scriptures in a way not seen before.

The Prophet under the New Testament is more of a corroborative ministry than sovereign.

Apostolic Preaching and Teaching

Apostolic preaching/teaching is characterized by its foundational and authoritative anointing. Apostles lay foundations (1 Corinthians 3:10). The foundations are the basics of the Christian faith. By basics, we do not mean that they are less momentous. All other truths must be built upon these basic foundational teachings.

Apostles are also "planters" (1 Corinthians 3:6). A planter starts a new work usually in an unplanted field. Apostles may be church planters, missionaries, or pioneers. A pioneer is the first person to do something.

1 Corinthians 3:10: According to the grace of God, which is given unto me, as a wise Master Builder, I have laid the foundation, and another buildeth thereon. But let every man take heed how he buildeth thereupon.

Apostles begin new work. They lay a "kingdom" foundation in the churches or ministries they are starting. The rest of the building cannot be adequately erected without these foundations. Therefore, the apostolic preacher/teacher must be equipped with a clear understanding of the kingdom of God and its guiding principles.

Apostolic preaching and teaching operate with the highest level of spiritual authority (Matthew 7:28-29).

Paul rebukes the Galatians for leaving the foundational truths he had taught them. This is an excellent example of apostolic correction. The epistles to the Corinthians are also good examples of apostolic authority and admonition.

Prophetic Preaching and Teaching

Prophetic ministry is the revelation of God's will. The prophet makes known the will of God in a timely and enthusiastic manner. To move in the prophetic is to uncover what is covered in the Word.

Prophetic preaching is the call to do God's will. This may come through a plea for personal and corporate holiness, or to God's specific revelation, plan, or strategy. The prophetic ministry of the Word establishes God's intentions, standards and issues a call to those intentions and standards.

Prophetic messages and ministry are for the local church and the entire body of Christ. The most significant error of prophets is the assumption that prophets must be discordant and disparaging in their administration. While this disposition is habitual among prophets or prophetic people, it doesn't legitimize the crudity. Don't justify the flesh; crucify it instead.

Evangelistic Preaching and Teaching

The evangelistic ministry is chiefly concerned with winning people to Christ. The skillful evangelist has a powerful anointing to convince people they need to be saved and gets excellent results.

Paul told Timothy that he must do the work of an evangelist (2 Timothy 4:5).

All ministers must develop evangelistic skills and be prepared to communicate the gospel culturally appropriately.

1 Peter 3:15: But sanctify the Lord God in your hearts: and be ready always to give an answer to every man that asketh you a reason of the hope that is in you with meekness and fear:

Every message should contain the basics of the gospel. (1) The depravity of man. (2) Christ died for our sins. (3) He was buried, and He rose again on the third day according to the Scriptures. (4) He is returning to establish his millennial kingdom and rule as the King of kings and the Lord of Lords and those who overcome the world, the devil and flesh as he overcame will rule and reign with him (Revelation 3:21).

Evangelistic preaching does two things: it presents the gospel of the kingdom to the lost calling them into justification through Jesus Christ. This ministry will impart to God's people a passion for the lost.

Pastoral Preaching and Teaching

- They feed the people of God (1 Peter 5:2). This feeding process requires the skillful preparation of God's Word to enable understanding and application.
- The pastor must spend much time laboring in God's Word so that he might hear the voice of the Lord and gain illumination.
- The pastor must prepare and arrange the truth he is presenting so that the people can grasp its meaning and application in their lives.
- Pastoral preaching and teaching must equip people to do God's will as they function in the calling of God upon their lives.
- Pastoral preaching and teaching must build the spiritual community of the church. He must invite the members to participate in the community. This will encourage the building of relationships. This sense of community is powerful.
- He must create an atmosphere of reproduction in which the members will be actively making disciples.
- Pastoral preaching and teaching are topical.
- The pastor will lead the congregation in lessons about a spiritual truth or discipline. It may be corrective teaching, or he may address specific areas of sin, failure, or weakness.

Teaching Ministry

Gifted teachers enjoy the study and research of the Bible more than they do the actual teaching of the lessons. They are more motivated to study than to teach. Since the primary work of the fivefold ministry is to make disciples, his teaching should be designed to that end.

He is not merely teaching to inform or instruct but to produce a response that is a pattern of life consistent with one who is a disciple - a follower of Jesus Christ.

The Apostle

Hebrews 3:1: Wherefore, holy brethren, partakers of the heavenly calling, consider the Apostle and High Priest of our profession, Christ Jesus;"

Jesus remains the exquisite exemplar of Apostolos. The messenger or one who is sent. We have his own statement, As the father has sent Me. Even so, I sent you.

John 20:21: "Then said Jesus to them again, Peace be unto you: as my Father hath sent me, even so send I you."

The true apostle is always one with a commission. Apostleship means far more than just being the Lord's Messenger boy. It is an office clothed with dignity and power, always first on the list of God's given ministries.

1 Corinthians 12:28: "And God hath set some in the church, first apostles, secondarily prophets, thirdly teachers, after that miracle, then gifts of healings, helps, governments, diversities of tongues." The apostle is sent by Christ in the same way that the Father sent him.

2 Corinthians 12:12: Truly the *signs of an apostle* were wrought among you *in all patience, in signs, and wonders, and mighty deeds.*

The lack of balance between the fruit and the gift is one of the principal criteria to distinguish between the false claimants to the apostolic office. The calling of an apostle will demand the death of the flesh that will lead to the fullest possible exhibition of all the fruit of the Spirit.

Galatians 5:22: "But the fruit of the Spirit is love, joy, peace, longsuffering, gentleness, goodness, faith," "Meekness, temperance: against such there is no law."

The magnificence of character will yield dynamic gifts. The manifestation of the fruit of the Spirit in the lives of the apostles is very apparent.

The personal experience of an apostle is very deep and real and not a mere tradition or hearsay in defense of his apostleship.

Paul writes in 1 Corinthians 9:1

Am I not an apostle? Am I not free? have I not seen Jesus Christ our Lord? Are not ye my work in the Lord? "The same type of qualification was evidently expected in all other claimants to the office.

Acts 1:22: Beginning from the baptism of John, unto that same day that he was taken up from us, must one be ordained to be a witness with us of his resurrection."

The Apostles' testimony and teachings must come with divine authority because of the consciousness of the commission.

I've received of the Lord, that which also I delivered unto you, says the apostle concerning the Lord's Supper (1 Corinthians 11:23).

The work of an apostle, above all else, was to lay the foundation (1 Corinthians 3:10; Ephesians 2:20).

In this sense, it is divinely fitting that the names of the twelve apostles of the Lamb are inscribed upon the foundation of New Jerusalem.

Revelation 21:14: And the wall of the city had twelve foundations and in them the names of the twelve apostles of the Lamb."

They laid the foundations as the earliest pioneers and preachers of the gospel (John 16:12-15).

I have many things to say unto you, but ye cannot bear them now. Howbeit when he, the Spirit of truth, is come, he will guide you into all truth: for he shall not speak of himself; but whatsoever he shall hear, that shall he speak, and he will show you things to come. He shall glorify me: for he shall receive of mine and shall shew it unto you. All things that the Father hath are mine: therefore, said I, that he shall take of mine, and shall shew it unto you.

Ephesians 3:5: "Which in other ages was not made known unto the sons of men, as it is now revealed unto his holy apostles and prophets by the Spirit;"

These revelations are now in the New Testament, the basis for all Christian faith and practice.

Apostolic calling demands that the apostle grasp the complexion and construction of the fivefold and be able to fully operate in all the offices. Thus, he shares the inspiration of a prophet. He does the work of an evangelist. He is familiar with pastoral care and can teach.

The apostles had the power to establish churches—this distinguished apostles from the evangelists. The evangelists could lead a revival with Salient fame, accompanied by a striking display of divine power, healing, signs and wonders. But he lacked the necessary gift for consolidating the result into a building form.

For example, the apostle is the contractor, and the prophet is the architect. An architect is responsible for visualizing designs. A contractor then implements that design.

If you are planning a significant renovation or want to build a new home, a contractor will say, "Call me first." An architect will say, "You should call me first." The reality is that architects, designers, and contractors all play a crucial role in the home-building process, and they complement each other. In short, you will need them all on board, so it is best to have them both right from the onset of the project – who you call first doesn't matter. Apostles need prophets and prophets need apostles.

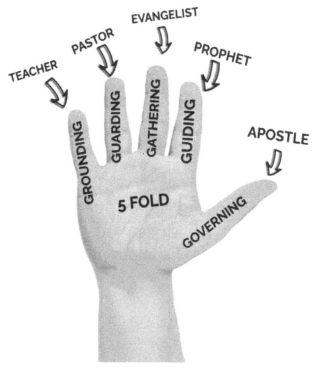

Figure 1

Paul and Barnabas, on the other hand, left behind fully functioning and deeply rooted assemblies with elders and deacons.

Acts 14:21-23

21 And when they had preached the gospel to that city and had taught many, they returned again to Lystra, and to Iconium, and Antioch,

22 Confirming the souls of the disciples, and exhorting them to continue in the faith, and that we must through much tribulation enter into the kingdom of God.

23 And when they had ordained them elders in every church, and had prayed with fasting, they commended them to the Lord, on whom they believed.

Acts 15:41: "And he went through Syria and Cilicia, confirming the churches."

Acts 16:5: "And so were the churches established in the faith and increased in number daily."

Philippians 1:1: "Paul and Timotheus, the servants of Jesus Christ, to all the saints in Christ Jesus which are at Philippi, with the bishops and deacons:"

1 Thessalonians 1:8: "For from you sounded out the word of the Lord not only in Macedonia and Achaia, but also in every place your faith to God-ward is spread abroad; so that we need not to speak anything."

1 Corinthians 12:28: "And God hath set some in the church, first apostles, secondarily prophets, thirdly teachers, after that miracle, then gifts of healings, helps, governments, diversities of tongues."

The apostles exercised a natural and unpremeditated authority. The apostle's authority was not something capricious. They were seasoned and mature leaders.

1 Corinthians 4:15: 'For though ye have ten thousand instructors in Christ yet have ye not many fathers: for in Christ Jesus, I have begotten you through the gospel."

Galatians 4:19: "My little children, of whom I travail in birth again until Christ be formed in you,"

1 Corinthians 9:1: "Am I not an apostle? Am I not free? have I not seen Jesus Christ our Lord? are not ye my work in the Lord?"

Acts 15:12: "Then all the multitude kept silence, and gave audience to Barnabas and Paul, declaring what miracles and wonders God had wrought among the Gentiles by them."

Acts 21:18: "And the day following Paul went in with us unto James; and all the elders were present."

Romans 15:20: "Yea, so have I strived to preach the gospel, not where Christ was named, lest I should build upon another man's foundation:"

2 Corinthians 10:16: "To preach the gospel in the regions beyond you, and not to boast in another man's line of things made ready to our hand."

The question that still befuddles many today concerning the apostle's ministry is its perpetuation. Can the New Testament standard be replicated in the church today?

Revelation 21:14: "And the wall of the city had twelve foundations and in them the names of the twelve apostles of the Lamb.

Is it possible for men today to have seen Jesus Christ our Lord in the literal sense as the New Testament apostles sufficed?

There is also the possibility of spiritual vision, such as Paul's, outside Damascus.

Acts 9:5: And he said, Who art thou, Lord? And the Lord said, I am Jesus whom thou persecute: it is hard for thee to kick against the pricks." Afterward, referred to in connection with this apostleship.

1 Corinthians 15:8-9: And last of all he was seen of me also, as of one born out of due time. For I am the least of the apostles, that am not meet to be called an apostle, because I persecuted the church of God.

We must remember that Paul regarded this experience as exceptional. Moreover, there no longer remains any foundations to be laid.

The Apostles had an obvious consciousness that it was being given to them to finally complete the divine revelation for this dispensation.

2 Timothy 1:13: "Hold fast the form of sound words, which thou hast heard of me, in faith and love which is in Christ Jesus."

2 Timothy 2:2: "And the things that thou hast heard of me among many witnesses, the same commit thou to faithful men, who shall be able to teach others also."

2 Peter 1:15: "Moreover I will endeavour that ye may be able after my decease to have these things always in remembrance."

Revelation 22:18-19: For I testify unto every man that heareth the words of the prophecy of this book, If any man shall add unto these things, God shall add unto him the plagues that are written in this book: 19 And if any man shall take away from the words of the book of this prophecy, God shall take away his part out of the book of life, and out of the holy city, and from the things which are written in this book.

Any supposed additional revelation today from self-appointed apostles is to be regarded with scornful suspicion.

Galatians 1:9: As we said before, so say I now again, if any man preach any other gospel unto you than that ye have received, let him be accursed."

In every generation, the whole body of Christ has been latched upon the foundation of the apostles and prophets.

Whoever claims to be an Apostle today can never pretend to be of the same stature as those of the original composition.

1 Corinthians 12:28: And God hath set some in the church, first apostles, secondarily prophets, thirdly teachers, after that miracle, then gifts of healings, helps, governments, diversities of tongues."

God has set these ministries within his church. Ephesians 4:11-13 reaffirms that they have been given for the building up of the Body of Christ, till we all come to the unity of the faith and to a perfect man.

The Office of the Apostle was not limited to the 12 Apostles because Barnabas was not one of the twelve yet, but he is called an apostle.

Acts 14:14: "Which when the apostles, Barnabas, and Paul, heard of, they rent their clothes, and ran in among the people, crying out,"

The title is also given to James, the Lord's brother, and the leader of the church at Jerusalem.

Galatians 1:19: "But other of the apostles saw I none, save James the Lord's brother."

Such apostles have a real place in the building up of the body of Christ and are legitimately expected in any generation.

In closing, I believe there are men today fulfilling a measure of apostolic benevolence; let no one deny them the recognition. The office consists not of the name but of power.

1 Corinthians 2:1-5: And my speech and my preaching was not with enticing words of man's wisdom, but in demonstration of the Spirit and of power: that your faith should not stand in the wisdom of men, but in the power of God.

The Office of The Prophet

There is a considerable murkiness in many people's minds concerning the real nature of the office of a prophet in the church today. Some people believe prophet is simply another name branding for the preacher. But this line of thought fails to recognize the essential place of direct inspiration and revelation in the New Testament.

Others think that a prophet is only a foreteller of the future. This also has an element of truth, but this is also deficient.

Others have distorted its potency and functions, branding it as a tool for guidance in the church or private affairs. The abuse of the office has also added a distressing smudge of confusion and prejudice against the office.

Unfortunately, we no longer use the title prophet to describe those bestowed with the office. The lack of dissemination of its cogency gives the impression that the Office has ceased to exist in the church today or is limited to those who use the title.

1 Corinthians 14:30: "If anything be revealed to another that sitteth by, let the first hold his peace."

Speaking from an immediate revelation is fundamental as relating either to future events or the mind of the Spirit.

Prophets are distinguished from teachers

Acts 13:1: "Now there were in the church that was at Antioch certain prophets and teachers; as Barnabas, and Simeon that was called Niger, and Lucius of Cyrene, and Manaen, which had been brought up with Herod the tetrarch, and Saul."

1 Corinthians 12:28: "And God hath set some in the church, first apostles, secondarily prophets, thirdly teachers, after that miracle, then gifts of healings, helps, governments, diversities of tongues."

Ephesians 4:11: "And he gave some, apostles; and some, prophets; and some, evangelists; and some, pastors, and teachers;"

Prophets are distinguished from evangelists in that Evangelists can preach but do not preach from an immediate revelation.

Prophet as the preacher provided a distinctive note of divine authority and power.

1 Corinthians 14:24: "But if all prophesy, and there come in one that believeth not, or one unlearned, he is convinced of all, he is judged of all:"

1 Corinthians 14:25: "And thus are the secrets of his heart made manifest; and so falling down on his face he will worship God, and report that God is in you of a truth."

When prophets speak scriptures become illuminated to them. A prophet is a powerful agent to promote revival. A true prophet does need preparation as much as any preacher, but it is the preparation of the heart. He must prophesy according to the proportion of faith given to him or her.

Romans 12:6: "Having then gifts differing according to the grace that is given to us, whether prophecy, let us prophesy according to the proportion of faith;"

His faith must be kept lively and strong, enlightened by the hours of communion with God. Prophets are very sensitive to the spiritual atmospheres around them.

The Prophet as a Foreteller

The New Testament also indicates a ministry of prophets that were spontaneous, inspired utterances in the assemblies, bringing exultation, edification, and comfort.

1 Corinthians 14:3: "But he that prophesieth speaketh unto men to edification, and exhortation, and comfort."

1 Corinthians 14:6: "Now, brethren, if I come unto you speaking with tongues, what shall I profit you, except I shall speak to you either by revelation, or by knowledge, or by prophesying, or by doctrine?"

1 Corinthians 14:30: "If anything be revealed to another that sitteth by, let the first hold his peace."

1 Corinthians 14:29: "Let the prophets speak two or three and let the other judge."

1 Corinthians 14:24: "But if all prophesy, and there come in one that believeth not, or one unlearned, he is convinced of all, he is judged of all:"

Then, there were cases of distinct foretelling conspicuously illustrated in the case of Prophet Agabus.

Acts11: 27- 30: And in these days came prophets from Jerusalem unto Antioch. 28 And there stood up one of them named Agabus and signified by the Spirit that there should be great dearth throughout all the world: which came to pass in the days of Claudius Caesar. 29 Then the disciples, every man according to his ability, determined to send relief unto the brethren which dwelt in Judaea: 30 Which also they did, and sent it to the elders by the hands of Barnabas and Saul.

Acts 21:11: "And when he was come unto us, he took Paul's girdle, and bound his own hands and feet, and said, thus saith the Holy Ghost, so shall the Jews at Jerusalem bind the man that owneth this girdle, and shall deliver him into the hands of the Gentiles."

The early church had confidence in the prophetic gift of Agabus, and rightly so! For that which He foretold came to pass, thus fulfilling the Old Testament test of Deuteronomy 18:22.

The Evangelist

The word evangelist occurs only three times in the New Testament. Philip the evangelist, (Acts 21:8; Ephesians 4:11) "And he gave some, apostles; and some, prophets; and some, evangelists; and some, pastors, and teachers;"

Do the work of an evangelist (2 Timothy 4:5).

The evangelist is a messenger of good tidings. Ephesians 4:11 makes it plain that the evangelist was part of the early church, a distinct and well-recognized ministry, separate from that of the apostles, prophets, pastors or teachers. Their favorite theme is salvation.

The whole bible, for them, seems to contain an integrated striking narrative, the gospel. They will often find gospel chronicles swaddled in the Old Testament records. Philip is the classic example. They are always ready to spawn creed from almost any portion of the Bible.

Philip had been chosen by the church and ordained by the apostles as a deacon in Acts Chapter 6. He found himself in Samaria preaching the gospel with glorious results.

They preach the gospel of necessity and spontaneously.

1 Corinthians 9:16: "For though I preach the gospel, I have nothing to glory of: for necessity is laid upon me; yea, woe is unto me, if I preach not the gospel!"

The evangelist is anointed to preach the gospel. His messages are designed to lead people to repentance and faith in the Lord Jesus Christ. They are accompanied by miracles that attract the attention of unbelievers and convict them of the truthfulness of his message.

There were undoubtedly many evangelists in the early church, but only one man is listed in the Book of Acts as an evangelist. His name was Philip: "And entering the house of Philip the evangelist, who was one of the seven, we stayed with him" (Acts 21:8).

And Philip went down to the city of Samaria and began proclaiming Christ to them. And the multitudes, with one accord, were paying attention to what was said by Philip, as they heard and saw the signs which he was performing. For in the case of many who had unclean spirits, they came out of them shouting with a loud voice; and many who had been paralyzed and lame were healed. And there was much rejoicing in that city (Acts 8:5-8).

Notice that Philip had one message—Christ. He proclaimed Christ a miracle worker, Son of God, Lord, Savior, and Soon-coming Judge. He urged people to repent and follow his Lord.

Philip was also equipped with supernatural signs and wonders that authenticated his message. One who stands in the office of an evangelist will be anointed with gifts of healing and other power gifts.

Many who travel from church to church and call themselves evangelists are not really evangelists because they only preach in church buildings to Christians and are not equipped with gifts of healing or miracles.

Their biggest miracle is getting people to fall over. These traveling ministers may be preachers or exhorters (Romans 12:8), but they do not have prerogatives to claim the office of an evangelist.

For further study concerning the office of evangelist, read Acts 8:4-40, a record of Philip's ministry.

Philip is our model evangelist. Miracles of healing are a prominent part of his ministry.

Evangelists need others. The sending of Peter and John to establish the glorious work commenced by Philip in Samaria is an example.

Acts 8:14: "Now when the apostles which were at Jerusalem heard that Samaria had received the word of God, they sent unto them Peter and John:

The varying ministries given by Christ are all dependent on one another to achieve the finest usefulness and most abiding results. But we see how Philip lacked discernment with all these spiritual gifts.

Acts 8:9: "But there was a certain man, called Simon, which before time in the same city used sorcery, and bewitched the people of Samaria, giving out that himself was some great one:"

Acts 8:13: "Then Simon himself believed also: and when he was baptized, he continued with Philip, and wondered, beholding the miracles and signs which were done."

He baptized Simon the witch upon belief, oblivious to the awful state of the man's heart in the sight of God.

Peter later received this discernment (Acts 8:18-23).

18 And when Simon saw that through laying on of the apostles' hands the Holy Ghost was given, he offered them money,

19 Saying, give me also this power, that on whomsoever I lay hands, he may receive the Holy Ghost.

20 But Peter said unto him, thy money perishes with thee, because thou hast thought that the gift of God may be purchased with money.

21 Thou hast neither part nor lot in this matter: for thy heart is not right in the sight of God.

22 Repent therefore of this thy wickedness, and pray God, if perhaps the thought of thine heart maybe forgiven thee.

23 For I perceive that thou art in the gall of bitterness, and in the bond of iniquity.

Secondly, it was not given to Philip to impart the Holy Spirit. Neither did he remain on in Samaria to do the pastor's work. He was divinely moved.

Acts 8:26: "And the angel of the Lord spake unto Philip, saying, Arise, and go toward the south unto the way that goeth down from Jerusalem unto Gaza, which is desert."

The evangelist who gathers the crowd can rarely meet their need for teaching so that they become established.

The evangelist's allotted task is to be continually on the move. Philip was married and had at least four children filled with the Holy Spirit.

In Acts 6:1-6: Philip was chosen to do the work of a deacon because of certain qualities in his character. The men chosen were to have a reputation of honesty, wisdom and a desire for the spiritual. Since they were to be making arrangements for the care of others, some leadership ability and a desire to work were probably considered as well.

Philip's life again appears on the pages of inspiration in Acts 8:5-13 and Acts 8:26-40. Both passages relate Philip's preaching of Christ to others, hence the phrase "Philip the evangelist" in Acts 8:8. The first part of Acts Chapter 8 tells of Philip preaching in Samaria after Saul began persecuting Christians in earnest. Recall for a moment that the Jews considered the Samaritans worse than dogs. Jews who had married Gentiles resettled in Canaan by the Assyrians after the defeat of the northern kingdom of Israel became known as Samaritans. Because the Samaritans were part Jewish and part Gentile, devout Jews would avoid these people at all costs.

This did not seem to matter to Philip. He, like Jesus, was concerned enough for their souls to put away prejudice to teach salvation (John 4:3-30). The end of chapter 8 tells of Philip's role in converting the Ethiopian eunuch. Though we have no way of knowing,

Philip was probably well off. He could support a household of at least four daughters, travel, and provide for Paul and his companions.

"And the next day we that were of Paul's company departed and came unto Caesarea: and we entered into the house of Philip the evangelist; which was one of the seven; and abode with him. And the same man had four daughters, virgins, which did prophesy" (Acts 21:8-9).

All four girls were unmarried and living in their father's household. We do not know the exact age of these daughters, but we know they were of an age of accountability and Christians. How can we know this? In Acts 2:17, Peter quotes the prophet Joel (2:28-29). These verses tell of a time when gifts of a miraculous nature would be given. The gift of prophecy is specifically mentioned.

Some of the most impactful events in Christian history were launched through evangelistic outreaches led by God-called evangelists.

Remember the impact of Whitefield, Moody, Finney, Sunday, Wesley, Edwards, Reinhard Bonnke, Billy Graham, and most significantly, the master evangelist Jesus Christ?

The Pastor

Ephesians 4:11 is remarkable as containing the only reference in the New Testament to pastors. Although this is probably the most widely recognized of all offices in the Christian ministry today, it must be remembered that the Greek word means shepherd.

The Greek word for "pastor" is poimen. 4166. Poimén shepherd, pastor.

https://biblehub.com/strongs/greek/4166.htm

The New Testament presents two church leadership offices—elder/overseer and deacon. Paul lists the qualifications for elder/overseer in 1 Timothy 3:1–7 and Titus 1:5–9. Notice that in the 1 Timothy passage, Paul refers to them as overseers (episcopos in Greek), and in Titus, he refers to them as elders (presbuteros in Greek). From this, it can be concluded that one office has different designations. The word elder refers to the life experience of the office holder, while the word overseer emphasizes the responsibility of the office holder to watch over the congregation and meet their spiritual needs.

In the New Testament, the words pastor, elder, and overseer can be used interchangeably, with each word emphasizing what contribution the leaders make to the Body of Christ.

The three words come together in 1 Peter 5:1–2 where Peter exhorts elders to shepherd the flock of God and serve as overseers, caring for the flock as they wait for the Chief Shepherd.

The term is found frequently in the New Testament and is only once translated as "pastors" (Ephesians 4:11). Every other occurrence of the word is translated as "shepherd." Most notably with the reference to Jesus.

John 10:11: "I am the good shepherd: the good shepherd giveth his life for the sheep."

1 Peter 2:25: "For ye were as sheep going astray; but are now returned unto the Shepherd and Bishop of your souls."

A pastor is essentially above all other things; as a shepherd of God's sheep, pastors are required to be men, more settled in a locality and residence, at least for a time in one place.

And this is what distinguishes them from Apostles and other ministers who are called to move around continually. In the early church, they were also termed as local elders.

Acts 11:30: "Which also they did and sent it to the elders by the hands of Barnabas and Saul."

Acts 14:23: "And when they had ordained them elders in every church, and had prayed with fasting, they commended them to the Lord, on whom they believed."

Acts 20:17: "And from Miletus he sent to Ephesus and called the elders of the church."

Acts 20:28: "Take heed therefore unto yourselves, and to all the flock, over the which the Holy Ghost hath made you overseers, to feed the church of God, which he hath purchased with his own blood."

But if the term elder had special reference to their age and standing, there was the more official title of overseer or Bishop, the word is the same in Greek, which conveyed a meaning of definite leadership and official position.

Philippians 1:1: Paul and Timotheus, the servants of Jesus Christ, to all the saints in Christ Jesus which are at Philippi, with the bishops and deacons:"

1 Timothy 3:1-7: This is a true saying, if a man desire the office of a bishop, he desireth a good work. 2 A bishop then must be blameless, the husband of one wife, vigilant, sober, of good behavior, given to hospitality, apt to teach; 3 Not given to wine, no striker, not greedy of filthy lucre; but patient, not a brawler, not covetous; 4 One that ruleth well his own house, having his children in subjection with all gravity; 5 For if a man knows not how to rule his own house, how shall he take care of the church of God? 6 Not a novice, lest being lifted up with pride he falls into the condemnation of the devil.7 Moreover he must have a good report of them which are without; lest he fall into reproach and the snare of the devil.

Titus 1:7: "For a bishop must be blameless, as the steward of God; not self-willed, not soon angry, not given to wine, no striker, not given to filthy lucre;"

1 Timothy 5:17: "Let the elders that rule well be counted worthy of double honor, especially they who labor in the word and doctrine."

They were commanded to feed a flock and take the oversight. 1 Peter 5:2 "Feed the flock of God, which is among you, taking the oversight thereof, not by constraint, but willingly; not for filthy lucre, but of a ready mind;"

It is necessary and expedient for them to give their whole time to the care of the flock. This is implied by Peter, warning that filthy lucre was not to be the motive for their service.

1 Peter 5:2: "Feed the flock of God, which is among you, taking the oversight thereof, not by constraint, but willingly; not for filthy lucre, but of a ready mind;"

Paul's reference is not to muzzle the ox that treads out the corn because the laborer is worthy of his hire. 1 Timothy 5:18: "For the scripture saith, thou shalt not muzzle the ox that treadeth out the corn. And the labourer is worthy of his reward."

The double honor of 1 Timothy 5:17: "Let the elders that rule well be counted worthy of double honor, especially they who labor in the word and doctrine."

This also carries the sense of reward for labor; they labor in the word and doctrine. Combining all these references, it is easy to grasp the nature of the type of ministry called pastors.

They were shepherds over the flock offering wise and competent oversight of the meetings of the assembly so that all things are done decently and in order.

1 Corinthians 14:40: "Let all things be done decently and in order." So that the doctrine is kept sound and convincing.

Titus 1:9: "Holding fast the faithful word as he hath been taught, that he may be able by sound doctrine both to exhort and to convince the gainsayers."

James 5:14: "Is any sick among you? let him call for the elders of the church; and let them pray over him, anointing him with oil in the name of the Lord:"

Matthew 24:45: "Who then is a faithful and wise servant, whom his lord hath made ruler over his household, to give them meat in due season?"

Hebrews 13:17: "Obey them that have the rule over you and submit yourselves: for they watch for your souls, as they that must give account, that they may do it with joy, and not with grief: for that is unprofitable for you."

Acts 20:28: "Take heed therefore unto yourselves, and to all the flock, over the which the Holy Ghost hath made you overseers, to feed the church of God, which he hath purchased with his own blood."

1 Peter 5:2: "Feed the flock of God, which is among you, taking the oversight thereof, not by constraint, but willingly; not for filthy lucre, but of a ready mind;"

Because a flock that is well fed is least likely to become unhealthy spiritually or give any trouble. The Ministry of men called to this work will always be primarily within the church.

It is the Holy Spirit that will make men overseers (Acts 20: 28). It is God who sets governments within the church.

1 Corinthians 12:28: Definite qualifications are to be looked for and demanded.

1 Timothy 3:1-7: God does not call a man for task for which he has no suitable gift or necessary qualifications.

Pastoral ministry, to be successful, does demand a real gift from God. It requires some measure of gift in conducting meetings, especially to maintain all things in the Spirit so that the wrong or the fanatical is detected and controlled and the good and true is given every encouragement and liberty.

It requires some measure of governing ability, the gift of government is required. A measure of tact and patience in dealing with individual problems of the diverse characters.

A transcendently important part of every true pastor's work is visitation (Acts 20:20).

Then there is the ever-present possibility of having to exercise discipline in the assembly. This requires great grace and a deep consuming love for God's sheep.

Not every brilliant preacher or teacher is a good pastor. Not every successful evangelist can become a shepherd. There are diversities of gifts. It is not a case of disparaging one ministry at the expense of another.

This New Testament office was probably filled with James. He appears to have exercised a position of Oversight and leadership in the church of Jerusalem (Acts 15:13,18 and 21). Tradition affirms that he seldom if ever left the city and that the integrity of his character was such that it caused him to be held in higher esteem, even by enemies of the church.

He's truly a notable and commendable pastor.

Acts 11: 22- 26

22 Then tidings of these things came unto the ears of the church which was in Jerusalem: and they sent forth Barnabas, that he should go as far as Antioch. 23 Who, when he came and had seen the grace of God, was glad, and exhorted them all, that with purpose of heart they would cleave unto the Lord.

24 For he was a good man, and full of the Holy Ghost and of faith: and many people was added unto the Lord. 25 Then departed Barnabas to Tarsus, for to seek Saul:

26 And when he had found him, he brought him unto Antioch. And it came to pass, that a whole year they assembled themselves with the church, and taught many people. And the disciples were called Christians first in Antioch.

His exhortation to the Converts to cleave to the Lord (verse 23), embodies the very essence of a pastoral ministry.

For if the keynote of the evangelist message is to come to Jesus. That of the pastor is Cleave to Jesus. Both messages are equally needed, though this is often not sufficiently recognized.

Acts 4:36: "And Joses, who by the apostles was surnamed Barnabas, (which is, being interpreted, The son of consolation,) a Levite, and of the country of Cyprus."

His attitude to Saul of Tarsus when the others treated him with suspicion.

Acts 9:27: "But Barnabas took him, and brought him to the apostles, and declared unto them how he had seen the Lord in the way, and that he had spoken to him, and how he had preached boldly at Damascus in the name of Jesus."

Then there were the angels of the seven churches referred to in Revelation chapters 2 and 3. These were also messengers of these assemblies, and it seemed most likely that the pastors were intended.

But above all these examples is the one who is called the Great Shepherd of the sheep.

Hebrews 13:20: And who is preeminently the pastor supreme pattern in all that pertains to this office, in patience in teaching, in giving an example for the sheep to follow. The Lord Jesus is indeed a good shepherd.

The greatest thing ever said about a pastoral ministry. This is the very essence of shepherding.

For the good pastor gives himself to death-to-self continually for the life of his sheep. The very antithesis is written concerning false shepherds, for they feed themselves.

Ezekiel 34:2-4: "Son of man, prophesy against the shepherds of Israel, prophesy, and say unto them, thus saith the Lord GOD unto the shepherds; Woe be to the shepherds of Israel that do feed themselves! should not the shepherds feed the flocks?"

Ye eat the fat, and ye clothe you with the wool, ye kill them that are fed: but ye feed not the flock.

4 The diseased have ye not strengthened, neither have ye healed that which was sick, neither have ye bound up that which was broken, neither have ye brought again that which was driven away, neither have ye sought that which was lost; but with force and with cruelty have ye ruled them.

The Teacher

The teachers held a well-defined and important place in the New Testament churches, this is evidenced by the fact that they are mentioned in all three of the lists of ministries, given respectively (Romans 12:6-8, 1 Corinthians 12:28, Ephesians 4:11).

Their ministry was combined with that of the pastor and the two offices are frequently united in one man.

Elders who were called to take a pastoral oversight of the assemblies had a special command to feed the flock (1 Peter 5:2). And it was desirable that such men should be asked to teach.

1 Timothy 3:2: While it will seem expedient for all the pastors to have at least some ability to teach, it does not necessarily follow that all teachers are also pastors.

The teacher can be called a roving minister, just like the apostle or the evangelist. And indeed, the more conspicuous his gift as a teacher, the more likely this is to be a scriptural case. Apollo's who traveled continually is an example in Acts 18:27.

1 Corinthians 16:12, Titus 3:13: Teaching requires a divine gift. This is of course implied in the passages quoted above. He has a gift differing according to the grace given Romans 12:6-7. It is God who set some in the church as teachers 1 Corinthians 12:28.

The man is not a teacher, merely by natural ability and inclination. There must be a divine stamp on the teacher. No ministry in the power of the Holy Spirit is ever dry. It will convey rivers of living water (John 7:38).

Paul describes the teaching ministry of Apollo's as watering (1 Corinthians 3:6). The saints will be left refreshed and revived (Acts 18:27).

Moreover, the only division caused by teaching in the power of the Spirit will be owing to definite unbelief and hardness of heart, in the hearers as in the ministries of our Lord and Paul and the apostles, there will be unnecessary divisions caused among sincere and simple-hearted believers.

True teachers will shun causing divisions except where it is unavoidable over some great fundamental issue.

His work is to build up the body not to divide but for such a ministry to be accomplished in power, it requires more than natural gifts. The teacher needs a special grace from God and those foremost gifts of the Spirit, which are essentially supernatural, in their real character, even though his appeal will be made to the logical faculties of his hearers and operate through the logical and reasoning faculties of his own understanding it must be enlightened by the Holy Ghost.

He may speak from notes and follow carefully prepared sequences. But at the heart of it all, it is a supernatural gift of the spirit.

God loves to honor his own word in whatever form it is preached. Nevertheless, for the most part, the ministry of the teacher will be less openly spectacular than that of these other brethren.

The teacher's work is not so much to evangelize, as it is to help those who are to believe through grace (Acts 18:27). He is usually called to water that which another is planted and to build upon the foundation already laid by another servant of the Lord.

1 Corinthians 3:6-10: Before God, the planter and the waterer are of equal value. Then the teacher must gladly carry his cross and happily and faithfully discharge his ministry as unto the Lord, and not unto men.

It has often been a regrettable fact that results of very successful evangelist campaigns have been largely wasted because not adequate provision was made for a pastor or teacher to follow on with their core equality.

The Apostles were careful to make provision for this line (Acts 8:14; Acts11:22; Acts14:21-23; Acts 15:36) etc.

If some assemblies are in danger, of stagnation, through lack of evangelical zeal, it is equally true that some others are in the same peril and perhaps, in a deeper sense, through lack of teaching, and soul food.

When a teacher ceases to be teachable himself, when he refuses to give due weight to the light and the experience of others also, when he is unwilling for his doctrine to be submitted for the approval of the whole body, then it becomes positively dangerous.

4

WHAT IS THE SCHOOL OF PROPHETS?

Schools of the Prophets is the name given to bands of prophets or "sons of prophets" living together for instruction and worship under Samuel, Elijah, and Elisha. Little is known about these schools, but they seem to have been important religious institutions in Israel and references to them are frequent (1 Samuel 10:11; 19:19–20; 2 Kings 2:3, 5; 4:38; 6:1). Not all the "sons of the prophets" claimed to have a supernatural gift; they were simply trained religious teachers, while some inspired prophets had received no training in the schools (Amos 7:14).

The Old Testament mentions a school of prophets in 1 Samuel 19:18–24, 2 Kings 2 and 4:38–44.

1 Samuel 19 mentions a company of prophets under Samuel's leadership. The "group of prophets" in 1 Samuel 19 was under the equipping ministry school of the prophet Samuel.

In 2 Kings 2, Elijah is traveling with Elisha, and a group of prophets from Bethel tells Elisha that Elijah will be taken from him that day (verse 3). Another group of prophets at Jericho repeats the prophecy (verse 5), and a third group of prophets near the Jordan River also delivers the same message (verse 7). After Elijah was taken up into heaven, Elisha sends fifty of these prophets to search for Elijah for three days (verses 15–18).

The School of the Prophets:

Prophets are first trained in the wilderness by the Lord. Then they must be instructed or study to show themselves approved as the scripture says.

2 Timothy 2:15: Do your best to present yourself to God as one approved, a worker who does not need to be ashamed and who correctly handles the word of truth.

This can be done by self-discipline. "Discipline yourself for the purpose of godliness" (1 Timothy 4:7).

Definition:

Spiritual Disciplines are habits and patterns of devotion.

Spiritual Disciplines are things a disciple of Jesus Christ does within the context of his relationship with Christ to become more like Christ.

"That I may know Him and the power of His resurrection and the fellowship of His sufferings, being conformed to His death; in order that I may attain to the resurrection of the dead. Not that I have already obtained it or have already become perfect, but I press on so that I may lay hold of that for which also I was laid hold of by Jesus Christ."

We will discuss Apprehending Christ in Chapter 22.

The Goal of Discipleship is to bring the Disciples into practical union with Christ through sanctification and the work of the Cross.

Prophets can also be taught by the imputed grace through the anointing of the Holy Spirit.

Philippians 3:10-12: [10] That I may know him, and the power of his resurrection, and the fellowship of his sufferings, being made conformable unto his death;

[11] If by any means I might attain unto the resurrection of the dead.

[12] Not as though I had already attained, either were already perfect: but I follow after, if that I may apprehend that for which also I am apprehended of Christ Jesus.

1 John 2:27: But the anointing which ye have received of him abideth in you, and ye need not that any man teaches you: but as the same anointing teacheth you of all things, and is truth, and is no lie, and even as it hath taught you, ye shall abide in him.

Or we can devote time in the temple, like Jesus did. Being the son of God, he did not despise those in authority but learned from them.

Luke 2:46: After three days they found him in the temple courts, sitting among the teachers, listening to them, and asking them questions.

It is, therefore, prideful and reckless to hypothecate and conclude that we have achieved ascendance, and no one can tell us anything new. Such pride has killed many beautiful vessels of God, ruining their ministries and making them drift into divination.

Samuel founded these schools of the prophets to serve as a voice of opposition against the corruption in that culture. They were radical inciters of righteousness, a resonance for moral excellence. They were men who feared God and walked in his divine counsel. Samuel gathered companies of young men who were pious, intelligent, and studious.

They were called the sons of the prophets. As they communed with God and studied his word and His works, wisdom from above was imputed to them.

In Samuel's day, there were two of these schools--one at Ramah, the home of the prophet, and the other at Kirjath-jearim, where the ark then was. Others were established in later times. (1 Samuel 19:18-24; 2 Kings 2:3, 5, 7, 12, 15) these schools were instituted to train prospective candidates for the prophetic and priestly offices.

The students at these schools sustained themselves by their own labor. Many of the religious teachers supported themselves by manual labor. Even so late as the time of the apostles, Paul and Aquila were no less honored because they earned a livelihood by their tent-making trade.

The passage most often connected to work in the book of Acts is Paul's tent-making in Acts 18:1-4. Although this passage is familiar, it is usually understood too narrowly.

In the familiar reading, Paul earns money by making tents to support himself in his real ministry of witnessing to Christ.

In a later chapter, we will talk about how those called in prophetic can sustain themselves as they serve God without the lure of the filthy lucre.

Students were taught how to pray, how to approach God, how to exercise faith in Him, and how to understand and obey Yahweh.

1 Samuel 19:18-24: They studied (scriptures) and interpretation of scriptures, along with sacred music and poetry.

1 Samuel 10:10: When they arrived at Gibeah, a procession of prophets met him; the Spirit of God came upon him in power, and he joined in their prophesying.

1 Samuel 19:20: So he sent men to capture him. But when they saw a group of prophets prophesying, with Samuel standing there as their leader, the Spirit of God came upon Saul's men, and they also prophesied.

1 Kings 2 and 4: Those in the prophetic were trained by Elijah or Samuel.

2 Kings 4:38: Elisha returned to Gilgal and there was a famine in that region. While the company of the prophets was meeting with him, he said to his servant, "Put on the large pot and cook some stew for these prophets."

2 Kings 5:22: "Everything is all right," Gehazi answered. "My master sent me to say, 'Two young men from the company of the prophets have just come to me from the hill country of Ephraim. Please give them a talent of silver and two sets of clothing.'"

In these prophetic schools' prophets were taught, tested and proven. They were brought up to exercise the office of a prophet, "preaching pure morality, repentance, holiness, reformation and heartfelt worship.

The Prophets:

Holy Men/Women of God

The prophets of the Old Testament were always calling the people to repentance and revealing God's will. The Holy Spirit, breathing freely into the spirit of the prophets, illuminated their souls and pervaded their thoughts, enabling them to declare divine truth in all its fullness.

Their inspiration consisted in the fullness of the influence of the Holy Spirit enabling them to accomplish their work. The control and guidance of the Holy Spirit guaranteed that their expression of truth was without error.

His or her job was to call the people back to God and to the fullness of the truth of God. Sometimes, the prophet's message involved reprimands to people and divulging the consequences of their indolence, ultimately calling them repentance and holiness.

Prophets and prophetesses are yielded men and women through whom God speaks. His message of love for the repentant sinner, warning, and rebuke for the rebels. Prophets must know the balance of embracing the repentant sinners and how to rebuke reprobates, Pharisees and rebels.

5. Image Formation

Jesus is our identity, and He lives His life through us, so our chief purpose in this life is to be like Him. In our daily walk with Jesus, we learn from Him and His spirit is helping us do His will over our own will. Thus, we are becoming more like Jesus. This is what it means to conform to His image. Romans 8:29: "Whom He (= God) foreknew, He also predestined to be conformed to the image of His Son (= Jesus), that He (= Jesus) might be the firstborn among many brethren."

Just as Christians have borne the image of the earthly Adam, they will also bear the image of Christ.

1 Corinthians 15:49: "As we have borne the image of the man of dust (Adam), we shall also bear the image of the heavenly Man (Christ)."

Those with a righteous heart are led by the Holy Spirit and are the children of God, members of His family, heirs of God and joint heirs with Christ; Jesus is the firstborn among His many brethren.

Romans 8:14-17: "As many as are led by the Spirit of God, these are children of God. For you did not receive the spirit of bondage again to fear, but you received the Spirit of adoption by whom we cry out, 'Abba, Father.' The Spirit Itself bears witness with our spirit that we are children of God, and if children, then heirs - heirs of God and joint heirs with Christ..."

In the Bible, to be a son of somebody means to have the character and nature of the person, so God's children are called to sanctification and holiness; as Father God is holy, they are called to purify themselves so to get closer and closer to God's holiness and bear once again His image in character and nature.

Ephesians 5:1: "Be imitators of God as beloved children."

Leviticus 11:44: "I am the Lord your God. You shall therefore sanctify yourselves, and you shall be holy; for I am holy..."

We conform to the image of Christ in holiness; we are being changed into His image from glory to glory, namely from victory over sin, darkness and the world as the Holy Spirit leads us.

2 Corinthians 3:18: "We all, with open faces beholding as in a mirror the glory of the Lord, are changed into the same image from glory to glory, even as by the Spirit of the Lord."

The Greek word for Sanctification in the New Testament is 38. Hagiasmos meaning holiness, and sanctification.

https://biblehub.com/greek/38.htm
https://biblehub.com/strongs/greek/38.htm

The root word for it is "hagiazō"/sanctify, which means "to separate from profane things, to set aside something as holy unto the Lord and dedicated to God, to be set apart, to purify by expiation and be free from sin, to purify internally by renewing of the soul, to cleanse, to dedicate to God."

The Biblical meaning and definition of the word Sanctification is the process of separating ourselves from the profane and corrupt things of this world, of consecrating ourselves to God, and then of purifying ourselves from sin through repentance and renunciation to renew our soul unto conformity with the spirit.

If a prophet does not submit to this process of conformation to the image of Christ, he will exhibit questionable personalities that do not reflect Christlikeness. This could lead to people questioning the prophet's disposition based on his carnal actions. It could also lead to divination.

In 2 Kings 2:23–24 Elisha, God's new messenger to the corrupt nation of Israel (the Northern Kingdom), had just returned from bidding Elijah, his predecessor, farewell. God had taken Elijah up to heaven in a whirlwind right before Elisha's eyes and promised to give him a double portion of Elijah's "spirit."

This spiritual power that Elisha sought was important, for Israel was rife with idolatry. This idolatry caused much suffering; this idolatry would eventually cause God's judgment to fall on the whole nation at the hands of the vicious Assyrians.

Elisha's job—to call the people to return to the true God and worship Him alone, to put away idolatry and all the vile practices associated with it—was important for the spiritual and physical well-being of the thousands of individuals in the nation. He needed credibility with the king, his fellow prophets, and with the people.

An odd incident recorded in verses 23–24 occurred near Bethel. Bethel was notable as one of the two centers for idolatrous worship in the Northern Kingdom. Israel's first king, Jeroboam, had instituted idolatrous worship as a political maneuver to keep his citizens from visiting Jerusalem. Jeroboam set up golden calves at Dan and Bethel (1 Kings 12:29) and ordained a program of counterfeit worship.

Eight kings and several dynasties later, Bethel had undoubtedly become a prosperous city thriving on commerce enjoyed by being a worship/tourist center. But there remained at Bethel a remnant of God-fearing people, represented by the "sons of the prophets" described in verse 3 of the same chapter.

Elisha would need the same credibility that Elijah once had to lead them and the people of Israel, yet they were already somewhat doubtful of him.

2 Kings 2:16–18 (KJV)

16 And they said unto him, behold now, there be with thy servants fifty strong men; let them go, we pray thee, and seek thy master: lest peradventure the Spirit of the Lord hath taken him up, and cast him upon some mountain, or into some valley. And he said, Ye shall not send.

17 And when they urged him till, he was ashamed, he said, Send. They sent therefore fifty men; and they sought three days but found him not.

18 And when they came again to him, (for he tarried at Jericho,) he said unto them, Did I not say unto you, Go not?

In this setting, as Elisha approached Bethel, no less than 42 "little children" came "out of the city, and mocked him, and said unto him, go up, thou bald head; go up, thou bald head" (verse 23).

Elisha "turned back, and looked on them, and cursed them in the name of the Lord." Then "there came forth two she bears out of the wood, and tare forty and two children of them" (verse 24).

Why would God allow two bears to maul little children for insulting Elisha? Was he impulsive and erratic?

We flinch in horror at the proposition of bears mauling little children at Elisha's command.

The Hebrew words used for Elisha's detractors include the Hebrew words qatan, na'ar, and yeled, with Strong's number 6996 (here translated "little").

Qatan means small in quantity, size, number, age, status, or importance. Na'ar means a boy or girl, servant, or young man—it is a word that can cover a range of ages from infant to young adult. Yeled likewise means a boy, child, son, or young man—essentially, someone's offspring.

In seeing how these words are used throughout the Old Testament, we know that they were "little children."

The reference to his baldness was likely an ordinary insult: " baldness on the back of the head, historically, "was considered a blemish among the Israelites and the Romans.

But the rest of the taunt from these "little children" hurled at the prophet was the taunt to "go up," which was a reference to Elijah's ride to heaven.

See a similar taunt made against Jesus here in Matthew 27:40, 42.

By shouting this challenge to Elisha, they were challenging his right to follow in Elijah's footsteps as God's designated representative to Israel—and declaring their intention that they wanted him to meet His Maker as well.

Elisha had to have credibility as God's designated representative. Sometimes there is a temptation among the prophetic to erroneously use the power of God to validate ego. False teachers today forbid people from criticizing them based on several verses that contain the phrase "touch not mine anointed."

They automatically claim they are "God's anointed" and argue that "touch" refers to speaking against them. Thus, they use these passages to make themselves "untouchable" in the eyes of those who follow them and attempt to instill fear into the hearts of anyone who opposes them.

Elisha did not have to curse them. Jesus was called names, but he did not curse his detractors—Matthew 27:14: And he answered him to never a word; insomuch that the governor marveled greatly

Matthew 26:63: But Jesus remained silent. Then the high priest said to Him, "I charge You under oath by the living God: Tell us if You are the Christ, the Son of God."

Matthew 27:12: And when He was accused by the chief priests and elders, He gave no answer.

Isaiah 53:7: He was oppressed, and he was afflicted, yet he opened not his mouth: he is brought as a lamb to the slaughter, and as a sheep before her shearers is dumb, so he openeth not his mouth.

Acts 8:32: The place of the scripture which he read was this, He was led as a sheep to the slaughter; and like a lamb dumb before his shearer, so opened he not his mouth:

God responded by doing something about Elisha's curse on the children, but this does not biblically validate cursing people who don't like and agree with you— Elijah his predecessor, was also used to calling fire on people.

The Two Fires

1 Kings 18:38: Then the fire of the LORD fell and consumed the burnt sacrifice, and the wood, and the stones, and the dust, and licked up the water that was in the trench.

The first fire does not destroy humans, it comes from God. Then the fire of the LORD fell, and consumed the burnt sacrifice, and the wood, and the stones, and the dust, and licked up the water that was in the trench.

But the second fire was Elijah's fire, The misuse of the gift to hurt people.

2 Kings 1:12: And Elijah answered and said unto them, If I be a man of God, let fire come down from heaven, and consume thee and thy fifty. And the fire of God came down from heaven and consumed him and his fifty.

"If I be a man of God" this is an ambivalent statement from Elijah. He is uncertain if he is the man of God. God already answered his prayer and confirmed it,

1 Kings 18:38: Then the fire of the LORD fell, and consumed the burnt sacrifice, and the wood, and the stones, and the dust, and licked up the water that was in the trench.

But now, he wants to misuse his gift to prove he is a prophet. This maltreatment of his prophetic office was rebuked later in the New Testament by Jesus.

In Mark 3, Jesus calls twelve men to be His apostles. Among them are "James's son of Zebedee and his brother John (to them he gave the name Boanerges, which means Sons of Thunder)" (Mark 3:17). This is the only place in Scripture that mentions the designation of the sons of Zebedee as the Sons of Thunder.

In one incident, Jesus and His disciples were traveling through Samaria on their way to Jerusalem when they ran into trouble. Jesus attempted to find accommodations for the night in one place but was met with opposition from the villagers simply because His destination was Jerusalem—a result of Jew-Samaritan prejudice. "When the disciples James and John saw this, they asked, 'Lord, do you want us to call fire down from heaven to destroy them?'" (Luke 9:54). But he turned, and rebuked them, and said, Ye know not what manner of spirit ye are of (Luke 9:55).

They were operating in a contrary spirit based on the rebuke from Jesus. This means that Elijah also operated in the same contrary spirit by calling fire on people.

Luke 9:56: "For the son of man is not come to destroy men's lives, but to save them. And they went to another village."

Jesus did not come to destroy lives but save them, but we see the same prophetic attitude of calling fire on people being rebuked by Jesus.

Elisha was not sanctioned to call the bears, and Elijah was not authorized to call the fire, but God granted it to tutor us about the misuse of the gift or office and the destructive consequence of spiritual infantilism.

The fire of the Lord only affected offerings, wood, stone, and dust and licking up the water on the trench. This is identified as the fire of the Lord. But there was another fire that Elijah wielded that did not proceed from the Lord.

2 Kings 1:10-12

10 And Elijah answered and said to the captain of fifty, If I be a man of God, then let fire come down from heaven, and consume thee and thy fifty. And there came down fire from heaven and consumed him and his fifty.

11 Again also he sent unto him another captain of fifty with his fifty. And he answered and said unto him, O man of God, thus hath the king said, Come down quickly.

12 And Elijah answered and said unto them, If I be a man of God, let fire come down from heaven, and consume thee and thy fifty. And the fire of God came down from heaven and consumed him and his fifty.

A prophet can release false fire that does not proceed from the Lord. God will honor it, but he does not endorse it. Prophets, if not careful, can misuse the fire of God to satisfy their ego.

What makes us angry? Do we, like the disciples, wish to call fire down from heaven? What if we would act, instead, to the contrary, as Paul writes, "If your enemy is hungry, feed him; if he is thirsty, give him something to drink; for by so doing, you will heap burning coals on his head. 21 Do not be overcome by evil but overcome evil with good" (Romans 12:20-21).

A Prophet's Disposition

- A prophet's candor and boldness can be viewed as harshness or insensitivity.

People will blame you for being controlling or even intimidating. People will tell you to tone it down. Soften your stance. They will tell you to sugarcoat your words. They will tell you to be tolerant and inclusive.

They will tell you that if you don't change, embrace the culture, and soften your message, no one will want to hear you.

- Your focus on right and wrong could be perceived as intolerant and legalistic.
- Your boldness and unrelenting passion can/will be blamed for impeding personal relationships.
- Your need to be alone with God will be misunderstood as being out of touch, being guarded, reclusive, and ignorant.

The message of a prophet is often dire. The prophet will embolden his or her hearers to repent. The prophet has hope mixed with anticipation of reformation, leading to God relenting on his judgments.

There is always a window of repentance promulgated by the prophet.

Prophets sometimes may present their messages poetically, with dramatic displays or evocative dreams. Prophecies sometimes are never direct.

Prophets must be lovers of God first, recipients of God's love. Then, they can love others and weave it within their delivery. Love undergirds every ministry and gift; the prophetic people are not an exception.

If you do not receive love from God, it will be difficult for you to show it to others. This explains why God will allow his prophets to fail awfully. Meekness will be your threshing floor. God will mortify your flesh until your self-image is dismantled.

1 Corinthians 13:4-13: "Love suffers long and is kind; love does not envy; love does not parade itself, is not puffed up; 5 does not behave rudely, does not seek its own, is not provoked, thinks no evil; 6 does not rejoice in iniquity, but rejoices in the truth; 7 bears all things, believes all things, hopes all things, endures all things. 8 Love never fails. But whether there are prophecies, they will fail; whether there are tongues, they will cease; whether there is knowledge, it will vanish away. 9 For we know in part, and we prophesy in part. 10 But when that which is perfect has come, then that which is in part will be done away. When I was a child, I spoke as a child, I understood as a child, I thought as a child; but when I became a man, I put away childish things. 12 For now we see in a mirror, dimly, but then face to face. Now I know in part, but then I shall know just as I also am known and now abide faith, hope, love, these three; but the greatest of these is love.

God uses the trials, the persecutions, and the dry seasons in our lives that seem like the desert to circumcise our hearts with His love and love for others. In the end, it's not about our prophetic gift or calling, who listens, who doesn't; it's all about loving as he does.

It is time to put away childish, immature thinking, selfishness, and self-seeking motives and to zealously pursue God out of a pure heart. God is love by his nature. This does not mean that the prophet is tolerant of sin. Love does not denote compromise.

In molding a prophet, God must take the entire person— body, soul, spirit, personality, weaknesses, and strengths- and then, through surrender, use that person to proclaim His message and accomplish a special mission.

The Prophetic is not for doormats and weaklings. Jesus warned about this.

How terrible for you! You make fine tombs for the prophets—the very prophets your ancestors murdered. You yourselves admit, then, that you approve of what your ancestors did; they murdered the prophets, and you build their tombs. For this reason, the Wisdom of God said, 'I will send them prophets and messengers; they will kill some of them and persecute others.' So, the people of this time will be punished for the murder of all the prophets killed since the creation of the world. "When Jesus left that place, the teachers of the Law and the Pharisees began to criticize him bitterly and ask him questions about many things, trying to lay traps for him and catch him saying something wrong" (Luke 11:47-54).

If Jesus is the holy, righteous, and unimpeachable man, what should lesser men or women with the prophetic gift expect if he faced this kind of reception? You will be persecuted. You will be rejected. You will be mocked. You are not an exception.

God's Castigatory Agents

In Israel's history, when the priests themselves often became corrupt and turned away from God, leading the people in the worship of idols, Prophets were raised to elevate the standard. When the priests failed to teach God's law to the people, kings, and judges failed to govern justly, God would broadcast his will intensely through prophets.

God sent his prophets to rebuke them when they were offering their children in the fires to Moloch and ritual prostitution with every imaginable lewd practice "on the high places, on the hills, and under every green tree" (2 Chronicles 28:4).

It is not easy to listen to a prophet if you do not have thick skin. They speak directly what God wants to say, not what people want to hear.

People love self-commiseration; they want their ears tickled. Come as you are; stay as you are. But true Prophets will point the church back to Calvary.

Amos 5:10: they hate the one who rebukes in the gate, and they abhor the one who speaks uprightly.

When the moral fabric of a culture or nation is decaying or declining, when nations or societies need spiritual realignment or reformation, God sends his Prophets.

God's Olive Trees

Prophets must be like olive trees. One characteristic of the evergreen olive tree is its high content of water. The water here is a symbol of the word of God (Ephesians 5:26). God does not work apart from His Word.

The Bible is God's written Word. Prophets, like the evergreen olive trees, must be full of God's word. Not just head knowledge. But revealed knowledge. Illuminated knowledge.

Like the olive trees that thrive in the wilderness, Prophets must be Survivalists. They must be like these evergreens; they must retain the high capacity of the living water, i.e., God's word, and be full of endurance even amid extreme heat, drought, snow, and cold of winter, which can be defined as trials of life.

Remember, the olives must be crushed to produce oil. Sometimes, God will lead prophets through crushing seasons. The olive press is used by God to crush past the flesh. Prophets must be yielded to the press and not the flesh.

The stronger the prophetic call one has on their life, the more wilderness, dying, winter, and desert time they will have to go through until true humility and love is worked in their lives and formed in their soul.

They may go through extraordinary trials and tribulations. The winters may be long, cold, and cruel, like the snow on an evergreen tree. Yet, outwardly, it is still a beautiful tree. The prophet must be able to embrace the seasons of death and the dying processes.

Welcome the cold of the snow and the heat of the summer. Submit and bow to the seasons of trials.

Personality Types:

Each person is a unique combination of four personality types. Over the centuries, these basic categories have gone by several names and designations, i.e., personality types A, B, C, and D, or sanguine, choleric, melancholic, and phlegmatic. Respectively.

But as Christians, we should inherit Jehovah's personality traits—his nature and not our nature. You need to embrace who you are in Christ instead of who you are in the flesh. Act in your true nature, not against it.

Who I Am in Christ

- I am blameless and free from accusation (Colossians 1:22).
- Christ Himself is in me (Colossians 1:27).
- I am firmly rooted in Christ and am now being built up in Him (Colossians. 2:7).
- I have been made complete in Christ (Colossians 2:10).
- I have been spiritually circumcised. My old, unregenerate nature has been removed (Colossians 2:11).
- I have been buried, raised, and made alive with Christ (Colossians 2:12,13).
- I died with Christ, and I have been raised up with Christ. My life is now hidden with Christ in God. Christ is now my life (Colossians 1:1-4).
- I am an expression of the life of Christ because He is my life (Colossians 3:4).
- I am chosen of God, holy and dearly loved (Colossians 3:12; 1 Thessalonians 1:4).
- I am a son of light and not of darkness (1 Thessalonians 5:5).
- I have been given a spirit of power, love, and self-discipline (2 Timothy 1:7).
- I have been saved and set apart according to God's doing (2 Timothy 1:9; Titus 3:5).
- Because I am sanctified and am one with the Sanctifier. He is not ashamed to call me brother (Hebrews 2:11).
- I am a holy partaker of a heavenly calling (Hebrews 3:1).
- I have the right to come boldly before the throne of God to find mercy and grace in a time of need (Hebrews 4:16).
- I have been born again (1 Peter 1:23).
- I am a living stone, being built up in Christ as a spiritual house (1 Peter 2:5).
- I am a member of a chosen race, a royal priesthood, a holy nation (1 Peter 2:9,10).

- I am a stranger to this world in which I temporarily live (1 Peter 2:11).
- I am an enemy of the devil (1 Peter 2:11).
- I have been given exceedingly great and precious promises by God by which I am a partaker of God's divine nature (2 Peter 1:4).
- I am forgiven on the account of Jesus' name (1 John 2:12).
- I am anointed by God (1 John 2:27).
- I am a child of God and will resemble Christ when He returns (1 John 3:1,2).
- I am loved (1 John 4:10).
- I am like Christ (1 John 4:10).
- I have life (1 John 5:12).
- I am born of God, and the evil one the devil, cannot touch me (1 John 5: 8).
- I have been redeemed (Revelation 5:9).
- I have been healed (Isaiah 53:5).
- I am the salt of the earth (Matthew 5:13).
- I am the light of the world (Matthew 5:14).
- I am commissioned to make disciples (Matthew 28:19,20).
- I am a child of God (John 1:12).
- I have eternal life (John 10:27).
- I have been given peace (John 14:27).
- I am part of the true vine, a channel of Christ's life (John 15:1,5).
- I am clean (John 15:3).
- I am Christ's friend (John 15:15).
- I am chosen and appointed by Christ to bear His fruit (John 15:16).
- I have been given glory (John 17:22).
- I have been justified, completely forgiven, and made righteous (Romans 5:1).
- I died with Christ and died to the power of sin's rule over my life (Romans 6:1-6).
- I am a slave of righteousness (Romans 6:18).
- I am free from sin and enslaved to God (Romans 6:22).
- I am free forever from condemnation (Romans 8:1).
- I am a son of God; God is spiritually my Father (Romans 8:14, 15 Galatians 3:26; 4:6).
- I am a joint heir with Christ, sharing His inheritance with Him (Romans 8:17).
- I am more than a conqueror through Christ, who loves me (Romans 8:37).
- I have faith (Romans 12:3).
- I have been sanctified and called to holiness (1 Corinthians 1:2).
- I have been given grace in Christ Jesus (1 Corinthians 1:4).

- I have been placed into Christ, by God's doing (1 Corinthians 1:30).
- I have received the Spirit of God into my life that I might know the things freely given to me by God (1 Corinthians 2:12).
- I have been given the mind of Christ (1 Corinthians 2:16).
- I am a temple, a dwelling place of God. His Spirit and His life dwell in me (1 Corinthians 3:16; 6:19).
- I am united to the Lord and am one spirit with Him (1 Corinthians 6:17).
- I am bought with a price; I am not my own; I belong to God (1 Corinthians 6:19, 20; 7:23) I am called (1 Corinthians 7:17).
- I am a member of Christ's Body (1 Corinthians 12:27; Ephesians 5:30).
- I am victorious through Jesus Christ (1 Corinthians 15:57).
- I have been established and sealed by God in Christ; I have been given to the Holy Spirit as a pledge guaranteeing my inheritance to come (2 Corinthians 1:21; Ephesians 1:13,14).
- God leads me in triumphal procession (2 Corinthians 2:14).
- I am to God the fragrance of Christ among those who are being saved and those who are perishing (2 Corinthians 2:15).
- I am being changed into the likeness of Christ (2 Corinthians 3:18).
- Since I have died, I no longer live for myself, but for Christ (2 Corinthians 5:14,15).
- I am a new creation (2 Corinthians 5:17).
- I am reconciled to God and am a minister of reconciliation (2 Corinthians 5:18,19).
- I have been made righteous (2 Corinthians 5:21).
- I am given strength in exchange for weakness (2 Corinthians 12:10).
- I have been crucified with Christ, and it is no longer I who live, but Christ lives in me. The life I am now living is Christ's life (Galatians 2:20).
- I am a son of God and one in Christ (Galatians 3:26, 28).
- I am Abraham's seed...an heir of the promise (Galatians 3:29).
- I am an heir of God since I am a son of God (Galatians 4:6,7).
- I am a saint (Ephesians 1:1; 1 Corinthians 1:2; Philippians 1:1; Colossians 1:2).
- I have been blessed with every spiritual blessing (Ephesians 1:3).
- I was chosen in Christ before the foundation of the world to be holy and am without blame before Him (Ephesians 1:4).
- I was predestined...determined by God...to be adopted as God's son (Ephesians 1:5).

- I have been sealed with the Holy Spirit (Ephesians 1:13).
- I have been redeemed and forgiven and am a recipient of His lavish grace. I have been made alive together with Christ (Ephesians 2:5).
- I have been raised up and seated with Christ in heaven (Ephesians 2:6).
- I am God's workmanship...His handiwork...born anew in Christ to do His work (Ephesians 2:10).
- I have direct access to God through the Spirit (Ephesians 2:18).
- I am a fellow citizen with the rest of God's family (Ephesians 2:19).
- I may approach God with boldness, freedom, and confidence (Ephesians 3:12).
- I am righteous and holy (Ephesians 2:24).
- I am a citizen of heaven, seated in heaven right now (Philippians 3:20, Ephesians 2:6).
- I am capable (Philippians 4:13).
- I have been rescued from the domain of Satan's rule and transferred to the kingdom of Christ (Colossians 1:13).
- I have been redeemed and forgiven of all my sins. The debt against me has been cancelled (Colossians 1:14).

Here are some traits that are commonly observed among prophetic people. These peculiarities can be used to benefit others, or they can be misused.

When a prophet walks in the Spirit (Galatians 5:25), his attitude and expression reflect the character of Christ. However, when a prophet walks in "the flesh," making carnal and soulish choices based on his sinful nature, his context and viewpoint will be expressed through ungodly traits (Galatians 5:16–17).

Expressing your impressions verbally

Peter spoke more often than any other disciple (Acts 2:14, 3:12, 4:8, 11:4).

Double-edged sword effect
Expose and restore.

God's mercy should undergird a prophet's motivation to expose sin; he or she should embrace God's perspective and restore those exposed.

If any man be overtaken in a fault, ye which are spiritual, restore such a one in the spirit of meekness; considering thyself, lest thou also be tempted" (Galatians 6:1). Exposure of sin is the first step of restoration.

Prophets should avoid impudent conclusions and carnal postulations. Don't doctor words. Don't fiddle with a hypothesis to prove your point.

Prophets can detect treachery and disguised malicious implements. Peter sensed deception in Ananias and Sapphira. His condemnation resulted in their deaths (Acts 5:3–10).

Don't react harshly to sinners. Don't call fire on sinners after exposing their sins. Seek remorse, and if there is penitence, restore with love.

Galatians 6:1 Brethren, if a man be overtaken in a fault, ye which are spiritual, restore such a one in the spirit of meekness; considering thyself, lest thou also be tempted.

Prophets are always quick to cut off people and disband those they deem unfit; this is a prideful attitude. Peter desired to cut off his offenders, and he asked Jesus how often he would have to forgive them (Matthew 18:21).

Prophets do not know how to separate the sin from the sinner. Therefore, he tends to reject them both with vigor. This can be misrepresented as anger. There needs to be a balance of truth and love.

Luke 7:47: "Wherefore I say unto thee, her sins, which are many, are forgiven; for she loved much: but to whom little is forgiven, the same loveth little."

You cannot reciprocate what you haven't experienced graciously. He who is forgiven many times loves much.

Prophets are very needed in today's church. They warn, scold, bless, heal, foretell, forth tell, call people to repentance and holiness, subdue atmospheres through God-breathed prayers and judge and counsel from the heart of God. But they need to reflect the nature of Christ.

My vision for this school is to equip and mentor prophets and prophetic people who yield to God and are committed to stand for truth and righteousness.

6. Definition of a Prophet

Prophet definition: My definition of a Prophet is: A yielded mouthpiece of God, who communicates by Divine Inspiration of God.

Other meanings from: https://www.biblestudytools.com/dictionaries/eastons-bible-dictionary/prophet.html

Heb. nabi, from a root meaning "to bubble forth, as from a fountain," hence "to utter," Compare Psalms 45:1). This Hebrew word is the first and the most generally used for a prophet. In the time of Samuel another word, ro'eh, "seer," began to be used (1 Samuel 9:9). It occurs seven times about Samuel. Afterward, another word, hozeh, "seer" (2 Samuel 24:11), was employed. In 1 Chronicles 29:29, all these three words are used: "Samuel the seer (ro'eh), Nathan the prophet (nabi'), Gad the seer" (hozeh). In Joshua 13:22, Balaam is called (Heb.) a kosem "diviner," a word used only of a false prophet.

The word nabi is the most frequently used.

When a prophecy comes forth, sometimes it is like a bubbling forth of a stream. When God brings forth the message through the yielded vessel, it bubbles forth from your spiritual man as an active living stream; when the soul is quiet and yielded enough, the words become so alive and powerful that the Lord scribes through the Yielded mouth of a prophet in words inspired and divine.

Luke 6:45: a good man out of the good treasure of his heart bringeth forth that which is good; and an evil man out of the evil treasure of his heart bringeth forth that which is evil: for of the abundance of the heart his mouth speaketh."

He that believeth on me, as the scripture hath said, out of his belly shall flow (bubble forth rivers of living water) John 7:38.

A prophet is a divinely inspired messenger who delivers a specific message from God for an individual or an entire nation. He is an inspired herald, a holy announcer, and a messenger with a divine message. This divine message must constantly be guarded by scripture, validated by love, and in line with God's redemptive purposes. God's Redemptive purposes are the things that Christ was manifested to accomplish on this earth.

In the Old Testament, in the book of Samuel, the Hebrew word ro'eh, which means seer, was used in 1 Samuel 9:9. Roeh means " A seer" or "vision." one who envisions.

Strong's Hebrew: 7203. ר (ro'eh) https://biblehub.com/hebrew/strongs_7203.htm

1 Samuel 9:9

Before time in Israel, when a man went to enquire of God, thus he spake, Come, and let us go to the seer: This scripture suggests that he who is now called a Prophet was before called a Seer.

In Greek, a prophétés: a prophet is simply an interpreter or forth-teller of the divine will, "one who speaks for another"—one who speaks for God and interprets God's will to the people. He is an "interpreter." For God.

Strong's Concordance 4396. Prophétés

https://biblehub.com/greek/4396.htm

In 1 Chronicles 29:29, three words are used:

Now the acts of David the king, first and last, behold, they are written in the book of Samuel, the seer, and the book of Nathan the prophet, and the book of Gad the seer.

"Samuel the seer (ro'eh), Strong's Hebrew 7200: To see, Nathan the prophet (nabi'), Strong's Hebrew 5030: A spokesman, speaker, prophet, Gad the seer" (hozeh). Strong's Hebrew 2374: A beholder in vision,

https://biblehub.com/1_chronicles/29-29.htm

Prophets have foresight and insight. They can both expound the word and expose it with deep insights, illuminating their hearers. Prophets also can foretell the future. But the foretelling must not be soulish, or self-generated. It must not veer from scripture; it must be grounded on scripture and incorporate the redemptive purposes of God.

God always uses the authentic, the Holy Spirit yielded vessels, but the enemy, the devil, will also bring forth the counterfeit, unholy, soulish or carnally yielded (false prophets) who are motivated or inspired by demons. It was the same in Old Testament Times.

God's Prophets always faced off with the counterfeit diviners.

Joshua 13:22: Balaam is called (in Hebrew) a qasam "diviner," this word is used mainly to refer to a false prophet.

Strong's Concordance 7080. Qasam: to practice divination.

https://biblehub.com/hebrew/7080.htm

Divination is so cunning, seductive, deceptive, and so evil. It is the counterfeit of a true prophet also known as a python spirit, familiar spirit, or seducing spirit. This spirit will deceive, seduce, imitate the authentic and confuse even the elect of God. Most Christians today are already convinced that diviners are true Prophets.

Acts 16:16: "And it came to pass, as we went to prayer, a certain damsel possessed with a spirit of divination met us, which brought her masters much gain by soothsaying:"

Strong's Greek 4436: From Putho; a Python, i.e., inspiration.

puthón: Python, a mythical serpent slain by Apollo, divination.

(pneuma Pythonos), the original Greek words translated "a spirit of divination," literally means "a spirit of Python."

Python, named after the Pythian serpent, is said to have guarded the oracle at Delphi and been slain by Apollo.

https://biblehub.com/greek/4436.htm

Acts 16:17-18: "The same followed Paul and us, and cried, saying, These men are the servants of the most high God, which shew unto us the way of salvation."

Was she right? Yes. These were true men of God preaching the right things.

Acts 16:18: "And this did she many days. But Paul, being grieved, turned and said to the spirit, I command thee in the name of Jesus Christ to come out of her. And he came out the same hour.

She kept repeating this "for many days" (Acts 16:18). Second, crying this out during "prayer" (Acts 16:16).

Paul discerned in his spiritual man through inner awareness that something was wrong.

Demonic spirits also enable today's psychics, witches and fortune tellers and say things that come to pass at least occasionally.

What did God say about His people seeking advice from psychics, witches, and fortune tellers? He called them "abominations" and strictly forbade them:

Deuteronomy 18:9-13

When thou art come into the land which the LORD thy God giveth thee, thou shalt not learn to do after the abominations of those nations." "There shall not be found among you any one that maketh his son or his daughter to pass through the fire, or that useth divination, or an observer of times, or an enchanter, or a witch," "Or a charmer, or a consulter with familiar spirits, or a wizard, or a necromancer." "For all that do these things are an abomination unto the LORD: and because of these abominations the LORD thy God doth drive them out from before thee." "Thou shalt be perfect with the LORD thy God."

Facebook and YouTube are rife and abundant with these false prophets and Apostles who masquerade as true workers of God, always ready to give you a special word of prophecy for a donation.

Remember, this diviner in Acts 16:19 also made money using this python spirit.

19 And when her masters saw that the hope of their gains was gone, they caught Paul and Silas and drew them into the marketplace unto the rulers,

1 Timothy 6:9-10: But they that will be rich fall into temptation and a snare, and into many foolish and hurtful lusts, which drown men in destruction and perdition.

For the love of money is the root of all evil: which while some coveted after, they have erred from the faith, and pierced themselves through with many sorrows.

Those in the prophetic are at risk of drifting into divination if their motives are impure and not truly yielded to God. Without proper accountability, they can become vulnerable to divination, deception or (mixture).

Dangerous Concoction's

What was the "death in the pot" in 2 Kings 4:39-41?

39 And one went out into the field to gather herbs and found a wild vine, and gathered thereof wild gourds his lap full, and came and shred them into the pot of pottage: for they knew them not.

40 So they poured out for the men to eat. And it came to pass, as they were eating of the pottage, that they cried out, and said, O thou man of God, there is death in the pot. And they could not eat thereof.

41 But he said, Then bring meal. And he cast it into the pot; and he said, Pour out for the people, that they may eat. And there was no harm in the pot.

There is an instructive analogy here. One went out to the field to gather herbs and noticed here that his target was herbs, not wild vines. He picked up a lot of wild vines and shredded them into the pot of pottage.

This verse reveals the intended ingredients for the pottage: wild herbs from the field. "Field" is the Hebrew sadeh, which refers to an open, uncultivated area of land where you can only find that which grows wild.

This carnal, undisciplined, and undiscerning gatherer went out and decided that wild vines could make a better stew than herbs. He was enticed by their soft and succulent appearance; their outward appearance and aromatic scent deceived him. But whatever he found in the field (a picture of the world or the flesh) were poisonous herbs.

1 John 2:16-17: For all that is in the world, the lust of the flesh, and the lust of the eyes, and the pride of life, is not of the Father, but is of the world. And the world passeth away, and the lust thereof: but he that doeth the will of God abideth for ever.

He was immature in spiritual matters; his senses were not yet trained, and he mistook the wild vine for an edible cucumber or squash.

Hebrews 5:14: But solid food is for the [spiritually] mature, whose senses are trained by practice to distinguish between what is morally good and what is evil.

He could not distinguish what is morally good and what is evil; he tried to gather man's ideas, false doctrines, and humanistic philosophies in an attempt to satisfy the spiritual appetites of a congregation. But what he collected was bitter and poisonous. If eaten in large amounts would tear up the digestive tract and could even cause death.

The world is full of poisonous ideas that may look harmless and even resemble the truth, but they are bitter and bring unhappiness to man. To recognize this and protect others from these bitter herbs, men need to be trained in the Word of God.

There was death in the pot. The wild herbs were picked from the field, without the discerning expertise of a master herbalist who could have known the difference between what was edible and what was not. So, the prophets cried out to the man of God,

The world and the flesh are full of diabolical and poisonous ideas, thoughts and attitudes. To the untrained, undiscriminating ear and eye, they sound and look good but are full of death and misery.

Elisha called for a meal (flour) and threw it into the pot, and by a miracle of God, the flour neutralized the poison.

"Meal" is the Hebrew word, gemah, a form of flour or meal. It was used of both a very coarse and very fine flour (Genesis 18:6) and of the ingredient for unleavened bread or cakes (Judges 6:19).

Meal or flour is used in making bread and Jesus Christ is the Bread of Life. Further, there were the Old Testament meal offerings which stood for the person of Jesus Christ, Only God's Word, which reveals Jesus Christ is the antidote to the death in the pot. Only Jesus Christ can give life.

Either we feed off God's life-giving Word, or we feed off the dangerous concoctions of poisonous words of the world.

Romans 8:5-7: For those who are according to the flesh set their minds on the things of the flesh, but those who are according to the Spirit, the things of the Spirit. 6 For the mind set on the flesh is death, but the mind set on the Spirit is life and peace, 7 because the mind set on the flesh is hostile toward God; for it does not subject itself to the law of God, for it is not even able to do so.

There was a mixture of lies and truth in the pot and it only yielded death. The problem among God's children is the mixture of the soul with the spirit. Whenever their spirit is released, their soul is released as well.

It is this mixture that disqualifies them from being used by God. The first qualification in the work of God is purity of the spirit. Matthew 5:8 KJV: Blessed are the pure in heart: for they shall see God.

Not a measure of power. Many people have great power, yet they pay no attention to the spirit. Although they may have the power to build, they are deficient in purity that sustains the power.

As a result, their work is bound to destruction. On the one hand, they build with power. On the other hand, they destroy with their impurity.

If you allow Beelzebub to influence your life, your oil will stink. Beelzebub is the Greek form of the name Baal-zebub, a pagan Philistine god worshiped in the ancient Philistine city of Ekron during the Old Testament times. It signifies "the lord of flies" (2 Kings 1:2).

Ecclesiastes 10:1: "Dead flies cause the ointment of the apothecary to send forth a stinking savour: so doth a little folly him that is in reputation for wisdom and honor."

These false prophets demonstrate God's power, yet at the same time, their character is infernal and diabolical. They operate two streams from within them, a filthy spirit is a mixed spirit (2 Corinthians 7:1).

Some people think that if they receive power from God, everything they do will be legitimized by heaven. But this will never happen. Whatever belongs to the soul will forever belong to the soul. The more we know God intimately, the more we will treasure the purity of his power.

We must cherish the purity of power. This purity is free from any soulish contamination. If a man or a woman has never experienced any dealings from God in his soul, it is impossible to expect the power that issues from him to be pure and divine.

Don't assume that your spiritual power is free from mixture. Many prophetic people infuse their own cleverness and personal feelings into their message to befuddle their duped hearers.

People can sense God's power on you. But at the same time, they can also discern the flesh when it sneaks into your words and wraps itself around the soul to strip the spirit of its efficacy. Your zeal can be mixed up with your sentiments.

The way to expel a mixture is through death to the flesh.

You will find God dealing with you in two ways. 1. The shattering of your soul (sanctification or the wilderness of the soul) 2. The Separation of the soul's sway from the spirit. (Dedication or consecration).

The natural man or the animal (your body) must be broken before the spirit man can be released. But when the spirit is released, it must not be mixed with soulish sentiments.

When your spirit is released in your ministering, it must not carry any sludge that emanates from self or the soul. This is a determinant of the quality of the Spirit released.

The true prophets proclaimed and declared without fear the message given to them. They did not soften it to soothe the susceptivity of the hearers. The seer beheld the pure visions given to them by God.

Numbers 12:6: And he said, hear now my words: If there be a prophet among you, I the LORD will make myself known unto him in a vision, and will speak unto him in a dream."

Here, God establishes some of the main means of communication with his prophets, it varies with many prophets, and we will tackle this subject later by hearing the voice of God.

A prophet is a yielded, dedicated, committed, and devoted spokesperson for God; he is only a voice. He is a yielded shofar in the mouth of God. God only blows through him. Without God, he has no sound. He must understand that fact or he will find himself in the divination camp giving soulish prophecies for sale. Prophet-lying instead of prophesying.

A prophet speaks in God's name and by his authority only. You cannot initiate or create your own words. God must write his story, paint his picture, and sing his song through you as you yield to him.

A prophet is the mouth by which God speaks to men; this was the concept in the Old Testament; the prophet had the privilege to hear from God and speak to men: Their words were inerrant.

Exodus: 7:1: And the LORD said unto Moses, See, I have made thee a god to Pharaoh: and Aaron thy brother shall be thy prophet.

Amos 3:7: surely the Lord GOD will do nothing, but he revealeth his secret unto his servants the prophets. This scripture is still used by many soothsayers to validate the Old Testament autonomy within the New Testament church. In the Old Testament, this was true. Under the new covenant, God speaks directly to his sheep through the Holy Spirit.

The scriptures below validate the importance of relying on the Holy Spirit in this new dispensation.

Hebrews 1:1: "God, who at sundry times and in divers manners spake in time past unto the fathers by the prophets."

Hebrews 1:2: "Hath in these last days spoken unto us by his Son, whom he hath appointed heir of all things, by whom also he made the worlds."

John 10:27: My sheep hear my voice, and I know them, and they follow me.

The true sheep of God know God's voice and follow and obey him. Their ears have been circumcised and they can discern the voice of God.

John 14:26: "But the Comforter, which is the Holy Ghost, whom the Father will send in my name, he shall teach you all things, and bring all things to your remembrance, whatsoever I have said unto you."

1 John 2:27: "But the anointing which ye have received of him abideth in you, and ye need not that any man teach you: but as the same anointing teacheth you of all things, and is truth, and is no lie, and even as it hath taught you, ye shall abide in him."

7. The Calling of a Prophet

In both the Old Testament and in the New Testament. Prophets never self-appointed themselves. Only false prophets would dare appoint themselves. It is dangerous to assume an office you have not been qualified for. Only God qualifies prophets.

Jeremiah 23:21: I have not sent these prophets, yet they ran: I have not spoken to them, yet they prophesied.

You cannot inherit Prophetic calling from the so-called senior fathers or prophets in the Lord, nor can you inherit it by human appointments. It is God himself that chooses and then calls a prophet. The initiative in making a prophet rest with God alone and all true prophets received a specific and personal call from God.

Jeremiah 1:5: before I formed thee in the belly, I knew thee; and before thou came forth out of the womb I sanctified thee, and I ordained thee a prophet unto the nations.

God forms, preordains, and sanctifies a prophet before His birth but a prophet neither starts his/her ministry immediately nor knows she/he is born a prophet.

Jesus was the son of God and God even before His birth, and He waited until He was about 30 years old to start His ministry. As Jesus waited for His appointed time to start His ministry, God waits until his appointed time to call a prophet and send her/him. The difference between Jesus and other prophets is that Jesus knew what He was born to do, and He knew His appointed time.

If God created you for the prophetic ministry, there is a time when He comes to reveal Himself and send you out.

Numbers 12:6: And he said, hear now my words: If there be a prophet among you, I the LORD will make myself known unto him in a vision, and will speak unto him in a dream.

The Call

The prophetic call comes to men and women at divergent stages in life. You must be called by God. Then, you submit to preparation, the olive press, or the wilderness experience. This is also called the death of the soul. This may take many years. Be patient and wait. Allow the potter to break you, mold you and shape you into his image.

Remember, the vessel must be blemished in his hands.

Jeremiah 18:4: and the vessel that he made of clay was marred in the hand of the potter: so he made it again another vessel, as seemed good to the potter to make it.

The word of God came to Jeremiah confirming that he was born a prophet of God. After that, God sent him out to the world.

Jeremiah's Call

Jeremiah 1:4-6: Then the word of the LORD came unto me, saying, Before I formed thee in the belly, I knew thee; and before thou came forth out of the womb I sanctified thee, and I ordained thee a prophet unto the nations. Then said I, Ah, Lord GOD! Behold, I cannot speak for I am a child.

Jeremiah 1:7-10: But the LORD said unto me, say not, I am a child: for thou shalt go to all that I shall send thee, and whatsoever I command thee thou shalt speak. Be not afraid of their faces: for I am with thee to deliver thee, saith the LORD. Then the LORD put forth his hand and touched my mouth. And the LORD said unto me, Behold, I have put my words in thy mouth. See, I have this day set thee over the nations and over the kingdoms, to root out, and to pull down, and to destroy, and to throw down, to build, and to plant.

Samuel's Calling

1 Samuel 3:1-3: And the child Samuel ministered unto the LORD before Eli. And the word of the LORD was precious in those days; there was no open vision. And it came to

pass at that time, when Eli was laid down in his place, and his eyes began to wax dim, that he could not see. And ere the lamp of God went out in the temple of the LORD, where the ark of God was, and Samuel was laid down to sleep.

1 Samuel 3:4-6: That the LORD called Samuel: and he answered, here am I. And he ran unto Eli, and said, here am I; for thou called me. And he said, I called not; lie down again. And he went and lay down. And the LORD called yet again, Samuel. And Samuel arose and went to Eli, and said, here am I; for thou didst call me. And he answered, I called not, my son; lie down again.

1 Samuel 3:7-9: Now Samuel did not yet know the LORD, neither was the word of the LORD yet revealed unto him. And the LORD called Samuel again the third time. And he arose and went to Eli, and said, here am I; for thou didst call me. And Eli perceived that the LORD had called the child. Therefore, Eli said unto Samuel, Go, lie down: and it shall be, if he calls thee, that thou shalt say, Speak, LORD; for thy servant hears. So, Samuel went and lay down in his place.

Ezekiel's Calling

Ezekiel 2:1-3: And he said unto me, Son of man, stand upon thy feet, and I will speak unto thee. And the spirit entered me when he spoke unto me, and set me upon my feet, that I heard him that spoke unto me. And he said unto me, Son of man, I send thee to the children of Israel, to a rebellious nation that hath rebelled against me: they and their fathers have transgressed against me, even unto this very day.

God confirms to a person that he or she was born a prophet at the right time and then sends the prophet out to the world.

If you are a true prophet of God, the word of God will come to you. Don't try to find the word by yourself.

Joel 1:1: The word of the LORD that came to Joel the son of Pethuel.

Hosea 1:1: The word of the LORD that came unto Hosea.

Ezekiel 1:3: The word of the LORD came expressly unto Ezekiel.

It took Jesus 30 years of preparation then only 3 years of ministry.

Isaiah 64:8: "But now, O LORD, thou art our father; we are the clay, and thou, our potter; and we all are the work of thy hand."

If you are called to be in the prophetic ministry. The Lord Our God will make himself known to you in a vision to announce your call. Then he will start speaking to you in dreams. He will also use other leaders to confirm this calling.

Numbers 12:6: And he said, hear now my words: If there be a prophet among you, I the LORD will make myself known unto him in a vision, and will speak unto him in a dream."

Job 33:15-18

In a dream, in a vision of the night, when deep sleep falls on people as they slumber in their beds, he may speak in their ears and terrify them with warnings, to turn them from wrongdoing and keep them from pride, to preserve them from the pit, their lives from perishing by the sword.

Dreams are images or visuals that come while in a state of sleep. God can divinely inspire them, or the enemy or soulish based on whom you are yielded to.

A vision is a spiritual revelation coming to an individual while awake. This revelation can come in the form of an open vision or a mental vision.

And Elisha prayed, "Open his eyes, Lord, so that he may see." Then the Lord opened the servant's eyes, and he looked and saw the hills full of horses and chariots of fire all around Elisha (2 Kings 6:17).

We can perceive visions in two ways. One is an open vision, and the other is a vision of the mind.

Open vision is a vision seen with your eyes wide open. It can be like a screen opens before you and you watch what is happening. Your natural eyes are opened to the spiritual realm and what is happening.

Visions are very vivid; you don't forget them. The visions of the Mind are the hardest to discern. Our soul can get in the way of truly hearing or seeing what God is wanting.

But God can speak to us with images in our mind. We can get a quick glimpse of something in our head, and then it quickly passes by, or sometimes it sticks around or is vivid.

When Paul was blind, he had a vision of Ananias coming and praying for him. This was a mental picture because his eyes could not see. This means that we have the ability within us to perceive or see pictures in our mind without our physical eyes.

Ephesians 1:18: The eyes of your understanding being enlightened; that ye may know what the hope of his calling is, and what the riches of the glory of his inheritance in the saints,

Romans 11:8: (According as it is written, God hath given them the spirit of slumber, eyes that they should not see, and ears that they should not hear;) unto this day.

Other scriptures: Jeremiah 5:21; Ezekiel 12:2; Matthew 13:13; Matthew 13:14; Mark 4:12

Ears can also be blocked in the spirit (Acts 7:51-53).

51 "You stiff-necked people! Your hearts and ears are still uncircumcised. You are just like your ancestors: You always resist the Holy Spirit! 52 Was there ever a prophet your ancestors did not persecute? They even killed those who predicted the coming of the Righteous One. And now you have betrayed and murdered him- 53 you who have received the law that was given through angels but have not obeyed it."

Jeremiah 6:10: To whom can I speak and give warning? Who will listen to me? Their ears are closed so they cannot hear. The word of the LORD is offensive to them; they find no pleasure in it.

"Uncircumcised ears" are those that hear the Word of God imperfectly, usually because they hear only what they want to hear, or they hear with such a strong prejudice that they reject the truth out of hand.

Interestingly, if God says something, it is likely that men will reject it, yet if a man says exactly the same thing, a high likelihood exists that the listener's mind will be much more open to what is said.

This shows how physically oriented we are. If we know something is coming from God, human nature always gets its guard up; it is already beginning to say, "No."

Regarding an uncircumcised heart, if what hinders a person from yielding to God is cut away—circumcised—the heart becomes open, pliable, and amenable to the Word of God. The effect is that he will submit.

Wait until you are released by God.

Those in the prophetic need to grow in trusting God and waiting patiently at the threshing floor of prayer or what we call the olive press. Let God lead you to your own Golgotha. Embrace your cross and die daily. Change is a process. Wait upon God.

Many people want change now but don't want to go through the waiting process. But the truth is, waiting is a must—God is going to make you wait until your flesh and vision is dead before you, and then he will make it alive in him before he can resurrect it again for you.

Patience is the fruit of the Spirit (Galatians 5:22).

It's developed only under trial, so we must not run from difficult situations. God uses those situations. But let endurance and steadfastness and patience have full play and do a thorough work, so that you may be [people] perfectly and fully developed [with no defects], lacking in nothing (James 1:4).

As we develop patience, the Bible says we finally feel completely satisfied—lacking nothing.

God calls us, then he gives us dreams, but He doesn't always allow us to see every unfolding and the exact timings of His plan. Not knowing the exact timing is very frustrating. When we entrust ourselves to Him, we can experience total peace and happiness even amid trials and testing.

Acts 13:2: As they ministered to the Lord, and fasted, the Holy Ghost said, separate me Barnabas and Saul for the work whereunto I have called them.

They were not petitioning God to bless them or their ministries. They were not even asking where to go for the next outreach or missionary work. They were loving on the Lord, ministering to him, fasting, and praying. Then God directed them to ordain men for ministry.

Prophet Moses was already an aging man in his 80s, and he received his call as he turned aside to behold a bush that blazed with flames and yet did not burn away (Exodus 3:1-4,17).

Prophet Isaiah saw a holy vision of the most holy God. That vision humbled him to confess his sinful speaking. After cleansing his lips, God challenged him to undertake the work of being a prophet; Isaiah's answer was, "Here am I; send me!" (Isaiah 6:1-9).

Prophet Hosea. God used his sad experience in his unhappy marriage life to prophesy to Israel. God called him first to experience in his home the unfaithfulness of his wife before he was ready to proclaim the continuing love and the unwearying patience of God towards his unfaithful people (Hosea 1:2, 11:8-9, 14:4).

Prophet Amos, working as a herdsman in his native Judaea, heard God calling him to leave those pasture lands and go to Israel to challenge the priests and rulers (Amos 7:12-15).

Prophet Micah was called to prophesy, but he tells how the anointing Spirit had come upon him, enabling him to speak God's word to both Israel and Judah (Micah 3:8).

Prophet Ezekiel shared being in exile with God's people in Babylon, sitting where they sat and becoming overwhelmed by what he saw until in the fourth month of the fifth year of their captivity, he was called to the prophetic ministry (Ezekiel 2:3-7, 3:14-15).

As you can see from these few examples, Prophets were not self-appointed. They were speaking because they had to; they were speaking what they heard, and they were obliged to pass it on (Jeremiah 20:9).

Some Titles Given to a Prophet

A man of God (1 Samuel 9:6), implying that as a man of righteous character he was more closely in touch with God than other men. (1 Kings 13:1, 2 Kings 4:9).

The servant of the LORD. This is another description going back to the time of Moses (Joshua 1:2), and it became the standard way of referring to all later prophets (2 Kings 17:13 and 23, Ezra 9:11, Jeremiah 7:25).

The messenger of the LORD. (Hagai 1:13, Malachi 3:1). 'Malachi' means 'my messenger'.

The man of the Spirit (Hosea 9:7; 2 Chronicles 15:1-2 and 24:20; Nehemiah 9:30; Micah 3:8).

My anointed one (Psalm 105:15). In Isaiah 61:1 the prophet claims that the Spirit of God had anointed him; an experience which years later Jesus declared had been fulfilled in his own experience (Luke 4:17-19).

A watchman. The prophet's responsibility is to first keep his eye on what is happening and then not fail to issue the appropriate warning to the people (Hosea 9:8, Ezekiel 3:17 and 33:1-9).

A trumpet-blower. (Jeremiah 6:17). The prophet's word must be loud and clear so that there can be no mistaking the urgency of his message (Isaiah 58:1, Jeremiah 4:5, Hosea 8:1, Joel 2:1 and 15, Amos 3:6).

Moses Syndrome

When God calls and then chooses individuals to serve as prophets. The first reaction may be one of unworthiness, unfitness, or even total unwillingness. They may feel unfit like Prophet Amos. Ineloquent like mosses. They may, like Jonah, try to run as far as possible in the opposite direction. They may even get to the lengths of accusing God of taking advantage of them (Jeremiah 20:7-8).

The prophets share one common obligation; they must pass on what God has revealed (Amos 3:8). This message may not be what most people want to hear (Isaiah 30:10). It may not even be the kind of message that the prophet himself likes passing on. As a watchman, you must be alert and watch carefully; as a seer, clean your eyes and see clearly; as a trumpeter, alert people loudly and effectively to the danger coming their way.

My speech and my preaching were not with persuasive words of human wisdom, but in demonstration of the Spirit and of power... —1 Corinthians 2:4

A message was given to Zerubbabel - a descendent of King David, who, having returned from the Babylonian captivity to govern Jerusalem, was the one chosen by God to start rebuilding the Jewish Temple. He was told by Zechariah the prophet that God would carry out the work - 'not by might nor by power, but by My Spirit,' says the LORD of hosts.

The Lord Himself will carry out His plans through you. Just learn to yield yourself, 'not by might nor by power, but by the Spirit alone.

We should be encouraged when we are intimidated by the task at hand, when our ministry is challenged. At times, we may find the task of the Lord or the ministry overwhelming and difficult when it is being rejected and opposed nevertheless, this Word from the Lord is as true for us today as it was so many centuries ago – God Who started a good work in us will complete it in the day of Christ Jesus... 'Not by might nor by power, but by My Spirit,' says the LORD.

Elijah Syndrome

Elijah had just destroyed the false prophets of Baal on Mt. Carmel. The fire had descended from heaven to validate his office and his God, the people of Israel acknowledged the Lord and the false prophets were all put to death. But this spiritual high was followed by a mixture of pride, fear, and failure in Elijah's life: the prophet was afraid and ran for his life from Queen Jezebel. The reason is made clear in 1 Kings 19:1–2: "Ahab told Jezebel all that Elijah had done, and how he had killed all the prophets with the sword. Then Jezebel sent a messenger to Elijah, saying, 'So may the gods do to me and more also if I do not make your life as the life of one of them by this time tomorrow.'

Elijah fled a day's journey into the wilderness (1 Kings 19:4). Elijah was so discouraged that he desired to die: "And he asked that he might die, saying, 'It is enough; now, O LORD, take away my life, for I am no better than my fathers'" (verse 4).

The Lord sent an angel to bring the prophet food and drink before and after sleeping. After his rest, Elijah took a forty-day journey to Mount Horeb to meet with the Lord (1 Kings 19:6–8). The Lord asked Elijah why he had fled to such a remote location.

Elijah's answer is telling: "The Israelites have rejected your covenant, torn down your altars, and put your prophets to death with the sword. I am the only one left, and now they are trying to kill me too" (verse 10).

Elijah elevated himself and saw himself as the lone prophet. He was now calling himself the only prophet. The only master prophet or even the predominant prophet. You may have heard many people calling themselves major 1 or Senior prophets. Elijah was making a fatal assumption here, and God was about to silence his pride and ego.

Jezebel seemed to be winning the fight; she got Elijah worked up in fear and pride, and Elijah had fled.

God does not use a discouraged Servant and does not like quitters. When Moses acted contrary to directives given to him by God to speak to the rock and not to strike the rock, he gave into his frustrations and anger, leading to God forbidding him from entering the promised land. He could see it from afar off but not enter it because he allowed anger and discouragement to get the best of him (Numbers 20:7-11).

Sometimes external matters can work their way into our soul and impede our obedience. The psychological issues altered his inward conviction. He gave into his flesh instead of obeying the spirit. This led to God selecting Joshua and Caleb to replace him. Joshua and Caleb were men of the spirit (Numbers 27:12-23, Joshua 14:6-15, Numbers 14:24).

During his conversation with God at Horeb, the Lord gave Elijah three important tasks. First, Elijah was to anoint Hazael as king over Syria (1 Kings 19:15). Second, he was to anoint Jehu as king of Israel (verse 16). Third, he was to anoint Elisha as the prophet to take his place (verse 16).

God would not let Elijah continue his earthly ministry because of his false assumptions and fearful attitude. God offered one important word of comfort to Elijah. It is a word of comfort but also a rebuke of sorts, God said, "Yet I will leave seven thousand in Israel, all the knees that have not bowed to Baal, and every mouth that has not kissed him" (1 Kings 19:18).

God is telling Elijah you are not the only one facing these challenges. I have seven thousand who have refused to bow to Baal, and they face the same pressure you face.

Elijah had thought he was the only one faithful to the Lord, and he took great comfort in the knowledge that thousands of others had not bowed to Baal. But because of his attitude, his ministry was done.

Every time I think of this story, I'm reminded that there is precedent in history, a pattern of preachers in the past who see themselves as some modern-day Elijah. They think that they are the only ones remaining and standing up for God; they have convinced themselves that they are the solitary paladins, ace in the hole, dernier resort.

Remember when God told Moses that he could not enter the Promised Land, but he would see it from afar? In Deuteronomy 32:51–52, God gives the reason that Moses was not permitted to enter the Promised Land: "This is because you broke faith with me in the presence of the Israelites at the waters of Meribah Kadesh in the Desert of Zin and because you did not uphold my holiness among the Israelites.

Therefore, you will see the land only from a distance; you will not enter the land I am giving to the people of Israel." God was true to His promise. He showed Moses the Promised Land but did not let him enter.

Branham's Claim to be Elijah.

William Branham was a true end-time prophet of God. His calling was authentic. Later in his ministry, he walked into error. No man or woman of God is immune to susceptibility.

Branham's followers identify him as the prophet Elijah of Malachi 4 and the seventh angel of Revelation 10. "The Word of the Lord has promised that He would send to the earth once again the spirit of Elijah in the form of that End Time Messenger who was the Angel to the Seventh Church Age in these final closing days of our time. They believe firmly that this promise was fulfilled in... William Marrion Branham." (The Revelation of the Seven Seals, Introduction, p. 19)

http://www.letusreason.org/Latrain26.htm

'He was Elijah the prophet, the seventh angelic messenger to the Laodicean Church Age (Footprints on the Sands of Time, p. 620).

I believe that God could have allowed a prophet to function in the spirit of Elijah. But that does not make you Prophet Elijah himself.

Branham believed that the Lord gave him the interpretations of the seals and that he was that 7th angel.

According to Branham, Wesley was the 6th angel - Revelation 9:14-15: "saying to the sixth angel who had the trumpet, "Release the four angels who are bound at the great river Euphrates." So, the four angels, who had been prepared for the hour and day and month and year, were released to kill a third of mankind."

Prophet Branham was indisputably a true prophet of God and a very humble man. But later in his ministry, he departed from truth embraced a false identity and was ensnared by the loner mentality and God removed him from the earth.

John Alexander Dowie

Alexander Dowie was a yielded anointed man of God. God used him greatly and very powerfully in the healing ministry until he called himself Elijah.

https://www.ministryexploit.com/history-biography-of-john-alexander-dowie/

Things began to crumble, and Dowie declared himself "Elijah the Restorer" or Elijah III. (First Elijah, then John the Baptist, then himself) He walked around dressed in an Old Testament-like priest's outfit. In 1905, he had a stroke and traveled to Mexico, where he bought a large tract of land for a "plantation paradise." In April 1906, the community and his family had finally had enough. Zion City was in financial ruin, his daughter had died, and his marriage had disintegrated. His wife claimed that he was promoting polygamy.

Dowie had a second stroke, which immobilized him. He was removed as the head of Zion, and lived a broken man for a few more months, until his death on March 11, 1907.

Here is the warning for those who want to be used by God. Don't let Elijah syndrome or your pride and ego get in the way and hinder you from entering your promised land.

Avoid grandiose titles and names. Avoid a superiority complex. Be a faithful man or woman of God, be humble and commit to God yield to him more of yourself and die more. The more the father uses you, the more you should cripple your flesh. We will not see an end-time move of God until we restore the message of the cross of Jesus, the message of death to self. We must see a marriage of Calvary and Pentecostalism.

8. Office Of A Prophet Vs. The Gift Of Prophecy?

One of the reasons there is confusion in the church today about the prophetic gift is the failure to distinguish between the "gift or office of the prophet" and the "gift of prophesying."

There is a difference between the Prophetic Ministry or ministering prophetically and the Prophetic Office. The first is a function, whereas the second is a position.

Romans 11:13: For I speak to you Gentiles, inasmuch as I am the apostle of the Gentiles, I magnify my office.

1 Timothy 3:1: This is a true saying, If a man desires the office of a bishop, he desires a good work.

In each of these cases, you will see that the term office is used to refer to someone who has been appointed to a position.

Paul clarifies this in 1 Corinthians 14:27-31. Paul refers to two kinds of prophetic ministry.

1. The first is what is communicated by vocal gifts.

Anyone who brings a message from the Lord by tongues, interpretation, or prophecy is prophesying.

2. Those who hold the office of a prophet are very separate from the ones above. You may all prophesy in the sense of bringing a word from the Lord for edification, but not all church members have the Prophetic Office.

Another passage that clearly shows the distinction is Acts 21:9. Philip the Evangelist was known to have daughters who prophesied. 9 And the same man (Philip) had four daughters, virgins, who prophesied.

10 And as we tarried [there] many days, there came down from Judaea a certain prophet, named Agabus. Philip had four daughters that exercised a prophetic ministry, but they were not classed as prophets. Agabus, however, held the prophetic office and was referred to as a prophet.

You may be able to prophesy, but this does not make you a prophet, only those who have been permanently appointed to the office of a prophet can be called by such a title. It is a fearful, and dangerous thing to title yourself with a title that God has not entrusted to you. There is a price attached to every call. Make sure you are willing to pay the price and wrestle with self and go through the trials associated with the prophet's office before assuming the office.

A prophet is a part of the fivefold ministry and a gift from Christ to the body of Christ. And the gift of prophesying is given by the Holy Spirit to individuals within the Church for the edification of the body as they yield themselves to God.

According to Ephesians 4:11-16, "He, Christ, gave some... i.e., prophets (Note the significance of the plural use of prophets emphasizing the importance of functioning in plurality for mutual accountability and judging of the prophesies given to the church) for the 1) perfecting of the saints, 2) for the work of the ministry, 3) for the edifying of the body of Christ. This passage clearly states that these equipping leaders were themselves a gift of Christ to His church and it was not just the gift of prophecy that was given.

1 Corinthians 12:28: "And God hath set some in the church, first apostles, secondarily prophets, thirdly teachers..." in the church. We see that it is God who set the Prophets in the Church. Those who claim that the Prophetic Office no longer exists should contend with this scripture's validity.

A prophet is an equipping leader. He is qualified according to function in the "office" of a prophet. "Office" implies position or rank. There are three uses of the word "office" in the KJV, which include:

Romans 11:13, Romans 12:4 and 1 Timothy 3:1

In Romans 11:13 Paul said, "I am the apostle of the Gentiles, I magnify mine "office" (Greek for diakonia meaning service, ministry). Romans 12:4 states, "For as we have many members in the one body, and all members have not the same "office. 1 Timothy 3:1 says, "This is a true saying if a man desire, the "office" (Greek word episcope meaning oversite) of a bishop, he desireth a good work."

The "office" is a descriptive function. The different Greek names given to represent the various leaders in the church (i.e. apostles, prophets, evangelists, pastors, teachers, deacons, etc.), simply describe who these leaders were and what their function was in the church.

The servant leaders described in Ephesians 4:11 were themselves gifts to the church. Their primary purpose was to serve and lead by example. Their primary function was 1) For the perfecting of the saints, 2) for the work of ministry, and 3) for the edifying of the body of Christ.

Those who serve in the function or "office" of a prophet, that is as a "gift" from Christ to the church. They operate in this gift as their primary ministry. Because the prophets are a "gift" to the church, the prophet consistently walks in that gift because that is who they are in the Body of Christ.

Make certain of your calling or you will be the most miserable of all men or women. Be sure that this is what God is calling you to do. Die to your flesh while you wait for God to release you. Don't release yourself only to be destroyed by the devil.

Prophesying

Now, concerning "prophesying." It is available to any believer in the Body of Christ. According to 1 Corinthians 12:7, "The manifestation of the Spirit is given to every man to profit withal." 1 Corinthians 12:8, "For to one is given by the Spirit."

In 1 Corinthians 12:11, it states, "But all these worketh that one and the selfsame Spirit, dividing to every man severally as he will." 1 Corinthians 12:18 says, "But now hath God set the members every one of them in the body, as it hath pleased him."

In 1 Corinthians 12:29 it says, "Are all apostles? (No') Are all prophets? (No') Are all teachers?" 'No')

Thus, we see that the "gift of prophesying" is available from the Holy Spirit to all believers in the Body of Christ. The "gift of prophesying" can be ministered by the Spirit through any yielded believer in the Body of Christ at any time the Spirit chooses. The persons who minister in the "gift of prophesying" do so by the unction of the Holy Spirit. Persons who are moved by the Spirit to prophesy may be led to prophesy "only one time" or "many times," depending upon how the Holy Spirit leads him or her.

The gift of prophecy is for edification, exhortations, and comfort.

1 Corinthians 14:3: but he who prophesies speaks edification and exhortation and comfort to men.

Prophecy is divinely inspired and anointed babble or utterance, a supernatural miraculous proclamation in a known language. It does not proceed from intellect but is a manifestation of the Spirit. Prophecy is the vehicle that transports the divine message to its desired destination. This will be explained further in the spiritual gift manual.

1 Corinthians 12:7: This ability to prophesy can be possessed and operated by all born-again Christians who are baptized of the Holy Spirit and are yielded to God.

1 Corinthians 14:31: For you can all prophesy in turn so that everyone may be instructed and encouraged?

I have witnessed personally church services where this gift was manifested cordially during consecrated worship. It is beautiful to behold; it is so orderly and so harmonious.

1 Samuel 10:5-6: Sometimes the gift will manifest when a true prophet or prophets are present (5) Afterward you will come to the hill of God where the Philistine garrison is; and it shall be as soon as you have come there to the city, that you will meet a group of prophets coming down from the high place with harp, tambourine, flute, and a lyre before them, and they will be prophesying.

1 Samuel 10:9-10: When Saul turned around to leave Samuel, God changed his heart, and all the signs came about that day. When Saul and his attendant arrived at Gibeah, a group of prophets met him. Then the Spirit of God took control of him, and he prophesied along with them.

And sometimes when hands are laid on you by an anointed minister, that gift can be activated and it will manifest.

Acts 19:1-6: And when Paul had laid his hands upon them, the Holy Spirit came on them, and they began speaking with tongues and prophesying.

Why is prophecy important?

There are five reasons why prophecy is so important in the local church:

- Prophecy brings life. Prophecy brought life to the valley of dry bones
- (Ezekiel 37:1-4).
- Prophecy gives clarity to spiritual vision. The Bible says, "Where there is no vision, the people perish.' The Lord gives vision through the prophetic word (Proverbs 29:13, 18).
- Prophecy edifies, warns, exhorts, and comforts (1 Corinthians 14:3).
- Prophecy brings revival and restoration. True prophecy brings restoration and revival (Acts 2:16-18).
- God uses prophecy to direct and guide (Acts 13:1-3).

Seven Ways to Judge Prophecy

- By their fruits you shall know them (Matthew 7:16-18,20).
- Does it glorify Christ (John 16:14; 1 Corinthians 12:3; I John 4:1-2)?
- Does it agree with the Scriptures (Isaiah 8:20)?
- Are their prophecies fulfilled? (Deuteronomy 18:22) Some prophecies are not of God, even though they may come to pass. The benchmark remains that all prophecies should exalt the Lord Jesus.
- Is the prophecy disjointed or confused? True prophecy is line upon line and precept upon precept (Isaiah 28:13).
- Do the prophecies produce liberty or bondage (Romans 8:15)?
- Prophecies should be witnessed with our spirit (1 John 2:20,27).

The first part of man, namely his spirit, the origin in man of all the Divine activity; this is the sphere and instrument of all the operations of God. God is a spirit, and only the spirit can have access to or fellowship with spirit.

- Only spirit can know spirit (1 Corinthians 2:9-11).
- Only spirit can serve the spirit. (Romans 1:9, 7:6, 12:11).
- Only spirit can worship God Who is Spirit. (John 4:23,24; Philippians 3:3).
- Only the spirit can receive revelation from God Who is the spirit (Revelation 1:10, 1 Corinthians 2:10). We shall return to this later.

God is determined to have all His dealings with man and fulfill all His purposes through man by means of his spirit; so, we can rely on the spiritual man inside to confirm what God is saying.

The Dual Principle of Essence
The Composition of Man

The creation of man was accomplished in two stages.

- The physical phase, which began with the first man, Adam.
- The spiritual state which began with the second Adam, Jesus Christ.

1 Corinthians 15:45-46: And so it is written, the first man Adam was made a living soul; the last Adam was made a quickening spirit. 46 Howbeit that was not first which is spiritual, but that which is natural; and afterward that which is spiritual.

Man was made from his creation and birth with a human spirit, which became an integral part of man, but he was still mentally and spiritually incomplete. He needed another Spirit, the Holy Spirit of God.

And when the Holy Spirit is received, God's Spirit itself bears witness with our spirit that we are children of God, Romans 8:16. The Spirit itself beareth witness with our spirit, that we are the children of God:

This is the begotten stage of man's spiritual creation.

This is clearly explained in 1 Corinthians 2:9: "But as it is written, Eye hath not seen, nor ear heard, neither have entered into the heart of man, the things which God hath prepared for them that love him."

This is spiritual knowledge mentioned here it has not entered the natural mind of man.

The natural mind can receive knowledge of material and physical things. It can have a sense of morality, ethics, art and culture. These are qualities not possessed by animals. Man acquired knowledge in the realm of good and evil.

Man acquired this knowledge from the tree of knowledge of good and evil.

He can know and perform what is good only on the human level, this is only made possible by the human spirit within man.

But this performance is limited to the human level of the human spirit. This essence is selfish, and rebellious. He can express love on the human level, but without the Holy Spirit of God he cannot possess or express love on the God level nor can he acquire knowledge of that which is spiritual,

1 Corinthians 2:10: But God hath revealed them unto us by his Spirit: for the Spirit searcheth all things, yea, the deep things of God."

But God has revealed spiritual things unto us by his Spirit. Notice that spiritual knowledge is revealed by a person called the Holy Spirit referred to here as God's Spirit.

God is the revealer. 1 Corinthians 2:11: "For what man knoweth the things of a man, save the spirit of man which is in him? Even so the things of God knoweth no man, but the Spirit of God."

The natural man with this one spirit is limited. The things of God knoweth no man but the Spirit of God. Only when the Holy Spirit enters combining with the human spirit can a man come to comprehend that which is spiritual?

But the natural man received not the things of the Spirit of God, for they are foolishness to him? Neither can he know them, because they are spiritually discerned.

1 Corinthians 2:14: "But the natural man receiveth not the things of the Spirit of God: for they are foolishness unto him: neither can he know them, because they are spiritually discerned."

That is why the most highly educated people are the most ignorant and limited in spiritual cognizance. They are confined to knowledge of the material, self-centered level, the knowledge of God, and the things of God are foolishness to them.

God says the wisdom of this world is foolishness with God (1 Corinthians 3:19).

1 Corinthians 3:19: "For the wisdom of this world is foolishness with God. For it is written, He taketh the wise in their own craftiness."

Job 5:13: He taketh the wise in their own craftiness: and the counsel of the forward is carried headlong.

As beasts are taken in a trap or birds in a snare or net, these crafty men, who are wise in their own opinion are entangled and taken in their own schemes; their knowledge trips them,

God's purpose in creating a man on earth.

- To restore the government of God on earth, and regulate or govern human life, through God's government by developing righteous and spiritual character.
- To develop the deposit of the kingdom of God inside of you and eventually grow into maturity and sonship in preparation to rule and reign with Christ in the millennia.

These two goals require that man reject Satan's ways and embrace God's ways. One-third of the angels who became evil could not be changed. Eternal things are not subject to change.

But physical matters are constantly changing.

God's grand plan for his spiritual creation included the word divesting himself of his supreme glory and taking on him the likeness of the human flesh as Jesus Christ, making it possible for God to reproduce himself in us.

Man can now be born into God's family. The first human, Adam, was created with the potential of qualifying to replace Satan on Earth's throne to restore the government of God but he needed to resist and reject Satan's ways, which were the foundation of an evil government.

Genesis 3:8: "And they heard the voice of the LORD God walking in the garden in the cool of the day: and Adam and his wife hid themselves from the presence of the LORD God amongst the trees of the garden."

God gave them responsibilities to accomplish.

- To Reflect His Image, God created Adam and Eve in His image (Genesis 1:27).
- To Tend and Keep the Garden, 'dress it' and 'keep it'" (Genesis 2:15, KJV). Using their "physical and mental faculties," they had to "preserve the garden in the same perfect state in which [they] had received it,"
- To Name the Animals (Genesis 1:20-26; 2:19). He brought them all to Adam "to see what he would name them; and whatever the man called each living creature, which was its name.
- To Take Charge of All Other Creatures, God appointed them to "have dominion over the fish of the sea, and over the fowl of the air, and over the cattle, and over all the earth, and over every creeping thing that creepeth upon the earth" (Genesis 1:26, KJV). The relationship of man to the rest of the creation was to be one of rulership. By transferring the ruling power over "all the earth" to Adam and Eve, God planned to make [them] His representatives over the earth.
- To Never Eat from One of the Two Special Trees in the Garden, "all kinds of trees grow out of the ground—trees that [are] pleasing to the eye and good for food." And Adam and Eve were free to eat from any of those except one (Genesis 2:9, 16-17).

In the middle of the garden stood the tree of life and the tree of the knowledge of good and evil (Genesis 2:9).

Meanwhile, the tree of the knowledge of good and evil was the one God prohibited Adam and Eve to eat from Genesis 2:16-17.

God did not want Adam and Eve to know evil.

To Multiply, Fill, and Subdue the Earth

After creating Adam and Eve, God blessed them to multiply, fill, and subdue the earth (Genesis 1:28).

This was a period of learning. Satan gave them time to learn then Satan came to the scene when the man and the woman decided to break the governing laws by violating divine established boundaries to live without the confines of God's laws.

God had instructed them in the governing knowledge of God and the spiritual laws. Satan was restrained from any contact with them until God first had taught them.

There is a similarity with Revelation 20:7-10.

Revelation 20:7-10: "When the thousand years are over, Satan will be released from his prison and will go out to deceive the nations in the four corners of the earth—Gog and Magog—to gather them for battle. In number, they are like the sand on the seashore. They marched across the breadth of the earth and surrounded the camp of God's people, the city he loves. But fire came down from heaven and devoured them. And the devil, who deceived them, was thrown into the lake of burning sulfur, where the beast and the false prophet had been thrown. They will be tormented day and night for ever and ever."

"Why will God release Satan at the end of the millennial reign of Jesus Christ?" To do the same thing he did in the garden, evaluate their knowledge of 1000 years under Christ.

At the beginning of the millennium, only believers will be alive (Revelation 19:17-21), some who live through the tribulation period, and some who come back with the Lord at His second coming. It will be a time of peace unparalleled in history (Isaiah 2:4; Micah 4:3). Jesus will be ruling on the throne of David.

The believers who live through the tribulation will be mortal. They will live and repopulate the earth during the millennial kingdom. Without the devastation of sin taking its toll.

All those who are born during the millennium will enjoy the benefits and blessings of Christ's reign on the earth, but they will still be born with a sinful nature, and they will still have to freely repent and believe the gospel, personally choosing Christ as Savior and Lord.

Yet, at the end of the millennial reign, Satan is loosed and can deceive a vast multitude to follow him in one final rebellion against the Lord of glory and His saints!

God is going to keep Satan away from the millennial period so that the people living on Earth can learn the necessary lessons. And then after that, he will be unleashed again to evaluate them to see if they have learned the lesson.

Adam did not have life inherent, self-containing life, but he had a human spirit that needed to be united with God's Holy Spirit. If his human spirit were united with God's Holy Spirit it could have given him eternal life. But God offered him immortal life through the tree of life.

God did not force or compel him to take it. He merely made it freely accessible. Adam was to eat all the trees of the garden except the one forbidden tree of the knowledge of good and evil.

What if Adam had taken from the Tree of Life?

There is one difference between the original Adam and a Christian today. Adam had not yet sinned, and no repentance was necessary. If he had chosen the Tree of Life, Adam would have received the Holy Spirit of the immortal God to join with his human spirit.

Adam was required to make a choice, He would have rejected the way of Satan, by taking from the tree of life. He would have received the Holy Spirit of God to unite with his human spirit.

This would have united him mentally and spiritually with God. Just as the converted spirit inside the begotten Christian. Christ in us is the hope of glory Colossians 1:27.

The mind of Christ is mentioned in Philippians 2:5. The very mind of God would have been in Adam, but instead, the mind and the attitude of Satan entered him and worked in him.

Ephesians 2:2: Satan as the prince of the power, the air does indeed actually work within humans.

Satan began to work in the mind of Adam even as God would have worked in his mind had he taken of the Tree of Life.

Christ is the author of eternal life (nor is there salvation in any other, Acts 4:12). No one except Christ is during paradise (Revelation 2:7) and of the street of the city (Revelation 22:2). Christ is in the midst of the church.

Jesus is like a Tree of Life in the sense that we have life in Him, which lasts forever. Jesus is like a Tree of Life. Those who believe in Him have eternal life through Him. Jesus is life.

The Ascendancy of the Spiritual Man Over the Natural Man

In the fall, the soul was allowed to take the ascendancy over the spirit; the spirit with conscience, communion, and intuition being subjected to the soul with its reason, desire, and volition. This ascendancy of the soul made man what he is afterward called;

the "natural" i.e., soulish (Gk. psukikos) man, and inasmuch as it was the reasoning and desiring and choosing that were inspired and prompted by the devil, and the capitulation was to him, and the spirit union with God was rejected and violated in all its claims. The result is that man is not only separated from God but is horizoned by a lower life than was intended in his natural state.

But more, he is then called "flesh"; this is the active law of his fallen condition. It is not something in him; it is himself, the real principle of his being, and it is always set over against "spirit," which is the real principle of life reunited with God by regeneration.

We will deal with this topic in a later chapter on Spirit, soul, and body.

The importance of breaking

John 12:24

Verily, verily, I say unto you, Except a corn of wheat fall into the ground and die, it abideth alone: but if it die, it bringeth forth much fruit."

Hebrews 4:12-13: For the word of God is quick, and powerful, and sharper than any two edged sword, piercing even to the dividing asunder of soul and spirit, and of the joints and marrow, and is a discerner of the thoughts and intents of the heart.

13 Neither is there any creature that is not manifest in his sight: but all thing s are naked and opened unto the eyes of him with whom we have to do.

1 Corinthians 2:11-14: For what man knoweth the things of a man, save the spirit of man which is in him? even so the things of God knoweth no man, but the Spirit of God.

12 Now we have received, not the spirit of the world, but the spirit which is of God; that we might know the things that are freely given to us of God.

13 Which things also we speak, not in the words which man's wisdom teacheth, but which the Holy Ghost teacheth; comparing spiritual things with spiritual.

14 But the natural man receiveth not the things of the Spirit of God: for they are foolishness unto him: neither can he know them, because they are spiritually discerned.

2 Corinthians 3:6: Who also hath made us able ministers of the New Testament; not of the letter, but of the spirit: for the letter killeth, but the spirit giveth life.

Romans 1:9: For God is my witness, whom I serve with my spirit in the gospel of his Son, that without ceasing I make mention of you always in my prayers.

Romans 7:6: But now we are delivered from the law, that being dead wherein we were held; that we should serve in newness of spirit, and not in the oldness of the letter.

Romans 8:4-8: That the righteousness of the law might be fulfilled in us, who walk not after the flesh, but after the Spirit.

5 For they that are after the flesh do mind the things of the flesh; but they that are after the Spirit the things of the Spirit.

6 For to be carnally minded is death; but to be spiritually minded is life and peace.

7 Because the carnal mind is enmity against God: for it is not subject to the law of God, neither indeed can be.

8 So then they that are in the flesh cannot please God.

Galatians 5:16-25

16 This I say then, walk in the Spirit, and ye shall not fulfil the lust of the flesh.

17 For the flesh lusteth against the Spirit, and the Spirit against the flesh: and these are contrary the one to the other: so that ye cannot do the things that ye would.

18 But if ye be led by the Spirit, ye are not under the law.

19 Now the works of the flesh are manifest, which are these, Adultery, fornication, uncleanness, lasciviousness,

20 Idolatry, witchcraft, hatred, variance, emulations, wrath, strife, seditions, heresies,

21 Envying's, murders, drunkenness, revellings, and such like: of the which I tell you before, as I have also told you in time past, that they which do such things shall not inherit the kingdom of God.

22 But the fruit of the Spirit is love, joy, peace, longsuffering, gentleness, goodness, faith,

23 Meekness, temperance: against such there is no law.

24 And they that are Christ's have crucified the flesh with the affections and lusts.

25 If we live in the Spirit, let us also walk in the Spirit.

26 Let us not be desirous of vain glory, provoking one another, envying one another.

Sooner or later, any honest and true servant of God will discover that self is the greatest exasperation and ruination to his own work or calling.

You begin to perceive that the old nature is not compatible with your spirit man. They cannot flourish together. The old nature seeks its own expression, while the spirit man seeks his own expression.

You begin to determine that the old nature cannot be subjected willingly to the rule of the Spirit without discretionary persuasion or a strict regimen and that the old nature cannot work according to God's highest demands.

You discover that the greatest hindrance to your work or service is the flesh, and that if the flesh is alive, it will frustrate you or even impede you from exercising your spirit.

Every son or daughter of God, those who have inculcated their senses, those who have vanquished and subjugated their carnal senses. Who are led by the spirit. These ones should be able to exercise their spirit to secure God's presence.

The Holy Spirit enables us to inculcate God's word by the Spirit, to impact the human condition by divine input from the Spirit, to convey God's mind through the Spirit, and to dispense and recover divine revelation within His Spirit.

Yet the frustration of the flesh makes it impossible to use your spirit. Many vessels of the Lord are currently shelved and rendered debilitated and infirm to perform the Lord's work, they have never been dealt with by the Lord in their flesh. The cross has not cut deeper into their experience. The sword of God's word has not yet punctured their fleshy armor with truth that transforms.

Without this kind of dealing, they are unqualified and incompetent for any spiritual work. The excitements become fleshly sentiments, zeal becomes schematic, and prayers become feeble.

God must baptize the yielded vessel with death. Your flesh must be disfigured, your pride must be mortified, and your self must be muted before you can become a useful vessel to the Lord.

9.
Common Fallacies Prophecy:

The gift of prophecy (1 Corinthians 12) and the Office of the prophet (Ephesians 4:11) are the same thing.

There is a gift of prophecy, there maybe even be prophetic people. But not everyone is a prophet. For example, you may wear a LeBron James shirt, but that does not transform you into LeBron James. You may prophesy, but prophesying and giving out words of knowledge does not qualify you to stand in the office of a prophet, much like wearing a Cleveland Browns Jersey does not qualify you to play for the Cleveland Browns. You must be called, signed, prepared, qualified, and released by God. There are no shortcuts.

To walk in the office of a prophet, you must have a clear call, not empty suggestions and feelings. Consistent manifestation, demonstration, and validation of your calling by the Holy Spirit are required. You must be tested and proven with time.

You must develop an intimate relationship with God and be able to manifest two of the revelation gifts (word of wisdom, word of knowledge, or discerning of spirits) plus prophecy.

But even if you have those, don't presume you are a prophet already. Prophets must be called by God directly and released by God himself or through tried and tested prophetic presbyters.

You still need character formation, growth, death to self-daily. Don't rush. Wait upon the Lord to call you or release you. Don't release yourself.

- **Prophecy is the same as the interpretation of tongues.**

The Bible says, "greater is he that prophesieth than he that speaketh with tongues" (1 Corinthians 14:5).

Both are inspired utterances. Tongues, of course, are inspired utterance in an "unknown" tongue. The interpretation of tongues is inspired utterance saying that which was spoken in tongues. Prophecy, on the other hand, is inspired utterance in a "known" tongue. The difference between interpretation and prophecy is that interpretation is dependent upon tongues, whereas prophecy is not.

- **Prophecy is only a prediction of the future (Foretelling).**

People think that "prophecy" means predicting (foretelling) what will happen in the future. Prophecy in the New Testament church carries no prediction aspect with it whatsoever, for "he that prophesies speaketh unto men to edification, and exhortation, and comfort" (1 Corinthians 14:3). Notice that there is no mention of the word prediction here. This does not mean that the prediction element is no longer needed. The office of a prophet mainly does prediction. Like Agabus, the prophet in the New Testament predicted famine.

Acts 11:28 and there stood up one of them named Agabus, and signified by the Spirit that there should be great dearth throughout all the world: which came to pass in the days of Claudius Caesar."

- **Prophecy is the same thing as preaching.**

The words "preach" and "prophesy" come from two entirely different Greek words. To "preach" means to proclaim, announce, cry, or tell.

Jesus said, "Go ye into all the world, and Preach the gospel…" (Mark 16:15). He didn't say to prophesy the Gospel.

The word prophecy as we defined earlier means to "bubble up, to flow forth," Teaching and preaching are preplanned, but prophecy is spontaneous.

- **Prophecy must be Acrimonious:**

The Bible is very clear on this topic of love. I know that many people in the prophetic are often accused of being controlling, intimidating, not loving, and very hard to deal with. But let us look at this scripture.

Though I speak with the tongues of men and angels but have not love, I have become sounding brass or a clanging cymbal. And though I have the gift of prophecy, and understand all mysteries and all knowledge, and though I have all faith, so that I could remove mountains, but have no love, I am nothing" (1 Corinthians 13:4-1).

There are many angry, carnal and hate-filled prophets Out there who are like clanging cymbals'. They are false prophets deceiving many people and being deceived themselves. They don't exhibit love. Their message is not love but mixed with hurt and rejections they have received in their lives; they are angry and unforgiving. They will mix their messages with all those personal issues, and this brings forth a very diluted and polluted brook. And they don't offer fresh living water. Mixtures are dangerous for prophets.

The more you grow in your prophetic call, the more wilderness and Gethsemane experiences you will pass through for great lessons that you will never learn in a seminary or institutionalized settings. Great spiritual riches are available in the place of death; God is creating a heart full of love, and his heart is full of it. Love drove him to the cross without hesitation. Love is not a license to sin.

The desert is a very rich place for developing love in the heart of a prophet; lessons are learned in the spirit as the flesh gives way to God in the dry wilderness. The desert will sharpen you and humble you until you are clothed in humility and love. The father wants to entrust his heart to his Prophets. Prophets must be like the green olive tree, which thrives in the wilderness, deeply rooted into the ground, deeply rooted in God, and can withstand any season yet remaining ever green.

Philippians 2:6-9: For He did not consider equality with God something to be grasped, but made himself nothing, taking the very nature of a servant, being made in human likeness. And being found in appearance as a man, he humbled himself and became obedient to death, even death on a cross! Therefore, God exalted him to the highest place and gave him the name that is above every name.

- **Prophecy should be castigatory.**

Prophets too often assume they know what is right and wrong. If you are tempted to dispense a critical word, it is probably not prophecy. It is criticism. If your prophecy hurts people, you are likely being urgent and not prophetic.

- **Prophecy is constantly rebuffed.**

Prophecy is not always spurned, but prophetic words must be subjected to spiritual judgement and liability. And therefore, we must expect that there will be those that will reject it or shun it. The Old Testament prophets often were rejected and scorned. Rejection is a common experience for people exercising prophetic. However, dwelling on rejections and seeking concurrence can lead to improbable suppositions.

Prophetic people are especially susceptible to rejection. This rejection can lead to bitterness, negativism, and misery – all things that make prophetic people useless for the ministry of the Holy Spirit. In rejection, we must open our hearts so that the love of God can flow in.

- **Prophecy must be Indignant and poignant.**

Don't allow the past wounds into your prophecy. Too often, the very thing we prophesied against is the very thing that is tripping us up in our personal life. This type of "prophecy" is dangerous because it often brings condemnation and not encouragement to others. Don't allow your anger or unresolved biased issues into the prophetic word. Avoid the hysterical submit under the movement of the Holy Spirit and be self-controlled. Know when the Holy Spirit is done speaking and know when the flesh begins to infringe upon your sentiments.

- **Discernment, the word of knowledge, is prophecy.**

Many times, prophetic people can spiritually perceive sinful dispositions, which they can confuse with the gift of discernment. Discernment is not prophecy. Prophecy needs discernment. Supernatural knowledge about people's lives or situations does not make one prophetic. Diviners and physics can do the same. The false prophet may look like a sheep, but they attack like the wolf. They seek to devour by causing people to either believe a lie or to put their trust in some other place than truly following Jesus or his word. This is what makes them dangerous.

- **Prophecy must lead to prominence, gain.**

The danger of Self-Promotion, fame, materialism, and worldliness always seeks out weak-willed prophets who are trapped by their wicked, unrestrained senses. They seek the pleasures of this life through their ministry platform while manipulating and taking advantage of others. This is not prophecy but divination and is very dangerous. Another trap I commonly see prophetic people fall into is the desire to be rich, popular and compelling in ministry." This is the opposite of the true Spirit of prophecy (Revelation 19:10).

Prophecy is meant to testify to the awesomeness of Jesus, not to the prophetic ministry or the personal facade of man.

10.
THE OLD TESTAMENT PROPHET (CLASSIFICATION OF THE PROPHETS)

Prophets of the Old Testament are usually grouped as writing and oral prophets. Within these two groupings is another classification based on size, and not on content, or on quality of inspiration. Four prophetic books were longer in content and therefore called "major prophets." It does not mean the "major prophets" were more important or significant in subject matter than the "minor prophets." The "minor prophets" signify shorter books and nothing more. Those who call themselves Major Prophets, or senior prophets or senior "papa" today are nothing but prideful narcissistic ignominious whited sepulchers clamoring for earthly validations.

- Major writing prophets: Isaiah, Jeremiah, Ezekiel, and Daniel.
- Minor writing prophets: Hosea, Joel, Amos, Obadiah, Jonah, Micah, Nahum, Habakkuk, Zephaniah, Haggai, Zechariah, and Malachi.

The Oral Prophets:

1. Enoch (Jude 14-15)
2. Noah (2 Peter 2:5)
3. Abraham and the Patriarchs (Genesis 20:7; 27:27-29; 49)
4. Moses (Deuteronomy 18:18-22; 34:10-12)
5. Miriam and Aaron (Exodus 15:20; Numbers. 12:1-8)
6. The Seventy (Numbers. 11:24-29)
7. Balaam (Numbers 22-24)

8. Joshua (Joshua 1, 23, 24)
9. Deborah (Judges 4-5)
10. Unknown prophet in days of Gideon (Judges 6:7-10)
11. Unknown prophet in days of Eli (I Samuel 2:27-36)
12. Samuel (I Samuel 3:20)
13. Schools of prophets under Samuel (Saul) (I Samuel 10:10-12; 19:20-24)
14. Gad (I Samuel 22:5; 2 Samuel 24:11-19; I Chronicles 29:29; 2 Chronicles 29:25)
15. Nathan (2 Samuel 7, 12; 2 Chronicles. 9:29; 29:25)
16. David (Acts 2:30)
17. Ahijah (I Kings 11:26-40; 14:1-18)
18. Man of God from Judah (I Kings 13)
19. Shemaiah (I Kings 12:21-24; 2 Chronicles 12:1-8)
20. Iddo the Seer (2 Chronicles 12:15; 13:22)
21. Azariah (2 Chronicles 15)
22. Hanani (2 Chronicles 16:7-10)
23. Jehu son of Hanani (2 Chronicles 19:1-3)
24. Elijah (I Kings 17-2; I Kings 2)
25. Micaiah (I Kings 22)
26. Unknown prophet encouraged Ahab (I Kings 20:13-15)
27. An unknown prophet rebuked Ahab (I Kings 20:35-43).
28. Jahaziel (2 Chronicles 20:14-17)
29. Eliezer (2 Chronicles 20:37)
30. Elisha (2 Kings 2-8)
31. Prophetic School of Elisha (2 Kings 9:1-13)
32. Zechariah son of Jehoiada (2 Chronicles 24:20-22)
33. Man of God forbade Amaziah's league with Israel (2 Chronicles 25:7-10)
34. Unknown prophet rebuked Amaziah (2 Chronicles 25:15)
35. Zechariah (2 Chronicles 26:5)
36. Oded (2 Chronicles 28:8-15)
37. Huldah the prophetess (2 Kings 22:12-20)
38. Urijah (Jeremiah 26:20-23)

Work in the Old Testament

In most cases, the prophets were not "professionals" in the sense of earning a living from their prophetic activities. God designated them for special duties while amid other professions. Some prophets like (Jeremiah and Ezekiel) were priests with the responsibilities described above. Others were shepherds, including Moses and Amos. Deborah was a judge adjudicating issues for the Israelites. Huldah was a teacher.

When the unified kingdom split in two, the ten northern tribes (Israel) plunged immediately into idol worship. Elijah and Elisha, the last among the former prophets, were called by God to challenge these idolatrous Israelites to worship Yahweh alone. The first literary prophets, Amos, and Hosea, were called to challenge the apostate northern kings of Israel from Jeroboam through Hoshea.

Because kings and people refused to return to God, God allowed the powerful empire of Assyria to overthrow the northern kingdom of Israel (2 Kings 17:1-23).

A prophet's primary function in the Old Testament was to serve as God's representative or envoy, communicating God's mind to his people. True prophets never spoke on their own authority or shared their personal opinions, but rather delivered the message God himself gave them. God promised Moses, "Now go; I will help you speak and will teach you what to say" (Exodus 4:12). God assured Moses, "I will raise up for [my people] a prophet like you . . . and I will put my words in his mouth. He will tell them everything I command him" (Deuteronomy 18:18).

The Lord said to Jeremiah, "I have put my words in your mouth" (Jeremiah 1:9). God commissioned Ezekiel by saying, "You must speak my words to them" (Ezekiel 2:7). And many of the Old Testament prophetic books begin with the words, "The word of the LORD that came to . . ." (Hosea 1:2; Joel 1:1; Micah 1:1; Zephaniah. 1:1; Jonah 1:1). Amos claimed, "This is what the LORD says" (Amos 1:3).

Prophetic ministry was not restricted to only men in the Old Testament. Moses's sister Miriam is called a "prophet" (Exodus 15:20), as are Deborah (Judges. 4:4) and Huldah (2 Kings 22:14–20). We occasionally read of groups or bands of prophets ministering in Israel (1 Samuel 10:5; 1 Kings 18:4), referred to as "the company of the prophets" (2 Kings 2:3, 5, 7; 4:38).

The Bible doesn't explain how the word of the Lord came to a prophet, although in addition to the audible and internal voice of God, there are several instances in which the Lord revealed his will through visions (1 Samuel 3:1,15; 2 Samuel 7:17; Isaiah 1:1; Ezekiel 11:24) or dreams (Numbers 12:6).

The divine inspiration and authority of the Old Testament prophetic voice is clearly affirmed in 2 Peter 1:20–21: "No prophecy of Scripture came about by the prophet's own interpretation of things. For prophecy never had its origin in the human will, but prophets, though human, spoke from God as they were carried along by the Holy Spirit."

Those who claimed to speak for God were held to a strict standard of judgment. Even should an alleged prophet perform a sign or wonder or accurately predict the future, if he says, "Let us follow other gods . . . and let us worship them" (Deuteronomy 13:2), he is to be rejected (Deuteronomy 13:3). Likewise, if the word he speaks "does not take place or come true, that is a message the LORD has not spoken" (Deuteronomy 18:22; see also Jeremiah. 14:14; 23:21, 32; 28:15; Ezekiel 13:6). The punishment for speaking falsely in God's name was death (Deuteronomy 18:20).

After Samuel anointed Saul and throughout the time of Israel', prophets largely advised the king, delivering words of warning, divine guidance, and encouragement.

Nathan's well-known rebuke of David for his adulterous relationship with Bathsheba and his complicity in the death of her husband is a case in point (2 Samuel 12).

Being a mouthpiece for the word of the Lord was often a dangerous calling. People frequently mocked, rejected, persecuted, and even killed God's prophets (2 Chronicles 36:16; Jeremiah 11:21; 18:18; 20:2, 7–10). Stephen, the first martyr of the new covenant, pointedly asked, "Was there ever a prophet your ancestors did not persecute" (Acts 7:52)?

II.
The Prophets of the New Testament

The most prominent prophetic voice in the New Testament, aside from Jesus himself, was John the Baptist (Matthew 11:9; Luke 1:76). On the day of Pentecost, Peter declared that unlike the more limited exercise of prophecy during the time of the old covenant, God would henceforth pour out his Spirit "on all people" (Acts 2:17). Peter said the result would be a fulfillment of God's words: "Your sons and daughters will prophesy, your young men will see visions, your old men will dream dreams. Even on my servants, both men and women, I will pour out my Spirit in those days, and they will prophesy" (Acts 2:17–18).

Prophetic ministry in the early church was widespread and diverse. A band of prophets traveled from Jerusalem to Antioch, and one of them, Agabus, "stood up and through the Spirit predicted that a severe famine would spread over the entire Roman world" (Acts 11:28). Prophets were active in the church at Antioch (Acts 13:1), Tyre (Acts 21:4), and Caesarea, where the four daughters of Philip prophesied (Acts 21:8–9). Prophecy, one of the gifts of the Spirit designed for edifying the body of Christ, was also utilized in the churches at Rome (Romans 12:6), Corinth (1 Corinthians 12:7–11; 14:1–40), Ephesus (Ephesians. 2:20; 4:11; see also Acts 19:1–7; 1 Timothy 1:18), and Thessalonica (1 Thessalonians 5:19–22).

Functions in the New Testament (Confirmation)

Work in the New Testament

Prophets — New Testament and Old Testament (There's a Difference)

Authoritarian Prophets

There are misunderstandings regarding the gift of the prophet in the New Testament Church; and there are false teachings on the subject as well.

The ministry has been used by quacks to put many into bondage. They use the gift of prophecy for the purpose of manipulating people. Manipulation like this is witchcraft and condemned in the New Testament. It's a form of repressive abuse where the prophet's words are viewed as the spoken Word of God to which the believer cannot disagree.

Prophecies can be very encouraging and provide strength to believers. For example, Acts 15:32 says, "Judas and Silas, who themselves were prophets, said much to encourage and strengthen the brothers."

To encourage 3870. parakaleó, beseech, call for, urge.

https://biblehub.com/strongs/greek/3870.htm

This is the purpose of the prophetic gift in the Church and reveals why it is so necessary – it encourages and strengthens believers.

The original Greek word for 'encourage' in this passage means "to beseech, call for, urge." a prophetic word can inspire believers and provoke them to go forward and fulfill God's call on their lives.

Strengthen 1991. Epistérizó confirm, strengthen.

'Strengthen' in this passage means "to confirm, to support further.

Confusing New Testament Prophets with Old Testament Prophets

Many confuse the office of the Old Testament prophet with that of the New Testament prophet, they're very different. In the Old Testament, what the prophet said was equal to the Word of the LORD.

Jeremiah 1:4-10 King James Version (KJV)

Then the word of the LORD came unto me, saying, Before I formed thee in the belly, I knew thee; and before thou camest forth out of the womb I sanctified thee, and I ordained thee a prophet unto the nations.

Zechariah 4:8: Moreover the word of the LORD came unto me, saying,

Ezekiel 7:1: "Moreover the word of the LORD came unto me, saying,"

The word of the Lord which came to Zephaniah... (Zephaniah 1:1).

Additionally, Amos, Habakkuk and Micah describe the word of God as coming to them as something that they SAW. It came as a vision.

Luke 3:1: "In the fifteenth year of the reign of Tiberius Caesar – when Pontius Pilate was governor of Judea, Herod tetrarch of Galilee, his brother Philip tetrarch of Iturea and Traconitis, and Lysanias tetrarch of Abilene – during the high priesthood of Annas and Caiaphas, the word of God came to John son of Zechariah in the desert."

That is why kings valued the word of God from the mouth of the prophets. The primary purpose of the Old Testament prophet was to lead and guide Israel through the Word of the LORD and, in fact, a lot of their words became Holy Scripture and are included in what we know today as the Old Testament.

Hebrews 1:1: "God, who at sundry times and in divers manners spake in time past unto the fathers by the prophets."

Hebrews 1:2: Hath in these last days spoken unto us by his Son, whom he hath appointed heir of all things, by whom also he made the worlds."

The words of a prophet had to be 100% accurate. If their words were proven to be false, they were to no longer be regarded as prophets and, in fact, were to be put to death (Deuteronomy 18:20-22).

If an Old Testament prophet missed it just once, they were done. Jesus Christ was the last person to operate in the anointing of an Old Testament prophet (Hebrews 1:1-2).

Jesus was the Prophet that the Hebrews were waiting for (Deuteronomy 18:15).

The New Testament prophet is different.

"But when he, the Spirit of truth, comes, he will guide you into all truth. He will not speak on his own; he will speak only what he hears, and he will tell you what is yet to come" (John 16:13).

Since it's the Holy Spirit's job to guide believers in the New Testament era, we don't need the gift of prophecy for this function. So, when a prophet prophesies over you, don't receive it unless the Spirit has already been leading you in this direction or bearing witness with your spirit.

In other words, prophecies in the New Testament are to confirm what the Holy Spirit has already been leading you to do. Sometimes the believer isn't sensitive to the movement of the Spirit. Prophecy can help reposition their hearing, but external help must ultimately match the internal voice.

There may be times when this is somewhat inapplicable because the prophecy is for warning. The purpose of this type of prophecy is to prepare you and encourage you to get through the negative situation.

This was the function of Agabus' prophecy to Paul when he warned him of the severe persecutions he was going to face in Jerusalem.

In the New Testament, you are not to be forced into bondage to the words of prophets. We have a framework in our spirit. You are to be led and guided by the Holy Spirit, not a prophet.

So, if some prophet prophesies over you and it doesn't bear witness with your spirit, throw it out! Never allow yourself to be manipulated into doing something you don't have a peace from God about doing!

Judging Prophecies in the New Testament Era

1 John 4:1: "Beloved, believe not every spirit, but try the spirits whether they are of God: because many false prophets are gone out into the world."

Test the spirits and examine the prophecy. If you must test the prophecy, then this means there's the possibility that it might be wrong.

How do you test prophecies?

- By the Word of God.
- By the leading of the Holy Spirit in your spirit.

If a prophet tells you something that you don't have peace with, don't accept it. But make sure it is not your flesh resisting the word.

1 Thessalonians 5:16-21: Be joyful always; (17) pray continually; (18) give thanks in all circumstances, for this is God's will for you in Christ Jesus.

(19) Do not put out the Spirit's fire; (20) do not treat prophecies with contempt. (21) Test everything. Hold on to the good.

Because the prophet is an earthling he might miss it, or it might be a matter of immaturity or inexperience. They have not yet fully learned to distinguish the vile (flesh) from the precious (spirit).

A prophet may pick something up in the spirit, but it may be wrapped up in their soulish inclinations.

This explains why Paul added, "Test everything. Hold on to the good," after instructing believers not to hold prophecies in contempt. Why? Because the prophecy can be partially right-on and partially off.

Say a prophet gives you a personal prophecy but only half of it bears witness with your spirit. Should you discard the entire prophecy? No. Paul says to hold on to what is good. The rest should be put on the shelf until you have an inner witness.

Philippians 4:7: "And the peace of God, which passeth all understanding, shall keep your hearts and minds through Christ Jesus."

Colossians 3:15: "And let the peace of God rule in your hearts, to the which also ye are called in one body; and be ye thankful."

Don't despise prophecies. Yet don't just blindly embrace everything, only accept what you have peace about, as confirmed by the Holy Spirit.

Don't throw out the person who prophesies. We need to give room for growth and maturation of their ministry by encouraging them to get the training that they need,

The Example of Agabus

Agabus was a New Testament prophet, a good and respected prophet. Notice how he successfully predicted a famine:

Acts 11:27-30: During this time some prophets came down from Jerusalem to Antioch. (28) One of them, named Agabus, stood up and through the Spirit predicted that a severe famine would spread over the entire Roman world. (This happened during the reign of Claudius.) (29) The disciples, each according to his ability, decided to provide help for the brothers living in Judea. (30) This they did, sending their gift to the elders by Barnabas and Saul.

As you can see, Agabus was a prophet. He came to Antioch from Jerusalem with some other prophets and prophesied a famine that would negatively affect the people of Judea. The great historian, Josephus, documented this famine as occurring around 46 A.D. when Claudius was the Roman emperor. So Agabus was right about the famine, and it was good that the Christians at Antioch believed his prophecy and compassionately sent an offering to Judea.

This indicates that Agabus was a renowned and respected prophet. Also notice that the believers "decided to provide help" (verse 29), They had a peace about it, so they generously gave.

Agabus was accurate. But this doesn't mean he was perfect.

Acts 21:8-11

Leaving the next day, we reached Caesarea and stayed at the house of Philip the evangelist, one of the seven. (9) He had four unmarried daughters who prophesied.

(10) After we had been there a number of days, a prophet named Agabus came down from Judea. (11) Coming over to us, he took Paul's belt tied his own hands and feet with it and said, "The Holy Spirit says, 'In this way the Jews of Jerusalem will bind the owner of this belt and will hand him over to the Gentiles.' "

Agabus picked up something about Paul in the spirit and proceeded to speak in faith.

Acts 21:12-14

When we heard this, we and the people there pleaded with Paul not to go up to Jerusalem. (13) Then Paul answered, "Why are you weeping and breaking my heart? I am ready not only to be bound, but also to die in Jerusalem for the name of the Lord Jesus." (14) When he would not be dissuaded, we gave up and said, "The Lord's will be done."

The other believers accepted Agabus' prophecy and took it in a negative sense, they assumed it wasn't God's will for Paul to go to Jerusalem to minister. They tried to discourage Paul from going, even to the extent of weeping! Yet Agabus never said it wasn't God's will for Paul to go to Jerusalem, he merely informed him of the intense persecutions he would experience by going there.

Acts 23:11: verifies beyond any shadow of doubt that it was God's will for the apostle to witness in Jerusalem.

11 And the night following the Lord stood by him, and said, be of good cheer, Paul: for as thou hast testified of me in Jerusalem, so must thou bear witness also at Rome."

The purpose of Agabus' prophecy was to warn Paul of the troubles he would face so that he'd have the grace to trust God and persevere when it happened.

After hearing the prophecy, Paul weighed Agabus' prophecy carefully, held on to the good, and decided to go to Jerusalem based on the leadership of the Holy Spirit. In other words, Paul had peace about going to Jerusalem despite Agabus' warning and despite the other believers' discouraging antics.

Agabus' prophecy prepared Paul for the severe persecutions he would face in Jerusalem, but the details of his prophecy weren't wholly accurate.

Agabus said that the Jews in Jerusalem would bind up Paul's hands and feet and deliver him to the Roman government, but this is not what happened.

Nine days after arriving in Jerusalem the Jews apprehended Paul to murder him, not to turn him over to the Romans; and the Romans actually saved Paul from the Jews.

The soldiers then bound him with chains and took him into custody, but as soon as they found out he was a Roman citizen they released him (Acts 21:30-33 and 22:25-30).

As you can see, Agabus was a respected prophet. He accurately predicted that Paul would suffer great persecution in Jerusalem, and he was right that Paul would be bound hand and foot. This warning helped prepare Paul for his mission and gave him the grace to persevere when persecuted, but some of the details of Agabus' prophecy were clearly off. Agabus spoke in faith; he missed some of the details.

This proves that New Testament prophets can miss it. This is why believers must test prophecies by the Word of God and the leading of the Holy Spirit.

The New Testament prophet may inherit a lot of characteristics of the Old Testament prophets; however, he does not have all their responsibilities and roles or functions.

The New Testament prophet does not have definitiveness, as a source of direct guidance to the people.

In the Old Testament God expected His people to call upon Him and He would then speak through a prophet to give guidance. Kings often asked the prophet to seek God on their behalf (2 Kings 3:9-12).

The New Testament prophet is called to a working relationship with the apostolic ministry or the five- fold ministry. This interaction provides enough checks and balances for both ministries.

A prophet will envision the masterplan and call the church and individuals into an understanding and receipt of God's plans and purposes.

God is always speaking. Unfortunately, the sheep is never listening, and the bible is very clear, "my sheep hear my voice" (John 10:27-30).

If we are his sheep, then we will hear his voice unless we are not his sheep. If we are not his sheep, then we are someone else's goats.

We should encourage people to seek the Lord Jesus through his Holy Spirit for themselves. Build a close intimate relationship with Jesus. And discourage them from exalting or relying on prophets. Real prophets are humble and will rebuke those who seek to glorify their prophetic ministry or gift; they will never allow God's glory to be shared.

John Baptist denied that he was Christ but, that he was sent to testify to the light to point to the light, he refused to share the glory with Christ (John 1:19-28).

This is the testimony of John. When the Jews from Jerusalem sent priests and Levites to him to ask him, 'Who are you?' he admitted and did not deny it, but admitted, 'I am not the Christ' (John 1:19-20).

The reason why the prophetic is popular at the present is because the sheep have become dull in hearing, stone deaf; they have become deaf and dumb in the spirit.

Ephesians 4:11;12: the prophets are also called to perfect the saints to do works of ministry. The prophet will equip the body by teaching the body how to hear the voice of God and how to see in the spirit.

In the New Testament, the Scriptures clearly teach repeatedly that Christians must get guidance from The Holy Spirit who indwells them (Romans 8:14).

John 10:27: my sheep hear my voice, and I know them, and they follow me:

New Testament Prophets

Jesus: And thou, child, shalt be called the prophet of the Highest: for thou shalt go before the face of the Lord to prepare his ways (Luke 1:76).

And there was one Anna, a prophetess, the daughter of Phanuel, of the tribe of Asher: she was of a great age, and had lived with a husband seven years from her virginity (Luke 2:36).

John the Baptist for I say unto you, among those that are born of women there is not a greater prophet than John the Baptist: but he that is least in the kingdom of God is greater than he (Luke 7:28).

Barjesus (false prophet) And when they had gone through the isle unto Paphos, they found a certain sorcerer, a false prophet, a Jew, whose name [was] Barjesus: (Acts 13:6).

Agabus And as we tarried [there] many days, there came down from Judaea a certain prophet, named Agabus (Acts 21:10).

Unknown One of them, [even] a prophet of their own, said, The Cretians [are] always liars, evil beasts, slow bellies (Titus 1:12).

Matthias, Barnabas, Paul/Saul, Simon Jude/Judas (brother of James)11.

Can Prophecy Fail?

In every generation, people have made predictions of things to come. Imminent events. Far-off events. And sometimes they have come to pass but sometimes they don't.

Prophecy is conditional. Most prophecy is to some degree conditional. Its exact fulfillment depends on certain stated, or unstated but tacitly understood, conditions which are in the province of humanity. Take the prophecy of Jonah against Nineveh.

God had literally forced Jonah, by the storm at sea and the sojourn in the great fish, to go and warn Nineveh of imminent destruction. Then God changed His plan when the Assyrians repented. Jonah was mightily displeased, although he knew all along that the threatened destruction was conditional: "... Was not this my saying, when I was yet in my country? Therefore, I fled before unto Tarshish: for I knew that thou art a gracious God, and merciful, slow to anger, and of great kindness, and repentest thee of the evil" (Jonah 4:2).

Jonah knew in advance that God would repent (change His mind) if the people repented. And even though Jonah may never have told the Ninevites it was conditional — at least it is not so recorded — the king understood it that way (Jonah 3:9).

Was the entire prophecy against Nineveh therefore scrapped because the Assyrians repented? It was not. Only the time element of it was changed. When they returned to their old ways, the punishment was again set in motion. It finally came to pass in 612 B.C. when Nineveh was destroyed.

13.
Prophets Office Vs Ministering in the Prophetic

The prophet, is an equipping servant-leader, he is qualified according to Scripture to function in what the KJV calls the "office" of a prophet, "office" implies position or rank there is three uses of the word "office" in the KJV, which include Romans 11:13, Romans 12:4 and I Timothy 3:1 ,

In Romans 11:13 Paul said, "I am the apostle of the Gentiles, I magnify mine "office") Romans 12:4 states, "For as we have many members in the one body, and all members have not the same "office" I Timothy 3:1 it says, "This is a true saying, If a man desire, the "office of a bishop, he desireth a good work."

In truth, the "office" is not a position nor a rank but rather a descriptive function. The servant leaders who are described in Ephesians 4:11 were themselves gifts to the church. Their primary purpose was to serve and lead by example. Their primary function was 1) For the perfecting of the saints, 2) for the work of ministry, 3) for the edifying of the body of Christ.

Those who serve in the function or "office" of a prophet, that is as a "gift" from Christ to the church. Because the prophets are a "gift" to the church, the prophet's function is a continuing prophetic ministry and they consistently walk in that gift because that is who they are in the Body of Christ.

The reliance on prophets was altered in the New Testament. Jesus sent to us the counselor, the Holy Spirit. He says in John 10:27 my sheep hear my voice, and I know them, and they follow me.

Under the New Testament, the sheep can hear the voice of God. Every believer now can hear God for themselves.

There is no more dependence upon a prophet for auditory perception. Everything must be judged and tested by scripture.

John 10:4: when he has brought out all his own, he goes on ahead of them, and his sheep follow him because they know his voice.

John 16:13: Howbeit when he, the Spirit of truth, is come, he will guide you into all truth: for he shall not speak of himself; but whatsoever he shall hear, that shall he speak, and he will shew you things to come.

1 Corinthians 2:9: But as it is written, Eye hath not seen, nor ear heard, neither have entered the heart of man, the things which God hath prepared for them that love him.

In the New Testament, GOD uses the prophet to confirm what God is already saying to his sheep. This means that God will often use you as a prophet to confirm the very word or illuminate the word he has already spoken to someone. This will give them confirmation and raise their faith.

The purpose and the role of the New Testament prophet, is not primarily to prophesy, foretell or forth tell:

- First, it is to train the body to hear the Lord for themselves as part of the fivefold equipping ministry. Second, it is to teach believers how to find and live in the perfect will of God. Thirdly, to call the body of Christ into order unto the perfection and maturation in Christ.
- Prophets also instruct and train people in the use of spiritual gifts, helping churches establish the right framework and protocol for the gift to operate, for the edification of the church.
- Through fasting and prayer with other fivefold leaders, identify and set apart those called into ministry as directed by the Holy Spirit. Prophets should edify, encourage, direct, correct and rebuke while in right standing with God, and instruct in righteousness.

2 Timothy 3:16: All Scripture is God-breathed and is useful for teaching, rebuking, correcting and training in righteousness,

Elders of Israel in (Numbers 11:16-29), "when the spirit rested upon them, prophesied; "this does not mean that they are prophets, but they had the ability to prophesy in a moment we want to make this distinction clear. Asaph and Jeduthun "prophesied with a harp."

(1 Chronicles 25:3). Miriam and Deborah were prophetesses (Exodus 15:20).

A Prophet communicates the mind and will of God to men (Deuteronomy 18:18, 19)

18: I will raise up for them a prophet like you from among their fellow Israelites, and I will put my words in his mouth. He will tell them everything I commend him for.

The whole Bible is a prophetic book, the whole of it, the whole counsel. It was written by men who received the revelation and inspiration, what God revealed to them they made known to us, the foretelling of the future and prediction prophecy that a lot of people lay emphasis on is just a part of the prophetic.

Prophets are called and raised by God, molded, and shaped to correct moral decay, religious abuses and the apostasy in the church; they are reformers. They proclaim the great moral requirement of God; they exalt holiness and inspire holy truths and principles connected with God's character.

Enoch, Abraham, and the patriarchs, as bearers of God's message (Genesis 20:7; Exodus 7:1; Psalm105:15), as also Moses (Deuteronomy 18:15; 34:10; Hosea 12:13), are ranked among the prophets.

Jesus was a prophet of our faith:

In any case, I must press on today and tomorrow and the next day—for surely no prophet can die outside Jerusalem! Here Jesus referred to himself as a prophet Luke 13:33.

Luke 24:19: "What things?" he asked. "About Jesus of Nazareth," they replied. "He was a prophet, powerful in word and deed before God and all the people."

Tests of a Genuine Prophet

1 Thessalonians 5:20 remember Christ's warning: "Beware of false prophets, who come to you in sheep's clothing, but inwardly they are ravenous wolves. You will know them by their fruits" (Matthew 7:15).

- When you start your prophetic ministry, many people will doubt you, ridicule and even mock you, but remember; the fruit of your life will speak a great volume to them. They did these very things with Jesus.
- We cannot be quick to judge people presumptuously. Christ was a great prophet but his own people, including the religious leaders of his day, rejected him and did not confirm his office.

Church leaders and scholars did not endorse Him. Some said that His miracles were caused by "Beelzebub (the lord of the flies), the ruler of the demons" (Luke 12:24). His brothers, who knew and lived closely with Him for many years, did not, at first, believe in Him (John 7:5). His disciples "murmured and complained amongst themselves" often regarding His teachings (John 6:61) and forsook Him after Gethsemane (Mark 14:50).

- Prophet's prophecy lies in My name.
- I have not sent them,
- Commanded them, nor spoken to them.
- They prophesy to you a false vision, divination, a worthless thing, and the deceit of their heart" (Jeremiah 14:14; 5:13, 31; 14:18; 23:21).

Do you realize the four steps of discovering a false prophet deeply embedded in this verse? First, these false prophets are prophesying lies in his name. This is shocking but very true that false prophets will use the name of Jesus outwardly to sugarcoat their corrupted message.

Matthew 7:22: Many will say to me on that day, 'Lord, Lord, did we not prophesy in your name, and in your name drive out demons and perform many miracles?' Matthew 7:23 Then I will tell them plainly, 'I never knew you. Away from me, you evildoers!'

So, these false prophets that the Lord calls evil doers will prophesy in the name of Jesus. They will do great miracles but still there is no relationship between them and Jesus. Realize that he tells them, I never knew you (lack or relationship). Secondly, he says that I never sent them, meaning they have called themselves and sent themselves. Thirdly, he never called them, nor has he ever spoken to them. Fourth, there is no truth in these people.

The result is lies and deception, delusions, and false visions; then we have divination coming in and they are now practicing witchcraft in the name of the Lord.

Always use the rule of three approach in the topic of judging prophets judging and prophecy:

- (1) Do not quench the Spirit.
- (2) Do not despise prophecies.
- (3) Test all things; hold fast to that which is good" (1 Thessalonians 5:19-21).

Isaiah 8:20: "To the law and to the testimony: if they speak not according to this word, [it is] because [there is] no light in them."

The true prophet's sayings are totally consistent with all that the Holy Spirit has already revealed in Scripture.

Jeremiah 23:14: "I have seen also in the prophets of Jerusalem a horrible thing: they commit adultery and walk in lies: they strengthen also the hands of evildoers, that none doth return from his wickedness. 16 Thus saith the LORD of hosts, hearken not unto the words of the prophets that prophesy unto you: they make you vain: they speak a vision of their own heart, [and] not out of the mouth of the LORD."

True prophets will reprove sins rather than compromise and tolerate sin.

Jeremiah 28:9: "The prophet which prophesies of peace, when the word of the prophet shall come to pass, [then] shall the prophet be known, that the LORD hath truly sent him."

True prophet's predictions must come to pass unless conditional prophecy requires a response. Prophets were instructed to use the benchmark of "fulfilled predictions" as one of the tests of a genuine prophet: "As for the prophet who prophesies of peace when the word of the prophet comes to pass, the prophet will be known as one whom the Lord has truly sent" (Jeremiah 28:9).

Making predictions, or foretelling, is only one aspect of a prophet's work. In fact, it is only a minor phase. In contemplating "fulfilled predictions," we must also understand the principle of conditional prophecy.

The instant I speak concerning a nation and concerning a kingdom, to pluck up, to pull down, and to destroy it, if that nation against whom I have spoken turns from its evil, I will relent of the disaster that I thought to bring upon it. And the instant I speak concerning a nation and concerning a kingdom, to build and to plant it, if it does evil in My sight so that it does not obey My voice, then I will relent concerning the good with which I said I would benefit it" (Jeremiah 18:7-10).

Prophets must understand Conditional prophecy principle or Controlled uncertainty, is a Biblical principle applied to statements of a predictive nature that concern or involve the responses of human beings whenever an unfolding of judgments or prophecy given depends upon human choice.

Jonah had to learn this lesson of conditionality the hard way. His prophecy of destruction did not take place: he was very angry but God did relent because this was a conditional prophecy. "God saw their works, that they turned from their evil way; and God relented from the disaster that He had said He would bring upon them, and He did not do it" (Jonah 3:10).

Matthew 7:15: "Beware of false prophets, which come to you in sheep's clothing, but inwardly they are ravening wolves. Ye shall know them by their fruits. ... Even so every good tree bringeth forth good fruit; but a corrupt tree bringeth forth evil fruit. A good tree cannot bring forth evil fruit, neither [can] a corrupt tree brings forth good fruit. ...Wherefore by their fruits ye shall know them."

True prophets lead people to repentance and humility before God. There is no pretense in them. They are not pietistic. They reflect Christ's personality, character, and nature. Their fruits are the fruits of the Holy Spirit. Love undergirds their message.

1 John 4:2: "Hereby know ye the Spirit of God: Every spirit that confesseth that Jesus Christ is come in the flesh is of God:" (Hebrews 4:15) Jesus was in all points tempted like as [we are, yet] without sin.)

- True prophets confess that Jesus came in our "fallen" human flesh, yet He won the victory over every sin and all sin, just as we can, through walking in holiness and truth.

Daniel 10:17: "For how can the servants of this my lord talk with this my lord? For as for me, straightway there remained no strength in me, neither is there breath left in me."

- True prophets have no strength or breath of their own while in vision, but supernatural strength from God.

John 1:15: "John bare witness of him, and cried, saying, this was he of whom I spoke, He that cometh after me is preferred before me: for he was before me."

- Other Prophets who are mature must confirm your calling bearing witness by the Spirit of God.

The fruit test is very important to confirm in these last days. It is found in the Sermon on the Mount, as it deals specifically with "false prophets":

- "Beware of false prophets, who come to you in sheep's clothing, but inwardly they are ravenous wolves. You will know them by their fruits. Do men gather grapes from thorn bushes or figs from thistles? Even so, every good tree bears good fruit, but a bad tree bears bad fruit. A good tree cannot bear bad fruit, nor can a bad tree bear good fruit. . . . Therefore, by their fruits you will know them" (Matthew 7:15-20).

Realize that Jesus says you will know them. He is putting distinction between him and them. A prophet's individual fruit will qualify him or her or disqualify him or her. But if you want to know whether they belong to God then you will know them by the principle of loving one another

John 13:35: "By this shall all men know that ye are my disciples, if ye have love one to another."

What kind of prophet do people hear and see in you? Do they hear you or God? Do they see your fruit or the fruit of God's spirit flowing out of you? Is the substance of your life reliable or consistent? Is it worldly or godly? Faithful or unfaithful? Do your teachings exalt the written Word, or do they turn people away from the word? Do you maintain sound doctrine consistent with the Biblical message? Do sinners find the Lord through your message? Are the redemptive purposes of the cross embedded within your sermons and practice?

Many today follow credentials of false prophets. They follow signs instead of signs following them. They prefer swindlers, coercionists, which amass great wealth through manipulation.

Prophets are also humans and prone to falling back into the flesh. Moses was a prophet who spoke with God "face to face" (Exodus. 33:11), but his prophetic gift did not guarantee that he would not make mistakes. Because of his exasperation and public exhibit of wrath, he was not permitted to enter the Promised Land.

Even though the prophet's message is what God wants communicated, his/her own ministry may not appear to make a positive impact. Think of Jeremiah and Isaiah. When these men lived, they seemed to be "failures." But not so today.

Think of Ezekiel's predicament: "As for you, son of man, the children of your people are talking about you beside the walls and in the doors of the houses; and they speak to one another, everyone saying to his brother, 'please come and hear what the word is that comes from the Lord.' So, they come to you as people do, they sit before you as my people, and they hear your words, but they do not do them; for with their mouth, they show much love, but their hearts pursue their own gain. Indeed, you are to them as a very lovely song of one who has a pleasant voice and can play well on an instrument; for they hear your words, but they do not do them. And when this comes to pass—surely it will come—then they will know that a prophet has been among them" (Ezekiel. 33:30-33).

You may be consistent, faithful, and loyal to God and committed to your calling to the highest Biblical standards, and still the world will not recognize you or even celebrate you. Will you still be content with that?

Conditionality Of Prophecy

Prophecy isn't always fulfilled all at once. For example, God promises David a son, a descendant who will rule Jerusalem forever. Parts of this prophecy are fulfilled in David's literal immediate heir, Solomon. But other parts of this prophecy went unfulfilled for a long, long time—while Christianity claims Jesus Christ was that promised king, Judaism still awaits a Messiah and deliverer.

We also must understand the principle of conditional prophecy. This principle is better understood through the words of Prophet Jeremiah (Jeremiah 18:7-10).

The instant I speak concerning a nation and concerning a kingdom, to pluck up, to pull down, and to destroy it, if that nation against whom I have spoken turns from its evil, I will relent of the disaster that I thought to bring upon it. And the instant I speak concerning a nation and concerning a kingdom, to build and to plant it, if it does evil in

My sight so that it does not obey My voice, then I will relent concerning the good with which I said I would benefit it."

Conditional prophecy always needs a response. It depends upon human choice; some aspects of prophetic fulfillment are necessarily conditional.

1 Samuel 2:30,31: Therefore the Lord God of Israel says: 'I said indeed that your house and the house of your father would walk before me forever.' But now the Lord says: 'Far be it from me; for those who honor me I will honor, and those who despise me shall be lightly esteemed. Behold, the days are coming that I will cut off your arm and the arm of your father's house, so that there will not be an old man in your house.'"

Jonah had to learn this lesson of conditionality the hard way: "Then God saw their works, that they turned from their evil way; and God relented from the disaster that He had said He would bring upon them, and He did not do it" (Jonah 3:10).

King Josiah is another example of conditional prophecy. He had led his people in an exceptional way in 2 Chronicles 34. Because of his faithfulness, the Lord promised, "I will gather you to your fathers, and you shall be gathered to your grave in peace" (vs. 28). But Josiah did not die in peace. He died in battle! What went wrong?

He did not obey God's instruction. God did not give him orders to attack Egypt. In fact, the king of Egypt sent a special message to Josiah, emphasizing that Josiah's God was directing Egypt in battle against Babylon: "God is on my side, so don't oppose me, or he will destroy you" (2 Chronicles 35:21).

Josiah could have obeyed God and listened to the confirming voice of Egypt's king. But he disguised himself, led his army into the Battle of Carchemish, and was killed. God's promise that Josiah would die a peaceful death was conditional upon continual obedience.

When we go against God's counsel, choosing to follow personal soulish and earthly inclinations, God does not save us or sustain us. If you do it without his leadership, don't expect him to bail you out or protect you.

14. Types of Prophets in the Bible

There are many kinds of prophets. All ministers do not have the same calling or emphasis of the ministry. Jeremiah, for example, was called the "weeping prophet," while Ezra, Nathan, and Gad were "writing prophets," the latter two of which wrote 2 Samuel and 1 & 2 Chronicles. There are prophets who are also teachers (Acts 13:1).

There are prophets who work with pastors within a local church as elders. Some prophets are presbyters giving oversight. Other prophets have a traveling ministry. Some are authors, some are psalmists, scribes and some are involved in activism. Prophets are also seers; they see things supernaturally in the Spirit that other people don't see. 1 Samuel 9:9

Prophets can hear things that are not intended to be heard by others; if God reveals it to them, they can even hear evil plans conceived in privacy and secrecy (2 Kings 6:8-12). Prophets pronounce judgment (Jeremiah 1:16,17) ...Prophets can Pronounce or warn of God's judgments. Revelations 11:3-13 ... Prophets expose sin: Nathan the Prophet exposed the sin of David (2 Samuel 11:1 – 12:13).

Catalyst prophets & Revivalist:

These types of Prophets will stir things up. Many of them are revivalist prophets.

Missionary Prophet:

Many of the prophets of the Old Testament and many today find themselves like the prophets of old confronting kings and taking an important role in national affairs. Some also addressed their words to foreign nations. They demonstrate the ministry of the

Prophet to the Nations. Surely the Sovereign Lord does nothing without revealing his plan to his servants the prophets (Amos 3:7).

The Ardent & Holy Prophets:

Jeremiah and Ezekiel (Ezekiel 2:6) do not be afraid... (Jeremiah 20:14) Some prophets appear clandestine; they are not avoiding people; they have been asked to play a role much larger than them. This will make them disengage from common issues; they choose to remain confidential as much as possible. They don't want mixture.

The Action and Power Prophets:

Elijah and Elisha, Jehu (1 Kings 17:1) Now Elijah the Tish bite, from Tishbi in Gilead, said to Ahab, "As the LORD, the God of Israel, lives, whom I serve, there will be neither dew nor rain in the next few years except at my word." The Bible reveals that Elijah and Elisha, Jehu were believed to be very action based rather than words. Their ministry is highlighted with many miracles, powerful acts and confrontations.

The Prophetic Teachers

Samuel, Moses, Jesus (1 Samuel 3:21) The LORD continued to appear at Shiloh, and there he revealed himself to Samuel through his word. (4:1) And Samuel's word came to all Israel. (Numbers 5:4) The Israelites did ... just as the LORD had instructed Moses (Matthew 7:29) because he (Jesus) taught as one who had authority ... These prophets developed a love of teaching, exposition and corrective teaching. The mark of a prophetic teacher is that they feel obligated to explain the purpose, intention, and spirit of the Scripture.

The Judging Prophets

Moses, Samuel, Elijah, Elisha, Deborah (Exodus 18:13) The next day Moses took his seat to serve as judge for the people (1 Samuel 17:15) Samuel continued as judge over Israel all the days of his life. (1 Kings 18:40) Then Elijah commanded them, "Seize the prophets of Baal. Don't let anyone get away!" ... (1 Kings 19:17) ... and Elisha will put to death any who escape the sword of Jehu. Prophets are still Judges today; it is there in the scripture. We just want to ignore it but even today, just like in the Old Testament, the prophets can be called to judge on matters pertaining to the Church and believers. Therefore, if you have disputes about such matters, appoint as judges, even men of little account in the church!

1 Corinthians 6:4-5: I say this to shame you. Is it possible that there is nobody among you wise enough to judge a dispute between believers?

The Presbyter Prophet

Moses and Jesus, the prophetic call/gift is not greater than the leadership gift. There are Pastors who are prophetic, they make regular use of prophetic content in their ministry. Pastors are considered leaders in the present-day church structure because they are on the pulpit every Sunday. Prophets are classified as leaders in the context of the five- fold ministry.

Visionary Insightful Prophets

Daniel, Isaiah, Samuel, Elisha, etc. (1 Samuel 3:1). The boy Samuel ministered before the LORD under Eli. In those days the word of the LORD was rare; there were not many visions. (3:19) The LORD was with Samuel as he grew up, and he let none of his words fall to the ground.

The Ordinary Practicing Prophet

Jeremiah and Amos (Jeremiah 1:17) (Amos 2:1) They are the closest thing resembling the New Testament Church prophet. They have a general prophetic style.

The Hidden Prophets:

1 Kings 18:4: While Jezebel was killing off the Lord's prophets, Obadiah had taken a hundred prophets, hidden them in two caves, fifty in each, and supplied them with food and water. This is a revealing verse for those who think that prophets were very rare. It shows that even though being a prophet in the reign of Ahab and Jezebel was likely to result in death, many were still willing to endure hardship. God told Elijah he had seven thousand more.

Psalmist And Scribe Prophets:

For the director of music. To [the tune of] "Lilies." Of the Sons of Korah. A maskil. A wedding song. My heart is stirred by a noble theme as I recite my verses for the king; my tongue is the pen of a skillful writer. Psalm 45:1 the Lord uses some Prophets to prophesy through anointed music, they scribe or prophesy through their mouths and instruments, and their songs are spontaneous anointed worship that is oiled by the glory of God.

15.

Going through your Gethsemane

Matthew 26:36-38 the Prayer in the Garden (Mark 14:32-42; Luke 22:39-46) Then Jesus came with them to a place called Gethsemane, and said to the disciples, "Sit here while I go and pray over there." 37 And He took with Him Peter and the two sons of Zebedee, and He began to be sorrowful and deeply distressed. 38 Then He said to them, "My soul is exceedingly sorrowful, even to death. Stay here and watch with me." Jesus willingly and deliberately took his disciples to Gethsemane (olive groove) where the olives were being squeezed (oil press).

Judges 9:8: The olive tree said, should I leave my riches of oil by which God and men are honored (anointed).

Judges 9:8-9: "The trees once went forth to anoint a king over them. And they said to the olive tree, 'Reign over us!' 9 But the olive tree said to them, 'should I cease giving my oil, with which they honor God and men, and go to sway over trees?'

Notice that the anointing will honor God and men. Allow God to press out your anointing so that you can have favor before God and men.

Psalm 45:7: you love righteousness and hate wickedness; therefore God, your God, has set you above your companions by anointing you with the oil of joy.

The olives were never planted in temple courts (inside religious cloisters) in Zechariah 4:3. The two olives in this verse stand for the two priestly and royal offices and symbolize a continuous oil supply. Verse 12- Joshua, Verse 14 – Zerubbabel (these two olives are people).

Zechariah 4:2-3: and he said to me, "What do you see?" So, I said, "I am looking, and there is a lamp stand of solid gold with a bowl on top of it, and on the stand seven lamps with seven pipes to the seven lamps. 3 Two olive trees are by it, one at the right of the bowl and the other at its left."

They were to do their work in the temple and in the lives of people, they had the spirit enabled ministry, so we see that the olives are people.

In this verse the priest are olives to supply oil, and they were not to be planted at the temple courts. They were to work there and in the lives of God's people.

Romans 11:17: Gentiles are termed as wild olive shoots that have been grafted in. Revelation 11:4 – The power for effective ministry or witness is provided by the Spirit of God.

The oil

To extract the oil from the olives, they must be crushed. Jesus did not allow all his disciples at the oil press. Some disciples sat far off. He took with him the Remnants, those closest to him, those intimate with him (Mark 5:37).

He did not allow anyone except for the remnants, the intimate ones, the close ones, the inner circle. (Intimacy with Jesus will take you where others can't go)

Acts 3:1: the remnants stayed close to each other long after he went. He unites remnants one to another in the spirit through their limps – (Jacob had a limp.) When you grapple with God and subsist, God will be marked with a limp (Genesis 32:24).

You can only speak of what you know. You can only reproduce who you are –

In Mark 9:2: Jesus took the intimate ones, and led them up on top of a mountain, all alone, and he revealed his glory to them. He was transfigured. He uncovered himself to them. He only shows forth his glory and secrets to the remnants privately and expresses himself through them publicly.

- He divulged secrets and revelations to the remnants privately (Mark 13:3).
- He entrusted to them intimate assignments (Luke 22:8).
- He can only entrust the handling of his body and blood to his remnants (Acts 4:1-3).
- The remnants tarried with him before he was arrested (Matthew 26:36).

When Jesus took his disciples to the oil press, some disciples were to sit at the press and wait with him while he was being pressed and crushed to release the Holy Spirit (v 37).

The remnants went along with Him to be pressed with Him. He began to be pressed to the point of death. The wrath of God was being released on him to crush him to produce oil (Holy Spirit), the anointing (Mark 10:38, Isaiah 53:10).

"Stay here and keep watch with me (intercede with me, be crushed with me)," he said. He distanced himself and fell to the ground to be crushed.

Jesus was the alabaster box full of fragrance that had to be poured out to the world. He was the cistern of heaven's oil, the Holy Ghost was veiled in him, and for him to be unveiled there was to be a crushing, the weight of heaven. The burden of God was put upon him.

Isaiah 53:9-11

9 And he made his grave with the wicked, and with the rich in his death; because he had done no violence, neither was any deceit in his mouth.

10 Yet it pleased the Lord to bruise him; he hath put him to grief: when thou shalt make his soul an offering for sin, he shall see his seed, he shall prolong his days, and the pleasure of the Lord shall prosper in his hand.

11 He shall see of the travail of his soul and shall be satisfied: by his knowledge shall my righteous servant justify many; for he shall bear their iniquities.

Jesus was praying, "Do not press me into this cup, the cup of wrath, yet not my will. You own me, and you deserve to draw oil from this obedient olive and save and heal the world."

The cup symbolizes deep sorrow and suffering.

Slumber hindered the disciples from walking in the spirit. They did not submit to the crushing. Sleep can equate to flesh. Their flesh had kept them from producing oil. This is a lack of surrender for one hour (v 41). A continuous life of prayer allows God to go past your flesh and touch your spirit (v. 42). He willingly accepted to endure persecution, and the hardships from the oil press to the cross.

He saw how they hailed him as king then nailed him – the beatings, the mocking, the nails, the crucifixion, but he surrendered his will to a higher will, and at that moment, oil flowed. The Holy Spirit was only some days away from swarming and flooding the earth on Pentecost.

Colossians 2:9: For in Christ all the fullness of the Deity lives in bodily form.

The body of Jesus was the headquarters of Jehovah God on earth. The veil of his flesh had to be pierced on the cross to uncover the fullness of the spirit.

Stephen was never promoted to glory until he learned submission under a hail of stones. He was willing to submit his will to a higher will. He yielded to the pressing.

When Jesus said, "Father, forgive them for they don't know what they are doing," he surrendered to a higher will (Acts 7:54-60).

Stephen saw heaven at the moment of yielding. Revelation comes when we yield to the press and not the flesh – we are the olives. If we are the olives, the master has to take us to the press frequently to crush us, to crush past our flesh to produce oil, anointing that honors God and men. The one who knows the price of the oil is the olive. (v 43)

Again sleep (aka. flesh) kept them from producing oil, their eye lids became heavy. Their flesh was too fat to yield; they could not yield their will. (v 44) He went away again to be crushed. (v 45) Sleep /flesh still kept them from yielding.

Flesh hinders the crushing, just as the olive skins or coat hinders the olive from producing oil. Jesus told them, "Look, the trouble has come upon you, the calamity, and the hardship. You could not see it. You did not yield to the will of God in the spirit. You could not see it come. You were in the flesh."

John 18:1: they went into the olive grove oil press (v 2). Jesus often took his disciples to the press to press them. That is why the remnants often get pressed – we are close to the Master. The Master frequents the press, so we will frequent with him because we are one with Him.

John 17:4: Jesus prayed I have brought you glory. I have been pressed so the world will receive the anointing, the Holy Spirit because I yielded to the press.

John 17:19: He prayed, Father, I have sanctified myself I have set myself apart by accepting the press.

Death to the flesh will reveal the spirit. When they took apart the Lamb of God, they revealed the Lion of Judah – the ripping of His flesh at Calvary revealed the Holy Ghost. For us to reveal the Holy Ghost, we must be pressed past our flesh, or flesh must be ripped to reveal glory. As we die to the flesh at the oil press, we get consecrated for God's work – the oil flows!

John 15:1: Jesus is the vine; everyone in him produces fruit. Christians who don't produce he cuts, but those who produce fruit – they are pruned. They are taken back to the press to produce more oil. (v 4) No Christian can bring more fruit if they don't abide in Jesus.

If they abide, then they can always frequent the press because the Lord loves the press. He loves the olive grove. The key to much fruit is to remain in Christ, and to frequent the press. Gethsemane is a place of productivity and divine activity.

John 16:7: unless I go away the Counselor will not come, unless I agree to be pressed, the anointing will not come. [v 16:7]

When a mother is pregnant and in labor pains it is painful but when the child is born the pain turns into joy.

Romans 5:3: We rejoice in suffering in the oil press. Romans 8:17 if we get pressed, we will share in his glory. Present pressings to produce oil cannot be compared to the anointing that will be revealed.

The Lord constantly and frequently takes his chosen remnants to the press to extract oil. We can see that not all the disciples went to the press, but the remnants. If you are close to him, then you go where he goes. He loved the olive grove. He loved the press, the hardships, the troubles, the afflictions which are the press he would use to produce oil from us.

The remnants are at the press right now being pressed to produce the oil, the fresh wine, and revelations – the remnants will be his sources of refreshment in this dying and thirsty world, wherever they go – a living spring of water of his spirit will be. So, we must love the press! It is painful, but God is honored with oil that the olives produce.

God's grace and strength is sufficient to do in and through us what he wills if we will submit ourselves. Exodus 15:2: "The Lord is my strength and my song; He has given me victory. This is my God, and I will praise him—my father's God, and I will exalt him! Joshua 1:9 "This is my command—be strong and courageous! Do not be afraid or discouraged. For the Lord your God is with you wherever you go."

16.
The Relationship with the Holy Spirit

Quality is hard without some sacrifice or denial, willingly choosing to be submitted to God. Without brokenness and humility there is no release. There is no leadership without servanthood. No resurrection life and empowerment without death.

A Passionate Pursuit of God is more valuable than titles and positions, more extravagant than riches and acknowledgements.

1 Corinthians 15:9-10: For I am the least of the apostles, that am not meet to be called an apostle, because I persecuted the church of God.

10 But by the grace of God I am what I am: and his grace which was bestowed upon me was not in vain; but I labored more abundantly than they all: yet not I, but the grace of God which was with me.

When we surrender to the Holy Spirit, we have chosen the path to death. Death to self. When self is detached or removed from your spiritual essence, then your true essence shines forth.

Death to Self

The essence of your existence has to do with the fact that you are a "living reality." When you lose the functions or vitality, you "no longer exist." You are diseased. So, the essence of "death" is the absence of "life." Therefore, when one dies "one ceases to exist."

To spiritualize this term when someone "spiritually dies or dies to self," self-ceases to exist. That soulish part of the person ceases to live to its own pleasure but yields its desires to a higher one. As such, you are no longer concerned with "your own will, emotions, mind or happiness," because you are no longer in the picture... God is in the picture when you no longer live but Christ lives in you. You are no longer the center of your own little universe... God encompasses all of it.

Many in this world want to live for self... but God's Word says die to self! Many people came to Jesus and asked to be His disciples, but most turned away because they were unwilling to pay the price of following Jesus. They did not want to make themselves "slaves of Christ" (Luke 14:26, 33; 16:13; Romans 12:1; 1 Corinthians 6:19-20; 1 Peter 1:18-19).

Jesus said, "He who loves his father or mother or himself more than me, he is not worthy of me" (Matthew 10:37-39). Thus, Paul said, "I have been crucified with Christ; it is no longer I who live, but Christ lives in me" (Galatians 2:20).

The intimate and sweet relationship with the Holy Spirit begins when we receive the gentle promptings and convicting invitations to come a little closer to God. The Holy Spirit will begin to give us heavenly divine burdens. We will be invited to the table of prayer and earnestly called upon to surrender both spirit, soul, and body wholly to God.

What does it mean to die to self?

Jesus described the "dying to self" process ("denying self") as part of following Him — "If anyone wishes to come after Me, he must deny himself, and take up his cross and follow Me" (Matthew 16:24); He then went on to say that "dying to self" is a positive, not a negative: "For whoever wishes to save his life will lose it; but whoever loses his life for My sake will find it!" (Matthew 16:25). In dying to the self-life, we discover an "abundant life" by depending on God, who provides much more than we can imagine. Jesus put it this way: Unless a grain of wheat falls into the earth and dies, it remains alone; but if it dies, it bears much fruit" (John 12:24; Galatians 5:22-23).

Unless you fall to the dust, humble yourself, and prostrate your soul on the altar of death, you cannot bring forth effective fruits. When we die to self we set aside "our wants and desires" our soulish inclinations and instead focus on God.

Dying to oneself is a concept that is unacceptable to many carnal Christians today. We want revivals and moves of God, but we fail to embrace the death that brings it.

The Christian life is an ongoing process of dying to self and living for Christ – seeking His will and kingdom and righteousness, rather than our own. But, as fallen humans, we are hard-wired to seek our own will above anyone else's... we want our way in life... and we all tend to see things from our point of view and define the world by how we see it.

Dying to self is a process of stripping away layers of sin encrusted upon our wicked soulish man. It is an integral part of the process of sanctification. It was the disciple's instinct to preserve their own lives that caused them to flee from Christ at His arrest.

The Christian life is not about us – it's all about Christ... you cannot be independent; it is a life of dependence upon God. It's about yielding our will to God's will ... it's about putting Christ first above everything else, no matter what it costs us... it's the realization that we are His servants; as such, our goal is to live for Him and glorify Him in everything we do.

The greatest hope for believers is to die to self so that we might live for Christ. You will realize that there is no way you can live for yourself and live for Christ. One essence or substance must yield.

Dying to self is not "optional." As believers we are to "take up our cross daily" and follow Christ. Paul says, "I die every day" (1 Corinthians 15:31).

God uses, trials, persecutions, poverty, loneliness, distress, failure, disappointments. God uses these things to teach us, cause us to lose our will, and let God take charge.

When we begin to die our pure faith trusts the word of God even when there is no indication of God's presence or blessing. As a prophet you must distrust yourself, your own wisdom, your strength, and look to Christ alone for what you need.

How Does One Die to Self?

We must remember that we cannot rid ourselves of the flesh on this earth. The flesh is attached to us – it is still apart of us. But we must willingly refuse to serve it. Through regeneration, we are cut free from the flesh though it desires to rule over us. We have been given the power to master it. But we can still refuse to submit our will to the Spirit, exercise self-will and choose to serve the old self.

To be in God's will, "Serving self" is not an option, so we must "serve the Spirit." Our spiritual growth comes as we recognize the death that dwells in the rebellious old carnal nature of the flesh, and urgently flee from the clutches of that death and embrace the power of the new life through the life of Christ imparted within our spirits at regeneration.

You need to acknowledge the flesh, reject promptings and urges, acknowledge the nature of the Spirit which is your true essence, and surrender one's total spirit, soul, and body to the Spirit's leadership.

We must get to the place where we can say to God, "Not my will, but Thy will be done?" Let's recount the story of Jesus being tempted in the wilderness – the Holy Spirit led Jesus into the wilderness to be tempted by the devil (Matthew 4:1-16; Hebrews 4:15-16). After Jesus "fasted" for forty days and nights, the tempter approached Him.

Jesus knew the only way to combat the enemy of God was through prayer, fasting & the Word. The devil was not successful in getting Jesus to succumb to his whims of temptations, because Jesus was strengthened in His resolve to withstand through prayer and fasting and the word.

Dying to self" – what does it look like in practice?

- Dying to oneself involves "seeking God's will" then obeying His will" over our own (Isaiah 1:18-20; Matthew 9:13; 12:7).
- Dying to self involves love. Our obedience needs to be motivated by "love" – we must strive to obey God because we "love Him," and we don't want to grieve Him or cause Him pain.
- Dying to oneself involves Choices – When someone cuts you off in traffic you must choose to let go instead of going off into fits of rage (the flesh).

Humility and obedience are the pathway to death. "Jesus humbled Himself and became obedient unto death" (Philippians 2:8). In death He fully surrendered His will to the will of the Father; in death He gave up self, with its natural reluctance to drink the cup… He gave up his life. If it had not been for His boundless humility, counting Himself as nothing except as a servant to do and suffer the will of God, He never would have gone to the cross… and we would still be in our sins.

All those who have been used greatly by God have gone through an experience of 'dying to self' as described in Galatians 2:20.

The Secret of The Fullness of God

Ephesians 1:14: The Spirit is the guarantee [the first installment, the pledge, a foretaste] of our inheritance until the redemption of God's own [purchased] possession [His believers], to the praise of His glory.

What then is the secret of his fullness and of His abundant life of peace, power, and love?

The answer is this: the absolute, unwavering surrender of our lives to God to do His will instead of our own. When we surrender our sins and believe we will receive the Holy Spirit and when we surrender our lives and believe we are filled with the Holy Spirit.

Matthew 16:24-27

Then said Jesus unto his disciples, if any man will come after me, let him deny himself, and take up his cross, and follow me. For whosoever will save his life shall lose it: and whosoever will lose his life for my sake shall find it.

Receiving the Spirit is God's answer to repentance and faith. The fullness of the Spirit is God's answer to surrender and faith. At Salvation, the Spirit enters. At surrender, the spirit that has already entered, takes full possession. The Supreme human condition of the fullness of the Spirit is a life that is wholly surrendered to God to do his will.

First, the situation or the sinner. He has but one nature, the old man. He is declared absolutely to be dead in trespasses and sin. He has the self-life, but not the God life within him. He walks in the flesh and the Spirit strives with him but not in him.

For only he who is in Christ has the spirit.

Romans 8:9: But ye are not in the flesh, but in the Spirit, if so be that the Spirit of God dwell in you. Now if any man has not the Spirit of Christ, he is none of his.

But now comes a wonderful change. You repent and believe on the Lord Jesus Christ. What happens is you are born again. Born from above, Born of God, Born of the Spirit. And what does this phrase signify? A new life. A divine life. The life of God.

John 3:7: "Marvel not that I said unto thee, Ye must be born again."

John 3:3: "Jesus answered and said unto him, Verily, verily, I say unto thee, except a man be born again, he cannot see the kingdom of God."

See The Kingdom, 3708. Horaó, behold, perceive, See Properly, to stare at, to discern clearly.

Luke 17:20: Once, having been asked by the Pharisees when the kingdom of God would come, Jesus replied, "The kingdom of God does not come with your careful observation, 21 nor will people say, 'Here it is,' or 'There it is,' because the kingdom of God is within you."

Luke 16:16: The law and the prophets were until John: since that time the kingdom of God is preached, and every man presseth into it.

Romans 14:17: For the kingdom of God is not meat and drink, but righteousness, and peace, and joy in the Holy Ghost.

Galatians 5:22: But the fruit of the Spirit is love, joy, peace, patience, kindness, goodness, faithfulness.

Matthew 6:33: But seek ye first the kingdom of God, and his righteousness; and all these things shall be added unto you.

Seek ye the spread and accomplishment of God's kingdom; seek ye personal conformity to his standard of righteousness.

In the first chapter of Philippians, Paul tells the church at Philippi that his prayer for them is that their love would abound with knowledge and discernment, that they would be pure and blameless as they wait for the day of Christ, and that they would be "filled with the fruit of righteousness that comes through Jesus Christ—to the glory and praise of God" (Philippians 1:9–11).

The fruit of righteousness, like all fruit, springs from a seed—in this case, the seed of grace implanted in the heart of all believers at the moment of salvation.

Romans 3:10–18: Paul describes the state of unredeemed man—not one of us is righteous (pure, holy, undefiled).

God himself in the person of the Holy Spirit has come to dwell in us. We have received the Holy Spirit. We now have what the sinner does not have, a new nature. But when the new life came in, did the old man go out?

This is not the case. The old life does not go out when the new one comes in. Now, as a believer, you have a dual nature. In you are both the flesh and the spirit, the old life and the new. These two coexist, both dwell in you, they struggle for the Mastership of your life.

The flesh lusteth against the Spirit, and the Spirit against the flesh. Each desire to fill him (Galatians 5:17).

For the flesh lusteth against the Spirit and the Spirit against the flesh: and these are contrary, the one to the other: so that ye cannot do the things that ye would."

It is no longer how you should receive the Spirit. That one is settled. You have received him, but you find a joint tenancy with the flesh hidden inside.

The question now is having two natures within you, or shall you be filled with one of them? You must allow the fullness and the abundant life of the Spirit to rule you.

How can you be filled?

By yielding yourself wholly to the one that Filled you.

You have the power of choice. You can yield to either. But whatever life you yield to, that life will fill you. Once you yielded yourself as a servant of the flesh, Romans 6:19, were you not filled with all the unrighteousness? Romans 1:29, Even now just in proportion, as he yields himself to the spirit.

Romans 6:19: Will you not be filled with the Spirit?

It is like using air freshener in a stinking house. Air fresheners help mask odors while gracing your space with a pleasant scent. Suppose that you had an 8 bedroomed stinking house, and every room was full of a pungent. What if you used the Electric Air Fresheners and put only 1 in the one of the bedrooms. Would you be able to eliminate the reeking smell?

If you open one bedroom but leave the rest closed, the other 7 rooms with their stinking stench will hinder life within your house. But how can you fill the house? You must yield the house wholly to him?

You must capitulate to the leading of the spirit. Throwing open every door, closet, chamber, and lodging to the fragrant breath of the spirit of God and yield wholly to the life-giving stream and refuse to yield yourself to the carnal streams of the flesh.

Even so is it with the Holy Spirit, though he has come into every believer inside and he abides there and will abide forever, yet every believer is also indwelt by flesh and the spirit.

And you may continue to yield to the flesh that will thwart and choke up and clog up the manifestation of the fullness of the Spirit which is within him. Even after the Spirit has been received, there must be mastership of self in our lives.

Matthew 16:24–26: "Then Jesus said to His disciples, 'If anyone desires to come after Me, let him deny himself, and take up his cross, and follow Me.

Philippians 2:12: Wherefore, my beloved, as ye have always obeyed, not as in my presence only, but now much more in my absence, work out your own salvation with fear and trembling."

Failure to yield to the spirit explains the lack of the fullness of the Spirit expressed in the church today.

The power of that self-life. The selfish disposition in an enmity to God. It's carnality. It's grieving and quenches the spirit. It's deadly; it will hinder the flourishing of the fruits of the Spirit.

This self-life is fierce and desperate, devastative; you must resist its effort to master you. The trouble is not the spirit or to be habited by the Spirit. Can you yield to him and give him the opportunity to express himself fully?

The remedy is clear, logical, inescapable; yield to the spirit. Resist the self-life to the Mastership of it and surrender to the Spirit that the law of the Spirit of life in Christ Jesus made us free from the law of sin and death.

Romans 8:2: "For the law of the Spirit of life in Christ Jesus hath made me free from the law of sin and death."

Galatians 3:21: "Is the law then against the promises of God? God forbid for if there had been a law given which could have given life, verily righteousness should have been by the law."

Paul, a bond servant of Jesus Christ, called to be an apostle, and set apart to the gospel of God (Romans 1:1).

Yield to him to do his will, not your own. I beseech you, brethren, by the mercies of God that you present your bodies as living sacrifices unto God,

To whom you yield yourself to obey, His servants you are (Romans 6:13, 16,19).

But now, being made free from sin and becoming servants of God, you have your fruit unto holiness verse 22 You know the power blessing, fullness fruitage of the Holy Spirit, to whom you have now yielded.

Notice the impressive repetition and significant position, Romans 6: his exhortation to yield ourselves to God follows Romans 5. That is, as soon as the believer is justified by faith and receives the Holy Ghost verses 5, he is urged to yield himself to God holy and absolutely.

Because of the twofold nature of the believer, whatsoever you are filled with, you must yield to it. Otherwise, you will go on living in the power and the fullness of the flesh.

Therefore, the absolute yielding of our life to God is the first great step after conversion, having received the Spirit. There is no other way in reason.

But woe unto us if we omit the one supreme condition. We fail to open the doors of the soul to let the floodgate of his presence into the dark rooms within our soul. Surrender and pivot. Let the ancient gate open releasing its fullness.

This is the pathway of those who walk in the blessed life of the Holy Spirit. There is a yearning after a richness and fullness of life in Christ which never ceases to haunt your soul.

His blessed voice now calls you to these lofty untrodden heights of intimate communion, privilege, and service. Every consecrated child of God knows this Fact. Surrendering to God is the supreme step that brings you into the fullness of a closer walk with God.

Your journey may have been marred with complications, trials, confusion, difficulty but surrender was the culmination. And this fullness of the Spirit was the outcome of such act.

The fullness and the power that marks your life will go hand in hand with an unqualified, unwavering surrender of life in its fullest sweep.

To do the will of Him that sent you, only such surrender can bring his fullness again. That surrender is the secret of fullness. The resistance of the flesh proves the secret of fullness.

We can lead meetings, perform for men, sow seeds, that self-will is the stronghold of the flesh and the act of surrender storms the stronghold of self. This what the spirit desires, and the flesh must resist.

When a man or a woman tries to make such a surrender. The flesh will immediately assail you.

What clamorous protest! What hostility! What fear! What an agonizing struggle! What deadly swooning of the soul at the mere thought of yielding to God.

That day on which a child of God decides to yield his will to God, you will stand appalled at the revelations of your own unwillingness to do God's will. You will be astonished and humiliated beyond measure at the desperate and the repeated onslaught of self-life driving you into fear and defeat.

Self-life is a deadly plague within you that you must extirpate under the mighty hand of God.

When God states a condition of blessing, no other thing can be substituted. This is why all your crying, waiting, petitioning and even agonizing before God has accomplished nothing. You have been praying instead of obeying.

Prayer is all right with obedience, but not instead of it. Obedience is better than sacrifice. It is better than prayer? God is petitioning us.

Romans 12:1: "I beseech you therefore, brethren, by the mercies of God, that ye present your bodies a living sacrifice, holy, acceptable unto God, which is your reasonable service."

He expects us to act. But we kneel and we begin to pray. Prayer is a good thing. Indeed it is. But not well spent If we don't obey.

Genesis 22:16: And what was this upon the doing of which the blessing of God came to him as never before? It was a yielding of his all to God in the surrender of his son,

No other thing will avail, constant prayer, all these will not avail anything. This yielded life is the very citadel of faith. God will not force it. When it comes, it will flood your life with this fullness of blessing.

How much more must God be grieved by our poor attempt to bribe him by giving him everything else except the one thing he wants ourselves? My son, give me thine heart. There is a giving, which is the giving of us and there is a gift of ourselves.

If our response to the lover of our soul falls short of the true hearted surrender of ourselves, we thereby show that we do not fully trust him. But this shows him the distrust haunting our surrender to him.

God cannot give fullness of the Spirit to him, who does not have such fullness of trust, as to yield his life to Him. The responsibility for this fullness of the Spirit is in your own hands.

The question now rests with you. God has already done all he can for us in giving Christ. He has blessed us with every spiritual blessing in the heavenly In Christ Jesus.

Do we want God to pour out the fullness of the Holy Spirit? He has done so in Christ.

In Him dwells all the fullness of the Godhead Bodily (Colossians 2:9). Do we want God to put us in Christ where the fullness dwells? He has done so. There is but one thing left and that is yours.

It is to yield yourself to Christ, to whom you are united, and to give him opportunity to pour forth His fullness in and through you. This you must do.

Do not attempt to throw the responsibility on God. He has pledged to give you His fullness as soon as you surrender your life wholly to him. He will not coerce you. You may say I have wrestled. I have agonized. You are calling on God to do something instead of obeying His command to do something yourself.

The question is, have you yielded? Have you taken your hands off your own life and consecrated it holy, unflinchingly, eternally to the Lord Jesus to be his loving bond slave forever?

It is a question of your receptiveness. You surrender. Is he worthy of trust? Of absolute trust? Then how far will you trust him? Will you yield to him? With self-abandonment, Will you throw yourself upon him? The only limit to His fullness is the limitation of your surrender.

There is a deadly snake deep within you that you must slay without mercy, the snake of self, unbelief. Slay it with a trustful act of surrender. Crush it before it digs its fangs deeper into your heart.

17.
Trichotomy Of Man.

Ipray God your whole spirit and soul and body be preserved blameless unto the coming of our Lord Jesus Christ (1 Thessalonians 5:23).

For the word of God is quick, and powerful, and sharper than any two-edged sword, piercing even to the dividing asunder of soul and spirit, and of the joints and marrow (body), and is a discerner of the thoughts and intents of the heart (Hebrews 4:12).

We are created in the image of God; we have a spiritual nature that is separate and distinct from the body in which it dwells.

The two following passages from the Bible establish the fact that man is a triune being composed of spirit, soul, and body:

I pray God your whole spirit and soul and body be preserved blameless unto the coming of our Lord Jesus Christ (1 Thessalonians 5:23).

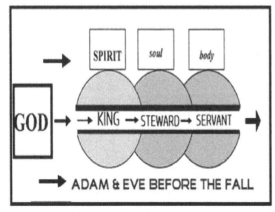
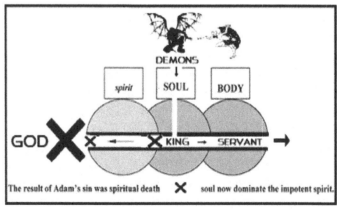

For the word of God (Christ) is quick, and powerful, and sharper than any two-edged sword, piercing even to the dividing asunder (Veil) of soul and spirit, and of the joints and marrow (body), and is a discerner of the thoughts and intents of the heart (Hebrews 4:12).

At salvation, the sword the word circumcises the old stubborn old heart to separate it from the spirit. God then habits the spirit.

1 Corinthians 6:17: "But he that is joined unto the Lord is one spirit."

In his unfallen state the 'Spirit' of man was influenced from Heaven. Still, when the human race fell through Adam, sin shut out the illumination and influence, the spirits influence that illuminated that chamber, pulled down the veil, the chamber of the spirit became a dark death chamber and remains so in every unregenerate heart until the Life and Light-giving power of the Holy Spirit floods that chamber with the Life and Light-giving power of the new life in Christ Jesus.

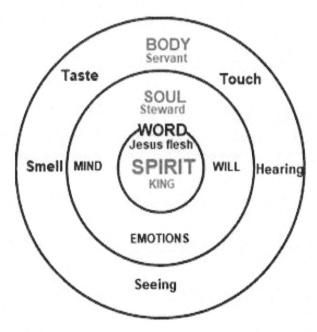

In the Garden of Eden: Eve saw that the tree was good for food, and that it was pleasant to the eyes, and a tree to be desired to make one wise, she took of the fruit thereof, and did eat. Genesis 3:6: the woman, Eve, saw that the tree was good for food the lust of the flesh, it was pleasant to the eyes the lust of the eyes, and a tree to be desired to make one wise, the pride of life. Eve was deceived, Adam disobeyed, sin came into the world, and death passed upon all men by sin, for that all have sinned...

1 John 2:15-17

Love is not the world, nor the things that are in the world. If any man loves the world, the love of the Father is not in him. For all that is in the world, the lust of the flesh, and the lust of the eyes, and the pride of life, is not of the Father, but is of the world.

The five senses; taste, touch, smell, hearing, and seeing, are the carnal mind – which is the enemy of God. These senses are what Satan uses to tempt us! The lust of the flesh includes tasting, touching, smelling, and hearing. The lust of the eyes is seeing. The pride of life is thinking you are special because of who you are, what you have, what you know, or what you look like.

The enemy uses these three things: the lust of the flesh, the lust of the eyes, and the pride of life to entice us to sin. Scripture shows this process at work in both the Garden of Eden and on the Mount of Temptation.

For to be carnally minded (minding the things of the flesh) is death; but to be spiritually minded is life and peace. Because the carnal mind (minding the things of the flesh) is enmity against God: for it is not subject to the law of God, neither indeed can be. So, then they that are in the flesh cannot please God...

Romans 8:6-8

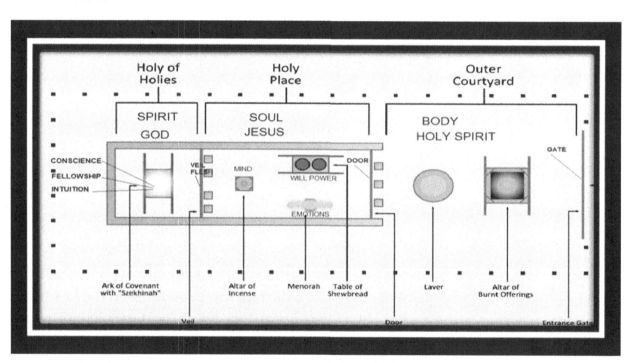

SPIRIT, SOUL, AND BODY

When you become born again your spirit and God's Spirit become one. Your human spirit fuses, joins and blends with the Holy Spirit to form a single entity called Spirit.

1 Corinthians 6:17: says but he who is joined to the Lord is one spirit with Him.

The soul, the Adamic nature, is battling the spirit nature. (saved nature/new creation)

At salvation, Hebrews 4:12 is fulfilled. The word living, moving and it is powerful and sharper than any two-edged sword and piercing to the dividing of soul and spirit, the spirit.

The word referred to here is Christ. Christ is the word of God. …and out of His mouth came a sharp two-edged sword; and His face was like the sun shining in its strength. (Revelation 1:16)

The two-edged swords were particularly deadly since they were able to cut from both sides of the blade.

So, at salvation, Christ cuts off the foreskin of the heart using this double-edged sword. Deuteronomy 10:16 Therefore circumcise the foreskin of your heart and be stiff-necked no longer.

Jeremiah 4:4: circumcise yourselves to the LORD, remove the foreskins of your hearts, O men of Judah and people of Jerusalem. Otherwise, my wrath will break out like fire and burn with no one to extinguish it, because of your evil deeds."

Spiritual circumcision must happen to each person who makes the New Covenant with God.

Under the New Covenant, God is calling a spiritual nation, composed of individuals, converted and regenerated by His Holy Spirit. God's people now are all to be "circumcised" spiritually. Physical circumcision is no longer necessary for religious purposes. It was a forerunner or type of what God really wanted, circumcision of the heart (Deuteronomy 10:16; 30:6; Jeremiah 4:4). Paul told the congregation in Rome that physical circumcision is of no spiritual benefit (Romans 2:25-29). Spiritual circumcision, though, is a process of conversion. That Christ circumcises us spiritually is made plain in Colossians 2:10-11. (10) And you are complete in Him, who is the head of all principality and power. (11) In Him you were also circumcised with the circumcision made without hands by putting off the body of the sins of the flesh, by the circumcision of Christ,

Colossians 2:11

In Him you were also circumcised in the putting off your sinful nature, with the circumcision performed by Christ and not by human hands.

Colossians 2:10-11 is talking about Hebrews 4:12 the word living, moving and it is powerful and sharper than any two-edged sword and piercing to the dividing of soul and spirit, the spirit.

Hebrews 4:12 is also what happened when God tore the veil. God allowed the flesh of his firstborn son to be cut or torn on that cross to make way for the life of God that resides in him to overflow and fill the whole earth.

His body was the veil Hebrews 10:20 by a new and living way, which he hath consecrated for us, through the veil, that is to say, his flesh.

God tore his flesh to allow us to receive life. The Life of God. John 1:4 in him was life; and the life was the light of men.

Genesis 2:7: And the LORD God formed man of the dust of the ground and breathed into his nostrils the breath of life; and man became a living soul.

1 Corinthians 15:45: so it is written: "The first man Adam became a living being," the last Adam a life-giving spirit. So, we see that Jesus is a life-giving spirit. John 1:4 in him was life; and the life was the light of men.

John 5:26: for as the Father has life in Himself, so also, He has granted the Son to have life in Himself.

1 John 1:2: and this is the life that was revealed; we have seen it and testified to it, and we proclaim to you the eternal life that was with the father and was revealed to us.

1 John 5:11: and this is that testimony: God has given us eternal life, and this life is in His Son.

Job 33:4: "The Spirit of God has made me, and the breath of the Almighty gives me life.

Adam's body had just been formed by God from the dust of the earth a lifeless human body lying on the ground. Then God "breathed" His own "breath of life" into the man's nostrils; God is the Source of life, and He directly placed life within man.

This breath of life is seen again in John 20:22, as Jesus imparts new life to His disciples. Jesus was the creator who imparted his life within Adam.

Now at salvation Jesus imparts life into our salvation experience. 1 Corinthians 15:45 so it is written: "The first man Adam became a living being"; the last Adam, a life-giving spirit.

Colossians 1:16: For by him were all things created, that are in heaven, and that are in earth, visible and invisible, whether they be thrones, or dominions, or principalities, or powers: all things were created by him, and for him.

Genesis 2:7: tells us that man became a living soul.

The word soul in Hebrew is nephesh, meaning "an animated, breathing, conscious, and living being."

So, what is the breath of God? It is God's resurrected life and power; it is Jesus himself the life-giving spirit. John 11:25 Jesus said to her, "I am the resurrection and the life. He who believes in me, though he may die, he shall live.

God gave this life within Adam to prepare him for communion with God. The Hebrew word for spirit is Ruach, which means "wind, breath, air, spirit."

Leviticus 17:14: the life of every creature is in its blood. That is why I have said to the people of Israel, 'You must never eat or drink blood, for the life of any creature is in its blood.' So whoever consumes blood will be cut off from the community.

If Leviticus 17:14 is true, then we can say that the Life of God resides inside the blood of Jesus. John 1:4 in him was life; and the life was the light of men.

Revelation 12:11: and they overcame him by the blood of the Lamb, and by the word of their testimony; and they loved not their lives unto the death.

Then Jesus said unto them, Verily, verily, I say unto you, except ye eat the flesh of the Son of man, and drink his blood, ye have no life in you (John 6:53).

His flesh is his suffering and the destruction of his flesh on the cross. Hebrews 10:20 by a new and living way, which he hath consecrated for us, through the veil, that is to say, his flesh.

If the veil was his flesh, then we must look at what happened to his flesh. It was torn and destroyed. So, to eat his flesh is to share in his suffering by putting to death our flesh.

1 Peter 4:13: but rejoice to the extent that you partake of Christ's sufferings, that when His glory is revealed, you may also be glad about exceeding joy.

Romans 8:17: and if we are children, then we are heirs: heirs of God and co-heirs with Christ–if indeed we suffer with Him, so that we may also be glorified with Him.

2 Corinthians 1:5: for just as the sufferings of Christ overflow to us, so also through Christ our comfort overflows.

2 Corinthians 4:10: we always carry around in our body the death of Jesus, so that the life of Jesus may also be revealed in our body.

Philippians 3:10: I want to know Christ and the power of His resurrection and the fellowship of His sufferings, being conformed to Him in His death,

To drink his blood is to partake of the life of God that is within his blood. It is to allow the life of God, the life-giving spirit, Jesus, to transform and conform our soul to his likeness.

1 Thessalonians 5:23: and the very God of peace sanctify you wholly; and I pray God your whole spirit and soul and body be preserved blameless unto the coming of our Lord Jesus Christ.

John 1:3-4: all things came into being through Him, and apart from Him nothing came into being that has come into being. In Him was life, and the life was the Light of men.

Revelation 13:8: and all that dwell upon the earth shall worship him, whose names are not written in the book of life of the Lamb slain from the foundation of the world. Matthew 25:34, Ephesians 1:4,

The Lamb hath been slain from the foundation of the world," because from "the foundation of the world "Hebrews 9:26 for then must he often have suffered since the foundation of the world: but now once in the end of the world hath he appeared to put away sin by the sacrifice of himself.

He was already sacrificed for the salvation of men, including Adam before the foundations of the world. His death "was foreordained before the foundation of the world," although manifest only in the last times.

We are all spiritual beings. Our first father was a spiritual being and a son of God.

Luke 3:38: which was the son of Enos, which was the son of Seth, which was the son of Adam, which was the son of God.

Hebrews 12:9: Furthermore, we have had human fathers who corrected us, and we paid them respect. Shall we not much more readily be in subjection to the Father of spirits and live?

Jesus who is called the second Adam in 1 Corinthians 15:45-49 we read that Jesus is the second Adam: "Thus it is written, 'The first man Adam became a living being'; the last Adam became a life-giving spirit. But it is not the spiritual that is first but the natural, and then the spiritual.

The first man was from the earth, a man of dust; the second man is from heaven. As was the man of dust, so also are those who are of the dust, and as is the man of heaven, so also are those who are of heaven. Just as we have borne the image of the man of dust, we shall also bear the image of the man of heaven."

1 Corinthians 15:45: First, Adam was a living being. Jesus is a life-giving being. Second, Adam was from the dust; Jesus, the second Adam, is from heaven. This passage shows that just as Adam was a natural being and Jesus was a spiritual being, so we likewise must be changed from a natural being to a spiritual being, transformed through Jesus Christ. Who is a life-giving spirit?

For as by a man came death, by a man has also come the resurrection of the dead. For as in Adam all die, so also in Christ shall all be made alive?"

1 Corinthians 15:21-22: This comparison and contrast demonstrate that through Adam, we experience death. But through Christ, we experience life.

1 Peter 1:20: He was chosen before the foundation of the world but was revealed at the end of the times for you.

Hebrews 2:14: Therefore, since the children have flesh and blood, He too shared in their humanity, so that by His death He might destroy him who holds the power of death, that is, the devil.

The Life of God. Is in the blood of Jesus… Leviticus 17:11 for the life of a creature is in the blood, and I have given it to you to make atonement for yourselves on the altar; it is the blood that makes atonement for one's life.

Deuteronomy 12:23: But be sure you do not eat the blood, because the blood is the life, and you must not eat the life with the meat.

For the life of all flesh is its blood, the life of all creatures consists in its blood; but only as long as the blood contains this life, for when it is dried up, or coagulated, life has passed away from it. When your spirit leaves your body, you die. Your spirit is the real you.

1Thessalonians 5:23: that your whole spirit, soul, and body be blameless until the coming of the Lord Jesus Christ.

Most Christians live in their soulish area and not in their spirit because they do not know the difference.

God Made Adam to be Spirit, Soul and Body.

His spirit was to be king of his life. God made his soul (mind, emotions and willpower) a servant. Lower that the spirit.

God doesn't reside in your mind. You find God within your spirit. You can have his influences from your spirit touching your mind. You can also put on the mind of Christ.

1 Corinthians 2:16: For who hath known the mind of the Lord, that he may instruct him? But we have the mind of Christ. You have the mind of Christ located within your spirit. So how can I have the mind of Christ?

Romans 12:2: And be not conformed to this world: but be ye transformed by the renewing of your mind, that ye may prove what [is] that good, and acceptable, and perfect, will of God.

Philippians 2:5: Let this mind be in you, which was also in Christ Jesus:

Man must have the life of God resident within the spirit, touching and affecting all the 3 departments of your being. SPIRIT, SOUL AND BODY. The body will only follow whoever rules man from the inside.

If it follows the mind, emotions, and your will, then the soul has become King. If the spirit is the king, then the SOUL (mind, emotions and will) will be servants to the spirit.

The body is a slave that takes orders from the (soul) servant or (Spirit) King.

Every human being must be born again in the spirit area of his life: a new nature, a new life and a new power comes into you and regenerates your spirit making it KING at salvation.

Most people live soulish lives. They live in their emotions, will, mind, and bodies following carnal senses.

The bible says that which is spirit is spirit, that which is body is body, and that which is soul is soul.

John 3:6: that having been born of the flesh is flesh, and that having been born of the Spirit is spirit. So, if we were spiritually born again at salvation then we are spiritual beings.

The body was made by God. The soul is the inside shell of the body. This part of man is his real self, his personality. The soul comprises intellect, emotions – the part that feels things and will power where man makes his decisions.

God made his spirit king in your life. If you quench the spirit, these 3 areas become disjoined, then your soul becomes king. And when your soul rules, people see the works of flesh on you.

God joined the body and soul together by His breath or word. And these two are to be subservient to the spirit. You don't have disease when the spirit is the king of your life. Your body functions at ease.

Proverbs 18:14: A man's spirit can endure sickness, but who can survive a broken spirit?

A man can endure anything if his spirit strong and empowered with the influence of the Holy Spirit

Proverbs 15:13: A joyful heart makes a cheerful face, but when the heart is sad, the spirit is broken.

The faculty of man called "spirit" enables the body to bear up against trouble and sickness.

Proverbs 17:22: A joyful heart is good medicine, but a broken spirit dries up the bones.

Once the spirit has become king, the soul is revived, and the body is free.

God has placed man's spirit inside the clay house, what we call body, behind the soul which is your thinking, feelings and will. Within your spirit God infuses his life. Divine interactions between your spirit and God's spirit takes place within your spirit.

1 Corinthians 2:9-10: But as it is written: "Eye has not seen, nor ear heard,

Nor have entered into the heart of man the things which God has prepared for those who love Him."

But God has revealed them to us through His Spirit. For the Spirit searches all things, yes, and the deep things of God.

1 Corinthians 2:11: for what man knoweth the things of a man, save the spirit of man which is in him? Even so the things of God knoweth no man, but the Spirit of God.

Spirit of God knows the things of God and our spirit knows the things of man. So at salvation, your spirit and the spirit of God fuse, join, and become one. 1 Corinthians 6:17 But he who is joined to the Lord is one spirit with Him.

God gave man's spirit the abilities to commune with deity. God will not commune with you through your soul or your body. The spirit must be king in your life before you can have a sanctified body or soul.

You can only think or perceive spiritually through your spirit. Until your spirit directs your will power, you cannot be the man or woman that God wants you to be.

The spirit is the communication center with heaven. That is where we get heaven's breaking news. It's a worship area. The sinner does not have it. When you have the spirit ruling, the soul is as a servant and the body as a slave, you have a perfect spiritual man or woman.

Only spirit can worship spirit. Only spirit can know/understand spirit. Only spirit can walk with spirit. Only spirit can be directed by spirit. Only spirit can serve spirit. Only spirit can receive revelation from spirit.

1 Corinthians 2:11: for who among men knows the thoughts of man except his own spirit within him? So too, no one knows the thoughts of God except the Spirit of God.

Proverbs 20:27: the spirit of man is the lamp of the LORD, Searching all the innermost parts of his being.

1 Corinthians 2:15: the spiritual man judges all things, but he himself is not subject to anyone's judgment.

Galatians 6:1: Brothers, if someone is caught in a trespass, you who are spiritual should restore him with a spirit of gentleness. But watch yourself, or you also may be tempted.

In the soul of man are three things; his mind/intellect, his emotions, where he feels, and his will power – this is the area of his rebellion.

James 4:1: what causes conflicts and quarrels among you? Don't they come from the passions at war within you?

When soul becomes king, everything is out of order with God. When Adam rebelled and disobeyed his God, his spirit died, and he had no more relationship and fellowship with God.

The human spirit is the born-again nature that comes to dwell in us now that we are born again.

What died in the Garden of Eden must come alive in CHRIST.

You don't make a commitment when you come to Jesus, you are born again. You are a new being. The human spirit within us is that born again nature.

The human spirit is your spirit fusing with God's Spirit; the thing that God put within you that was lying dormant. Then your spirit becomes the king of your life. Ephesians 2:1 as for you, you were dead in your transgressions and sins,

If you are not born again, you are walking around dead. Only your soul and body is alive. Ephesians 4:23 tells us man's spirit is the renewed spirit.

Romans 14:17: The kingdom of God is within you.

The kingdom of God is His righteousness, peace, and joy in the Holy Spirit within us. You do not seek peace – it is within you. We are joyful when the spirit is within us. The human personality becomes a dwelling place of God. God dwells upon your spiritual nature and expresses himself through your personalities.

You send forth God's Spirit through your spirit. Romans chapter 7 tells you the spirit must conquer that soul.

Hebrews 4:12: The word is dividing soul and spirit. The bible is the only thing that can divide soul and spirit. The dividing process – spiritual man and natural man can only be divided by the sword of the Spirit; that is the Word of God.

The three-compartment parts of the Tabernacle portray the three parts of man; the outer courts – the body of man, the Holy place – where the soul of man is and the Most Holy place – the spirit of man; the altar of incense can be the mind of man, the menorah lamp could be the emotions and the table of showbread could be the will.

There were three entrances to the Tabernacle; the gate to the outer court Exodus 27:16-19 – this, of course, is the body, it is open and it is big, the most exposed part of you; then there was a door to the Soul. Then the third entry is the veil which had no door at all, so the spirit is the hardest of all to get into.

Only the high priest could pass through the veil, only once. This means only God can minister to the spirit. There were three kinds of light in the tabernacle; the sun – the outer court, open to the elements, but the holy place only had the lamp stands – the mind, the emotions, and the will. But the Holy of Holies was lit by the Shekinah Glory of God, a divine supernatural light from God.

Romans 7:22: For in my inner being I delight in God's law; 7:23 but I see another law at work in me, waging war against the law of my mind and making me a prisoner of the law of sin at work within me.

Then Romans chapter 8 shows what Paul said about life in the spirit. (1) There is therefore now no condemnation for those who are in Christ Jesus. 2 For the law of the Spirit of life has set you free in Christ Jesus from the law of sin and death.

We have to decide each day if we are going to live in soul or spirit. The mind will accept a thought sometimes and even entertain it. Refuse to practice it by refusing to act on it. At that point, the spirit is ruling and commanding the mind to obey.

When we fast, we subdue our body, it gets weaker. The longer we fast we subdue our soulish nature.

Our willpower breaks down. Our mind does away with wanting to do this and that. Your emotions are stilled, then your spirit takes over and starts guiding and directing you.

So spiritual fasting has the soul, body and spirit all mixed up in it. When your spirit assumes its kingship, you are ready for action to be what the Lord wants you to be.

18.
Perfecting the Hearing, Circumcising the Ears and Eyes

As a prophet or prophetess, your eyes and ears are going to be very important. Therefore, cleaning or circumcising them and keeping them pure is very important.

In whom also ye also are circumcised with the circumcision made without hands, in putting off the body of the sins of the flesh by the circumcision of Christ" (Colossians. 2:11).

As we learned in the previous study entitled, "Spirit, Soul & Body man was created in God's image, therefore he is, as God is, a triune being, spirit, soul and body (1 Thessalonians. 5:23).

A simple analogy would be a basketball which has a leather cover (body) a rubber bladder (soul) and is filled with air (spirit).

The Bodily Form of the Soul

The soul has an invisible bodily form inside the physical body. Consider (Revelations 6:9-11). Notice that after death the disembodied soul retains a definite shape which could be clothed with a robe. The soul of the rich man in hell (Luke 16:22-24) still has his senses, sight, sound, touch, and taste.

We also learned that prior to the Fall, Adam's total being was in union with God. The light of the Holy Spirit passed through Adam's spirit unimpeded, reaching into his soul and influencing his mind, will, and body. Before the fall Adam was in harmony with his Creator, his spirit, soul and body were influenced by the power of God.

He was a spiritually minded being with free will, to which all things were possible. There was only one limitation placed upon Adam (Genesis 2:16-17).

As we shall see, a crucial change occurred when Adam and Eve exercised their God-given free will to disobey. A split second after the creature chose to defy his Creator an inward fatality occurred. Adam and Eve's spiritual union with God was the first casualty of their disobedience...the departure of the Holy Spirit's influence on their spirit rendered them spiritually dead, separated from God.

As a result of the "Fall" Adam and all his descendants were then, "dead in trespasses and sins..." (Ephesians 2:1). This death not only affected the spirit of man, but also the soul and body.

Effect of the "fall" on the physical Body

From this point on, Adam's physical body would gradually begin to deteriorate and eventually die, "for dust thou art, and unto dust shalt thou return" (Genesis 3:19).

Effect on the Soul

Without the light of the Holy Spirit to guide them (due to spiritual death), their fallen flesh becomes the dominating life force.

Prior to Adam's transgression, his soul was free from his flesh. When he sinned and died spiritually his soul became joined to his flesh.

Before the fall, the priority and order were spirit, soul, and body...the spirit was the master, the soul, the steward and the body, the servant.

After the fall the order was reversed...the body became the master, the soul remained the steward and the spirit became the servant.

Adam's soul and body have merged...the soul is now joined to the body of fallen flesh which has become the dominant life force.

Spirit, Soul, and Body upon Salvation

When a person, under the conviction of the Holy Spirit, repents of their sin and by faith trusts in Jesus' substitutionary death on their behalf, the word of God states that they are, "born again" (John 3:3). Jesus' explanation of the second birth to Nicodemus (John 3:3-8) reveals that He was referring to a spiritual re-birth "born of the Spirit" (v. 8).

The reason that Jesus is called the "last Adam" (1 Corinthians 15:45) is because He came to undo the curse of the first Adam. When Adam sinned, he immediately experienced a spiritual death, (Genesis 2:17) later followed by a physical death (Genesis 5:5). Upon salvation a reversal occurs...the spirit is first quickened then the body at a future time (Romans 8:23).

Adam's disobedience resulted in death. His entire being (spirit, soul, and body) was affected. The obedience of the "last Adam" restored life to that which was lost. Jesus' death, burial, and resurrection redeemed mankind...spirit, soul, and body. "For as one man's disobedience many were made sinners, so by the obedience of one shall many be made righteous" (Romans 5:19).

Therefore, if any man be in Christ, he is a new creature..." (2 Corinthians 5:17).

The miracle of the second birth as described in (Titus 3:5) "...according to his mercy he saved us, by the washing of regeneration, and renewing of the Holy Ghost..." Regenerated, restored to a former state...that which was dead is brought back to life! "And you hath he quickened, [made alive] who were dead in trespasses and sins..." (Ephesians 2:1) [Emphasis mine]

Salvation involves a supernatural operation whereby the believer is placed into the body of Christ through a spiritual baptism (1 Corinthians 12:13). This baptism involves a "circumcision made without hands" (Colossians 2:11) by which his soul is literally cut away from the body of flesh. In the process, the Holy Spirit indwells man's spirit, permanently sealing him (Ephesians 1:13), so that two spirits become one (1 Corinthians 6:17-19).

In God's eyes, every born-again believer has been "crucified with Christ" (Galatians 2:20), thereby uniting them to His death, burial and resurrection.

At this point, the believer is, "complete in him, [in Christ] which is the head of all principality and power..." (Colossians 2:10) [Emphasis mine]

The "circumcision made without hands" is a supernatural operation made by the Holy Spirit cutting free the redeemed soul from, "the body of the sins of the flesh."

Thereby restoring the priority and order of spirit, soul, and body (1 Thessalonians 5:23) and creating a sanctuary within the believer separate from the corrupt body of flesh. This is the only way the Holy Spirit could indwell man without being joined to his sinful flesh! Under the Old Testament, God dwelt in a tabernacle made with hands (Exodus 25). In the New Testament, He dwells in the tabernacle made without hands (within the believer). This is why the word of God refers to a saved person's body as the "temple of the Holy Ghost" (1 Corinthians 6:19, 3:16-17).

Christ in you, the hope of glory" (Colossians 1:27).

As a result of this spiritual operation every born-again believer has two diametrically opposed forces within. The Bible refers to them as the "new man" and the "old man" (Ephesians 4:22-24). The new man is led by the Spirit and the old man by the flesh.

Abraham, though ninety-nine years of age, was circumcised (consecrated) on the same day as Ishmael, who was thirteen.

Genesis 17:24: And Abraham was ninety years old and nine, when he was circumcised (consecrated) in the flesh of his foreskin. (When he was consecrated from his flesh).

Slaves, whether home-born or purchased, were circumcised.

Genesis 17:12: And he that is eight days old shall be circumcised (he that is 8 years in faith) among you, every man child in your generations, he that is born in the house, or bought with money of any stranger, which is not of thy seed.

Genesis 17:14: and the uncircumcised man child whose flesh of his foreskin is not circumcised, that soul shall be cut off from his people; he hath broken my covenant.

It was a sign and seal of the covenant of grace and the national covenant between God and the Hebrews. (1.) It sealed the promises made to Abraham, which related to the commonwealth of Israel, national promises. (2.) But the promises made to Abraham included the promise of redemption.

Galatians 3:14: that the blessing of Abraham might come on the Gentiles through Jesus Christ; that we might receive the promise of the Spirit through faith, a promise which has come upon us. The covenant with Abraham was a dispensation or a specific form of the covenant of grace, and circumcision was a sign and seal of that covenant. It had a spiritual meaning. It signified purification of the heart, inward circumcision effected by the Spirit.

Deuteronomy 10:16: Circumcise therefore the foreskin of your heart and be no more stiff-necked.

Deuteronomy 30:6: And the LORD thy God will circumcise thine heart, and the heart of thy seed, to love the LORD thy God with all thine heart, and with all thy soul, that thou mayest live.

Under the Jewish dispensation, church and state were identical. No one could be a member of one without also being a member of the other. Circumcision was a sign and seal of membership in both.

Every circumcised person bore thereby evidence that he was one of the chosen people, a member of the church of God as it then existed, and consequently also a member of the Jewish commonwealth.

In the Bible, God revealed to us a spiritual principle and experience called circumcision. To understand the Spiritual truth, it is first necessary to look at the dynamics of circumcision as God revealed them in the Old Testament.

Jesus' death on the cross accomplished much more than simply forgiving sins. It made it possible for you to become like Christ. For you to become Christ-like you must get rid of the old flesh nature that is sinful. This is where the spiritual principle of circumcision comes in. Circumcision is the cutting away of the flesh.

Matthew 6:22: The eye is the lamp of the body.

So, if your eye is clear, your whole body will be full of light.

What your eyes see affects the operation and function of your soul. Your eyes should only allow pure things into the temple. Your body is the temple.

The lamp of the tabernacle was the menorah. We can compare menorah here with the eye. Menorah is one of the oldest symbols of the Jewish faith, a seven-branched candelabrum used in the Temple. The priest lit the menorah in the Sanctuary every evening and cleaned it out every morning, replacing the wicks and putting fresh olive oil into the cups.

Since God dictated the creation of the Menorah from 100 percent pure gold, we must strive for a "solid gold relationship with God" regarding our motives and behavior. In other words, our shining character traits on the inside should reflect our holy actions on the outside, and vice versa.

In this way, the Menorah teaches us to bring out every soul's inner motive under God's holy light so that we shine internally and externally.

The priest lit the menorah in the Sanctuary every evening and cleaned it out every morning, replacing the wicks and putting fresh olive oil into the cups.

Matthew 6:22: The eye is the lamp of the body.

So, if your eyes are clear, your whole body will be full of light.

Light your eyes every evening and clean them every morning- Let your eyes behold his holiness in the evening. Consecrate your eyes. Dedicate your eyes to God in the evening and pray for God to cleanse it in the morning and protect it from beholding evil and guile.

Replacing wicks means cultivating your relationship with God and removing the corruption and the inward evil desires that choke the effectiveness of the light in you. Putting in fresh oil means that you allow your relationship with Jesus to remain fresh for the light to be effective.

The lamp of the tabernacle was the menorah. We can compare the menorah here with the eye. The Menorah's structure also inspires us to embrace holiness. The Menorah begins with a central stem that branches outwards, just as our demeanor, behavior, personality, and especially good deeds should branch out and influence others to illuminate the world around us.

Job 7:18: For you examine us every morning and test us every moment. As by the eye the bodily members learn its environment, and naturally, almost automatically, tends to adjust itself to it, so is it with the gaze of the soul. The soul perceives and tends to accommodate itself to the things of this world.

But we are not of this world. John 17:16 they are not of the world, just as I am not of the world.

Jesus is saying we are not of this world. Therefore, we should fix our gaze on our world. Our world is not this one.

Colossians 3:2: Set your affection on things above, not on things on the earth.

2 Corinthians 4:18: So we fix our eyes not on what is seen, but on what is unseen. For what is seen is temporary, but what is unseen is eternal.

Hebrews 12:2: fixing our eyes on Jesus, the pioneer and perfecter of faith. If we set our eyes upon things in heaven, heaven will affect our soulish perspective. Our soul will perceive things of God, and tends to accommodate itself to the things of heaven. If our eyes are set on the things of this world, then the things of this world will darken and influence our soul and rob it of the light or effectiveness. If we want to have a strong spiritual eye then we must guard it making sure that it is only beholding only, ***whatever is true, whatever is noble, whatever is right, whatever is pure, whatever is lovely, whatever is admirable--if anything is excellent or praiseworthy--think about such things. Philippians 4:8***

As the bodily eye is not itself light, but only an instrument for receiving and imparting light, so our eyes when disciplined can relay good light into the soul. If therefore thine eye be single. The word "single" here can also mean if your eye is dedicated. Psalm 119:130: The entrance of your words gives light; It gives understanding to the simple. If therefore thine eye be single (dedicated) clear, pure. This means not looking two ways.

Singleness of purpose, looking right at its object as opposed to having two ends in view (Proverbs 4:25-27). The man who looks with a good, sound eye, walks in the light, seeing every object clear; so a simple and persistent purpose to serve and please God in everything will make the whole soul consistent and bright in God.

1 Samuel 16:7: But the Lord said to Samuel, "Do not look on his appearance or on the height of his stature, because I have rejected him. For the Lord sees not as man sees. Man looks on the outward appearance, but the Lord looks on the heart."

Samuels's eyes were at first influenced by what traditions had taught him about how warriors should look like. They were muscular men with a strong personality.

But that was not the Lord's criteria. 1 Corinthians 1:27 But God chose the foolish things of the world to shame the wise; God chose the weak things of the world to shame the strong.

Psalm 101:3: I will not set before my eyes anything that is worthless. I hate the work of those who fall away; it shall not cling to me.

David makes a personal vow to not set his eyes before anything vile or worthless. The word worthless in Hebrew means worthless or wicked.

I will set no wicked thing before mine eyes, either the eyes of the body, which are the inlets of lust, "I will not propose to my heart;' "in my thought'. The eye picks the target that the soul craves.

That is, I will not set up an evil thing in my imagination, to dwell upon in my thoughts, and take delight and pleasure in meditating upon it; or set it before me, to imitate as a pattern, to work by, and copy after:

Psalm 16:8: I have set the LORD always before me: because he is at my right hand, I shall not be moved.

Matthew 5:28: But I say to you that everyone who looks at a woman with lustful intent has already committed adultery with her in his heart. (The soul has struggled with lust, therefore the motivation of the soul to the eye is not the admiration of the beauty of God's creation from a pure heart. Instead it is perversion of lust.

Titus 1:15,16: "To the pure, all things are pure. But to those who are defiled and unbelieving, nothing is pure, but both their mind and their conscience are defiled. They profess to know God, but by their deeds they deny him, being detestable and disobedient, and worthless for any good deed."

If your eyes are pure or clean, then you will see everything in the nature of their purity as God intended.

Psalm 119:18: Open my eyes, that I may behold wondrous things out of your law.

Even when reading the word, we need the illumination of God to understand the wondrous things therein. Our desires and motives and even the posture of our soul could affect the ability to see an illumination in the word.

The more our soul is yielded to God, the more his light shines through our eyes allowing us to see wondrous things in the word.

Proverbs 21:4: haughty eyes and a proud heart, the lamp of the wicked, are sin.

Proverbs have a lot to say about eyes, and it links them here to a proud heart. "Haughty eyes," produce sin." So, if you want wisdom, you don't want haughty eyes.

The word haughty comes from an old Anglo-French word, haut, which means "high," and which comes from the Latin word altus, from which we get our word altitude. Putting all that together, we find that haughty eyes look down at other people, as if the one looking down is "higher up" than others.

So, you can see the proud heart can influence the eyes to look down on people. Racial discrimination is the same.

If we cannot see people, the way God sees them then we have a biased eye.

The moment we see someone of another race, we will either see them as God's beautiful creation, or our biased soul steps in and influences our judgement. As you can see, our eyes pick the scene, but it is up to our heart to redirect our focus and soul.

At the heart of this again is the problem of comparing—we don't just look down; we look down at other people as if they are lower or lesser than we are.

Matthew 5:29: If your right eye causes you to sin, tear it out and throw it away. For it is better that you lose one of your members than that your whole body be thrown into hell.

So, we are called to discipline the eye. Control the light that comes through it… make sure, it is God's light. Just like the menorah draws oil, the source of light from the middle branch.

We must base our vision from God. Then our light will be his light. The light in our eyes will be his light.

Job 31:7: If my step has turned aside from the way and my heart has gone after my eyes, and if any spot has stuck to my hands,

Psalm 13:2-3: How long must I take counsel in my soul and have sorrow in my heart all the day?

How long shall my enemy be exalted over me? Consider and answer me, O Lord my God; light up my eyes, lest I sleep the sleep of death,

Psalm 38:10: My heart throbs; my strength fails me, and the light of my eyes—it also has gone from me.

When you lose the light or influence of God through your eyes, your soul will be plunged into darkness and relying on your soul will lead to heart throbs and strength failing.

Job 31:1: "I have made a covenant with my eyes; how then could I gaze at a virgin?"

You have to sometimes make a vow not to look at the exposure of sin.

Psalm 119:37: Turn my eyes from looking at worthless things; and give me life in your ways.

Realize that the life of God is hidden in the ways of God. If your eyes are focused on worthless things, it will lack the life of God. This means that you will have death ruling your visual perspective.

Psalm 32:8: I will instruct you and teach you in the way you should go; I will counsel you with my eye upon you. God's eyes upon your eyes, Greater is he that is within you.

This is God's eyes upon your eyes leading you in his ways. This means that God has overtaken the soul. Therefore, even your eyes are controlled and directed by God, only seeing what he sees.

Psalm 33:18: Behold, the eye of the Lord is on those who fear him, on those who hope in his steadfast love.

Ye are of God, little children, and have overcome them: because greater is he is in you, than he that is in the world (1 John 4:4).

James 1:27: Religion that is pure and undefiled before God, the Father, is this: to visit orphans and widows in their affliction, and to keep oneself unstained from the world.

Keeping your eyes from the corruption of the world

1 Peter 3:3-4: Do not let your adorning be external—the braiding of hair and the putting on of gold jewelry, or the clothing you wear— but let your adorning be the hidden person of the heart with the imperishable beauty of a gentle and quiet spirit, which in God's sight is very precious.

Isaiah 6:10: Make the heart of this people dull, and their ears heavy, and blind their eyes; lest they see with their eyes, and hear with their ears, and understand with their hearts, and turn and be healed."

Philippians 4:8: Finally, brothers, whatever is true, whatever is honorable, whatever is just, whatever is pure, whatever is lovely, whatever is commendable, if there is any excellence, if there is anything worthy of praise, think about these things.

John 12:40: "He has blinded their eyes and hardened their heart, lest they see with their eyes, and understand with their heart, and turn, and I would heal them."

Isaiah 5:21: Woe to those who are wise in their own eyes, and shrewd in their own sight!

You could be wise in your own eyes. That means the light in your eyes is governed by self and flesh.

Isaiah 43:8: Bring out the people who are blind, yet have eyes, who are deaf, yet have ears!

2 Peter 2:14: they have eyes full of adultery, insatiable for sin. They entice unsteady souls they have hearts trained in greed. Accursed children!

Song of Solomon 4:7: you are altogether beautiful, my love; there is no flaw in you.

Job 17:7: My eye has grown dim from vexation, and all my members are like a shadow. Weak, worn out, unstable, fleeting, ready to pass away.

When the eyes are vexed upon wrong things the result is weak, worn out, unstable, fleeting, and ready to pass away.

Lamentations 5:15-17: Joy has left our hearts; our dancing has turned to mourning....16 The crown has fallen from our head. Woe to us, for we have sinned! 17 Because of this, our hearts are faint; because of these, our eyes grow dim.

The heart—not only the eyes, are the channels but the heart the fountain head of lust.

Job 31:7: "Mine heart walked after mine eyes."

Luke 11:35: Be careful, then, that the light within you is not darkness.

Proverbs 20:27: The spirit of a man is the lamp of the LORD, searching out his inmost being.

The spirit of man, breathed into him at first by the Creator (Genesis 2:7), and afterwards quickened and illumined by the Divine Spirit, is the "candle of the Lord," given to man as an inward light and guide. Searching all the inward parts of the belly. That is, of the inmost heart of man; testing all his thoughts, feelings, desires, by God's law, approving some, condemning others, according as they agree with it or not. The word "belly" is equivalent to "heart" or "soul" in Job 15:2; Job 15:15; Job 32:19; John 7:38.

Matthew 6:23: But if your eye is evil, your whole body will be full of darkness. If then the light within you is darkness, how great is that darkness!

1 Corinthians 2:11: For who among men knows the thoughts of man except his own spirit within him? So too, no one knows the thoughts of God except the Spirit of God.

Matthew 6:22: The eye is the lamp of the body. So, if your eye is clear, your whole body will be full of light. What your eyes see affects the operation and function of your soul, your eyes should only allow pure things into the temple. Your body is the temple.

19.
Intimacy First

The dimensions of the spirit are realms revealed only to eagles that desire to sample the lofty heights. Only those who will walk with him like Enoch. This requires intimacy and unreserved dependable, reckless abandonment to the Holy spirit. In these dimensions earthly entanglements will be cut off in the flames of intimacy,

The groom is the refining fire. He forges and perfects the bride in his refining fire, engulfing her in fiery trials and perfecting her faith as gold.

Job 23:10: "But he knoweth the way that I take: when he hath tried me, I shall come forth as gold."

The bride reflects the groom; this formation leads to a glorious transformation.

Relational Worship

Apostle Paul described true worship perfectly in Romans 12:1-2: "I urge you therefore, brethren, by the mercies of God to present your bodies a living and holy sacrifice, acceptable to God which is your spiritual service of worship. And do not be conformed to this world but be transformed by the renewing of your mind that you may prove what the will of God is, that which is good and acceptable, or well pleasing and perfect."

This passage contains all the elements of true worship.

In this passage is a description of the manner of our worship: "present your bodies a living and holy sacrifice." Presenting our bodies means giving to God all of ourselves.

The reference to our bodies here means all our human faculties, "May your whole spirit, soul and body be kept blameless at the coming of our Lord Jesus Christ" (1 Thessalonians 5:23).

Make it your goal to have a deep, intimate relationship with God. Let Him into every area of your life. When you decide to serve God with your whole heart and make Him first in your life, your soul will prosper, and your joy and peace will increase.

Remember to lean on Him more than anything else, and tell Him, "God, I want to do this, but I can't do it without You." He doesn't expect you to live for Him in your own strength or ability.

The whole ministry of Jesus flowed out of an intimate relationship with the Father. Jesus Himself said, "Most assuredly, I say to you, the Son can do nothing of Himself, but what He sees the Father do; for whatever He does, the Son also does in like manner. For the Father loves the Son and shows Him all things that He Himself does" (John 5:19-20).

Jesus walked with the Father and was led continually by the Holy Spirit. During intense ministry demands, He would often withdraw from the crowds in order to pray, and we would do well to follow His example (Luke 5:15-16).

When Jesus called the twelve apostles, He established this same pattern: "Then He appointed twelve, that they might be with Him and that He might send them out to preach, and to have power to heal sicknesses and to cast out demons" (Mark 3:14-15). Before they were called to minister to others, they were called to be with Jesus. Ministry to the Lord comes before ministry for the Lord.

Our first call is to know God intimately and grow in relationship with Him. All other ministry activities—including healing the sick, casting out demons, prophesying—are secondary to that and should flow out of that relationship.

Jesus not only modeled a life of prayer and relationship with the Father, He taught it as well: "But you, when you pray, go into your room, and when you have shut your door, pray to your Father who is in the secret place; and your Father who sees in secret will reward you openly" (Matthew 6:6).

Jesus instructs us to spend focused time with God in the "secret place." This personal time with God is invaluable. Our highest aim should be to know God Himself and live a life of devotion and obedience to Him.

Rather than minister to others, seek to minister to the Lord. Prioritize your time in the secret place above all else. Don't lose your primary focus: relationship with God. This always comes first!

20.
WALKING IN THE SPIRIT

Our lives are a manifestation of what we think about God." "The man who is not led by the spirit is a slave to his environment."

Now faith is the assurance of things hoped for, the conviction of things not seen… And without faith it is impossible to please Him, for he who comes to God must believe that He is and that He is a rewarder of those who seek Him" (Hebrews 11:1, 6).

Walking in the spirit requires you to look past your natural circumstances and trust God completely.

"And I, brethren, could not speak to you as to spiritual men, but as to men of flesh, as to infants in Christ. I gave you milk to drink, not solid food; for you were not yet able to receive it. Indeed, even now you are not yet able. For you are still fleshly. For since there is jealousy and strife among you, are you not fleshly, and are you not walking like mere men" (1 Corinthians 3:1-3)?

"Concerning Him [Jesus] we have much to say, and it is hard to explain, since you have become dull of hearing. For though by this time you ought to be teachers, you have need again for someone to teach you the elementary principles of the oracles of God, and you have come to need milk and not solid food. For everyone who partakes only of milk is not accustomed to the word of righteousness, for he is an infant. But solid food is for the mature, who because of practice have their senses trained to discern good and evil" (Hebrews 5:11-14).

There are Four Kinds of Men (1 Corinthians 2-3)

1. Natural (lost) man - Non-believers
2. Infants in Christ- Baby Christians
3. Men of Flesh or Carnal Christians

The Soulish Man lives within the Five Natural Senses

1. Touch 2. Smell 3. Sight 4. Hearing 5. Taste

The Soulish Man relies on his mind, will, and emotions and does not know how to align his carnal soul to the Holy Spirit who lives within him.

4. The Spiritual Man

Within the spiritual man there is Conscience, Discernment, Communion Examples and Illustrations of Walking in the Spirit

- John 3:6: "That which is born of the flesh is flesh, and that which is born of the Spirit is spirit."
- Mark 2:8:   Jesus, aware in His spirit..."
- Matthew 14:22-33 "The disciples saw Him walking on the sea ..."
- Luke 24:13-35 "Then their eyes were opened, and they recognized Him."

Walk by the Spirit, and you will not carry out the desire of the flesh. For the flesh sets its desire against the Spirit, and the Spirit against the flesh; for these are in opposition to one another, so that you may not do the things that you please.

But if you are led by the Spirit, you are not under the Law (Galatians 5:16-18).

Seeing Spiritual Things

To see spiritual things, we must be born again.

- We must be filled with the Holy Spirit.
- We must be spiritually mature.
- We must have a spiritual mind.
- Natural things are (1) visible and (2) temporary.
- Spiritual things are (1) invisible and (2) eternal.

- Natural things have natural power.
- Spiritual things have spiritual power.

Some Guidelines for Walking in the Spirit

1. Be born again (John 3:3).
2. Be filled with the Holy Spirit (Romans 8:9; 1 Corinthians 2:9-16).
3. Be spiritually mature (1 Corinthians 3:1-3).
4. Be spiritually minded (Romans 8:5-8).
5. Have no condemnation (Romans 8:1).
6. Walk in freedom from fear (Romans 8:15).
7. Pray in the Spirit (Romans 8:26).
8. Develop and operate in your spiritual gifts (1 Corinthians 12:1).
9. Be led by the Spirit by following His promptings (Romans 8:14).
10. Do not be entangled in the world (2 Timothy 2:4).
11. Master spiritual disciplines (1 Timothy 4:7).
12. Learn the spiritual discipline of waiting (Romans 8:25).

Learn to Wait on God

Signs or Patterns that will show that you are not waiting on God.

- Debt
- Dependence on others
- Broken relationships and repeated conflict
- Unfinished projects
- Repeated moves and changes (church to church, job to job)
- Broken or un-kept vows
- Being discontent
- Reliance on formulas or methods ("how-to" books, etc.)
- Stress (not resting)
- Feelings of insecurity, doubt, fears, worthlessness
- Forcing or manipulating people or things in your life

"He commanded them ... to wait for the promise of the Father ..." (Acts 1:4).

God's Pattern and Purposes for Us in Waiting:

- God finished Creation with the Sabbath (Genesis 2:1-3).
- God made the Sabbath for Man and Not Man for the Sabbath (Mark 2:27).
- God's Purpose in the Sabbath was to establish a Pattern for Man to Rest in the Finished Work of Christ (Hebrews 4:9-11).
- Divine Order (God's Pattern) = God works, Man rests.
- Exodus 33:14 = the purpose of having a relationship with God is to experience God's presence.
- The purpose of God's presence in our lives is to give us rest!

7. Walking in the Spirit means that we must choose presence over process, relationships over results, rest over works (Exodus 33).

How to Walk in the Spirit

1. Have no condemnation (Romans 8:1).
2. Store up treasures in Heaven (Matthew 6:19).
3. Serve one Master (Matthew 6:24).
4. Live one day at a time (Matthew 6:25-27, 34).
5. Trust God for every need (Matthew 6:28-32).
   - Learn the difference between wants and needs.
   - Jesus defined needs as being food and clothing.
6. Be kingdom minded (Matthew 6:33-34).
7. Learn Contentment (Philippians 4:11-13).
8. Fill your life with God's Word (John 8:32).
9. Become Alert to the Promptings of the Holy Spirit.

Becoming Alert to the Promptings of the Holy Spirit

1. They are inward urgings to do God's will.
2. They are only understood by our spirit as we have been filled by the Holy Spirit.
3. They are usually opposite to our basic desires and inclinations.
4. They are always in harmony with the total message of the Scriptures.
5. They almost always involve less control on our part.
6. They always require faith.

How to Walk in the Spirit

1. Resist the devil (James 4:7).
2. Do not grieve the Holy Spirit (Ephesians 4:30).
3. Master your fleshly desires (Galatians 5:16-17).
4. Develop Discernment (Philippians 1:9).
5. Discover and accept God's design and boundaries for your life.

Here are some Godly limitations protect us and define us:

- Parents
- Time in History
- Gender
- Family
- Nationality
- Race
- Birth Order
- Mental Abilities
- Physical Features
- Personality

21.
THE TWO OFFICES OF MINISTRY

How to Minister from the Secret Place (Part One) Ezekiel 44:4-31.

What does God want us to know?

He wants us to know that according to Divine Order the words we speak, the prophecies, teachings, the ministrations must flow out of the (secret place the most holy place).

What does God want us to do?

He wants us to move from the carnal things (the natural) into the most holy place (the spiritual).

How can we move from natural things to spiritual things?

There is a story of the two priests named Zadok and Abiathar, they served under King David. Their story reveals three choices they had to make in their experience. These three choices revealed the true content of their hearts. Matthew 6:21 "For where your treasure is, there will your heart be also."

The Story of Zadok and Abiathar

Abiathar's name means **father (of) abundance**, Zadok's name means **Righteous, Just.**

This is a story of Kings and Priests.

- The Role of the Priest is to Provide Spiritual Leadership to the People.
- The Role of the King is to Provide Natural Leadership to the People.
- Kings are to Use Their Power and Resources to Support the Spiritual Leadership and Ministry of the Priests.
- Priests and Kings Both Serve God, But Differently (1 Samuel 22:17-23; 2 Samuel 15:24-31; 1 Kings 1:5-8; 2:26-27).

The Story of Zadok and Abiathar (1 Samuel 22:17-23; 2 Samuel 15:24-31; 1 Kings 1:5-8; 2:26-27).

- The Priests ministers to God by administering Spiritual Things.
- Kings Serve God by administering natural things.
- Priests are equivalent to the Spiritual essence of our ministries.
- Kings are equivalents to the natural reality of our ministries.
- Kings Serve Priests by contributing natural resources.
- Priests Serve Kings by contributing spiritual blueprints.

The Three Priestly Choices:

Which King Will I Serve?

The Story of Zadok and Abiathar

- First Choice: Who will be King? David or Saul (God's Choice or Human Imposition)
- Choice Between Brokenness or Self-Will
- Saul is a Priest-killer.
- Saul interposed himself into the Priest's Office. (self-appointment)
- Principle: When carnal and worldly things rule over your spirit two things will happen: They will kill your anointing and essence of your ministry (or spiritual) service; they will interpose and corrupt your spirit.

Both Zadok and Abiathar Chose David. 1 Samuel 22:17-23; 2 Samuel 15:24-31; 1 Kings 1:5-8; 2:26-27 **(when your spirit and soul are in harmony, God will always be expressed rightly through your expression).**

The Story of Zadok and Abiathar

- Second Choice: David or Absalom?
- Choice Between Grace and Works (Romans 11:6)
- And if by grace, then it is no longer of works; otherwise, grace is no longer grace. But if it is of works, it is no longer grace; otherwise, work is no longer work.
- Absalom seized the throne from David (flesh).
- David did not fight back (Spirit).
- Principle: When flesh rules over our spirit, flesh will exalt work (performance) over grace (The Anointing). Both Zadok and Abiathar Chose David. 1 Samuel 22:17-23; 2 Samuel 15:24-31; 1 Kings 1:5-8; 2:26-27 **(when your spirit and soul are in harmony God will always be expressed rightly through your expression).**

The Story of Zadok and Abiathar

Third Choice: Solomon or Adonijah?

- Choice Between God's Ways Versus Man's Ways.
- Adonijah publicly declared himself to be King (self-promotion, self-reliance).
- God privately chose Solomon (God's divine grace and favor).
- Principle: When flesh rules over the spirit, they will activate vanity, and introduce a mixture, promoting the flesh over the spirit.

Zadok Chose Solomon. Abiathar Chose Adonijah. 1 Samuel 22:17-23; 2 Samuel 15:24-31; 1 Kings 1:5-8; 2:26-27 **(when your spirit and soul are in harmony, God will always be expressed rightly through your expression).**

The Story of Zadok and Abiathar

You can only choose to serve one King. The King you choose to serve dominates your experience. Whoever you choose to serve will rule over you! If you choose to serve the fleshy things, you will be ruled by the fleshy things of this world. If you choose to serve the spiritual, you will be ruled by the spiritual things which are above (1 Samuel 22:17-23; 2 Samuel 15:24-31; 1 Kings 1:5-8; 2:26-27).

This is simply a choice between the Spirit and the Flesh. The Way of the Spirit is the Way of the Cross (Matthew 16:21-27). To Choose the Spirit is to Choose the Cross, denial and death to self.

Ezekiel 44:4-31 shows us the Fruition of the Choices Abiathar and Zadok Made. It also tutors us about the dual aspects of any ministration:

- Your soul, body, mind, will and emotions, the entire human faculty stands before the people while ministering.
- Your spirit stands before God while ministering.

What does God want us to know?

He wants us to know that according to the Divine Order the body (or outer court) ministry must be influenced by what flows out of the spiritual ministry.

What does God want us to do?

He wants us to move from the outer court (the fleshly things) into the most holy place (the spiritual). **When your spirit and soul are in harmony, God will always be expressed rightly through your expression.**

Abiathar = the Cursed Priesthood (Jeremiah 17:5-10)

Thus, saith the LORD; Cursed be the man that trusteth in man, and maketh flesh his arm, and whose heart departeth from the LORD.

Zadok = the Blessed (or Faithful) Priesthood

What does God want us to know?

He wants us to know that according to Divine Order, the spiritual must flow out from the most holy place or our spirit outwards toward the (outer court), the flesh.

What does God want us to do?

He wants us to move from the fleshy things towards the spiritual.

How will we do this? By the choices we make every day! God wants us to choose him all the time just like Jesus demonstrated.

John 8:29: "And he that sent me is with me: the father hath not left me alone; for I do always those things that please him."

John 5:19: Then answered Jesus and said unto them, Verily, verily, I say unto you, The Son can do nothing of himself, but what he seeth the Father do: for what things soever he doeth, these also doeth the Son likewise.

Let us today choose which King we shall serve. Let us choose to serve the Spirit of God.

22.
SPIRITUAL DISCIPLINES

Proverbs 25:28: "He that hath no rule over his own spirit is like a city that is broken down, and without walls."

Discipline yourself for the purpose of godliness" (1 Timothy 4:7).

Definition: Spiritual Disciplines are habits and patterns of devotion. Spiritual Disciplines are things a disciple of Jesus Christ does within the context of his relationship with Christ to become more like Christ.

For bodily exercise profiteth little: but godliness is profitable unto all things, having promise of the life that now is, and of that which is to come (1 Timothy 4:8).

We need more spiritual exercises than we need physical exercise.

1 Corinthians 9:24: Know ye not that they which run in a race run all, but one receiveth the prize? So run, that ye may obtain.

1 Corinthians 9:25: And every man that striveth for the mastery is temperate in all things. Now they do it to obtain a corruptible crown; but we an incorruptible one.

Apprehending Christ

That I may know Him and the power of His resurrection and the fellowship of His sufferings, being conformed to His death; in order that I may attain to the resurrection of the dead. Not that I have already obtained it or have already become perfect, but I press on so that I may lay hold of that for which also I was laid hold of by Jesus Christ" (Philippians 3:10-12).

Forgetting what's Behind and Reaching Forward is our goal of Apprehending Christ.

What is our present compelling goal?

Being United Together with Him

1. We have been crucified together with Christ (Galatians 2:20).
2. Buried Together with Christ (Romans 6:4).
3. We have been raised up together with Christ (Colossians 3:1).
4. We suffer together with Christ (Romans 8:17).
5. We are glorified together with Christ (Romans 8:17).
6. We will be caught up together with Christ (1 Thessalonians 4:17).
7. We will be enthroned together with Christ (Revelation 3:21).

There Are Four Laws of Apprehending Christ

1. Responsibility: This is the principle of liability or reporting to Authority
2. Following: The Principle of the Lordship of Jesus in your life.
3. Subjugation: The Principle of the Cross.
4. Discipling: The Principle of Reproduction.

The Goal of Prophetic Discipleship or mentoring is to bring the prophet into practical union with Christ through the Cross.

Two Key Thoughts to Keep in Mind:

- The disciple is not learning a subject; he is following a Master. His goal is conformation to Christ's image.
- Discipleship is not a series of studies but a growing awareness of Christ.
- The mind of man cannot apprehend the things of God because they are spiritually discerned (1 Corinthians 2:9-16).
- Spiritual disciplines are designed to promote spiritual awareness by strengthening the spirit of man (Galatians 5:16-17).
- Man's spirit is renewed as he or she master's spiritual disciplines and feeds on the Word of God (2 Corinthians 4:16; Colossians 3:10).

Purpose # 2: The Purpose for Spiritual Disciplines:

Discipline yourself for the purpose of godliness." Spiritual disciplines are designed to produce character qualities associated with godliness.

Discipline means (a) to exercise naked (to hide nothing) (b) to exercise vigorously in any other way (body or mind), (c) to "master" yourself = be lord over yourself. 2. Godliness = (a) to be devout, (b) a God-ward attitude that does what is well-pleasing to God. (c) God-fearing.

What are the characteristics of godliness?

1. Moral excellence (2 Peter 1:5) Character - moral strength; self-discipline
2. Spiritual Fruit (Galatians 5:22-23)

    - Godliness is the fruit of spiritual formation.
    - Spiritual formation is the goal of discipleship.

Eight Steps to Spiritual Formation - 2 Peter 1:5-8

1. Faith - belief and faithfulness.
2. Moral Excellence - moral goodness, modesty, purity, etc.
3. Knowledge - general understanding.
4. Self-Control - mastering your passions and desires.
5. Perseverance - not being moved from one's faith or purpose.
6. Godliness - piety towards God.
7. Brotherly Kindness - love for Christian brothers and sisters.
8. Love - agape; deeper, unconditional love for all men.

The Nature and Operation of Spiritual Disciplines

- They are patterns and habits.
- They must be done regularly.
- They must be developed or improved upon in our lives.
- They are deliberate choices we make.
- They involve the discipline (or control) of our mind, will, and emotions.
- They strengthen our spirits by denying our fleshly desires.
- They produce character and spiritual formation.

Three Categories of Spiritual Disciplines

1. Personal Disciplines:
2. Disciplines of Abstinence (Going without Something)
3. Corporate Disciplines (Things You Do with Others)

Personal Disciplines

1. Prayer - Communicating with God.
2. Bible Study - Understanding the Word of God.
3. Giving – Spirit led giving.
4. Serving - Having a ministry or serving with a ministry.
5. Fasting - Abstaining from food.
6. Meditation – Musing or going deeply into passages of Scripture.
7. Evangelism - Sharing your faith with another person or group.
8. Stewardship - Surrendering my possessions to the Lord.
9. Journaling - Recording your thoughts and events in a book.
10. Living by Faith – Walking in the Spirit.

Prayer:

Communicating with God.

- Communication requires speaking the same language:

What language does God speak?

- His Word!

Prayer requires:

- Honesty
- Faith

Bible Study:

2 Timothy 2:15: "Be diligent to present yourself approved to God as a workman who does not need to be ashamed, accurately handling the word of truth."

- Hearing
- Reading, Studying, Memorizing
- Meditating

All Scripture is inspired by God and profitable for teaching, for reproof, for correction, for training in righteousness; so that the man of God may be adequate, equipped for every good work" (2 Timothy 3:16-17).

Giving God wants you to be financially free!

- Choosing to serve God rather than money (Matthew 6:24).
- Trusting God totally for every need (Deuteronomy 8:18).
- Obeying Biblical teachings concerning money (John 14:21-23).
- Staying out of debt (Romans 13:8).
- Working diligently (2 Thessalonians 3:10).
- Establishing God's priorities in your life (Haggai 1:9).
- Choosing a good name rather than riches (Proverbs 22:1).
- Learning contentment (Philippians 4:11-12).
- Paying your bills (Romans 13:7).

Giving:

God's Four Purposes for Money:

1. To Provide Basic Needs
2. To Confirm Direction
3. To Enable Us to Give to others
4. To Illustrate His Power in Our Lives!

Tithes and Offerings

What is a tithe? A tithe is 10% of your total increase.

Isn't the tithe a part of the Old Testament law and therefore not required of New Testament believers?

The tithe is older than the law (Abraham paid tithes to Melchizedek hundreds of years before the Law was given to Moses – Hebrews 7:6).

In the New Testament the Tithe and the offerings were replaced by Holy Spirit led giving. There are no more percentages. But we give under the direction of the Holy Spirit, Spirit-led giving. We are not under compulsion. God loves a cheerful giver.

2 Corinthians 9:: Every man according as he purposeth in his heart, so let him give; not grudgingly, or of necessity: for God loveth a cheerful giver.

1 Chronicles 29:17: I know also, my God, that thou triest the heart, and hast pleasure in uprightness. As for me, in the uprightness of mine heart I have willingly offered all these things: and now have I seen with joy thy people, which are present here, to offer willingly unto thee.

The law was written for the lawless and the disobedient. But now we have received the spirit of obedience, the spirit of Christ.

1 Timothy 1:9-10

9 Knowing this, that the law is not made for a righteous man, but for the lawless and disobedient, for the ungodly and for sinners, for unholy and profane, for murderers of fathers and murderers of mothers, for manslayers, 10 For whoremongers, for them that defile themselves with mankind, for menstealers, for liars, for perjured persons, and if there be any other thing that is contrary to sound doctrine;

Tithes and Offerings

What is the purpose for tithing?

- To support God's work (Malachi 3:8).
- To learn to fear the Lord (Deuteronomy 14:22-23).
- God blesses those who tithe (Proverbs 3:9-10).

There are many kinds of fasts:

- Full Fast - denying yourself food or drink (other than water) for at least 36 hours.
- Partial Fast - denying yourself food or drink (other than water) for less than 36 hours.
- Substitutionary Fast - eating a modified diet.

- Fasting as a Discipline - regular fasting designed to discipline the flesh and strengthen the spirit.
- Corporate Fasting - fasting with others.

Fasting

Fasting is a spiritual discipline that involves going without food for a set period of time.

- One day per week.
- Two days per week.
- Several 10-day periods.
- One 21-40 day fast per year.

Fasting

What does the Spiritual Discipline of Fasting Accomplish in the Life of the Disciple?

Fasting strengthens the inner man (the spirit) of the disciple of Christ. Why does Fasting work? Fasting denies the flesh and brings it under the control of the spirit.

Purposes for Fasting

1. Strengthening the spirit (Luke 4:1-2,14)
2. Intercessory prayer (Deuteronomy 9:18)
3. Seeking discernment of God's will (Judges 20:23-27)
4. Mourning (1 Samuel 1:1-7)
5. Confession and repentance (1 Samuel 7:1-6)
6. Worship (1 Samuel 9:11-13)
7. Grief (1 Samuel 20:34; 31:13)
8. Supplication (2 Chronicles 20:1-3)
9. Seeking God's will and guidance (Ezra 8:21-23)

Suggestions on Fasting Properly

1. **Going without food is a serious matter.**

    - Fasting should be avoided or limited by those who have serious health concerns.

2. One of the greatest benefits of regular fasting is the cleansing effect.

- Nothing is healthier for the human body than a once-a-week habit of fasting.

3. The following suggestions may be helpful: -

- Fast regularly and drink plenty of water. - The best kind of fasting schedule is: One 24–36-hour period per week.
- A 7-10 day fast one or more times a year - If you feel led to go on an extended fast of 3 days or longer, you should prepare for it at least one month before by modifying your diet and fasting regularly.

4. Some additional tips: - Never eat heavily before or after a fast. - Break an extended fast with liquids, and then gradually build up to mild vegetables (well-cooked) or fruit. - Spend as much time in prayer as you can during your fast.

5. Your prayer time should double in length if you are able. - Keep a very moderate schedule during the fast. Avoid work (if possible) and recreation. - Spend as much time in the Bible as you can. - Keep your fast as much of a secret as you can. - There are seasons to fast regularly and there are times when Fasting

6. Meditation: Going Deeply into Passages of Scripture

1. The Bible teaches that there is a direct link between keeping the Word of God and receiving the blessings and promises of God:

- God's anointing is upon His Word (Isaiah 55:8-11).
- God's blessing is upon His Word (Psalm 119:2).
- God has magnified His Word above all things (Psalm 138:2).

Meditation.

The Bible teaches that obedience to God's Word will produce:

- Prosperity (Deuteronomy 11:1,7-9)
- Wellness (Deuteronomy 7:12-15)
- Life (Deuteronomy 27)
- Blessing (Deuteronomy 28)
- Success (Joshua 1:7-8)

- Fruitfulness (Psalm 1)
- Wisdom (Psalm 119:99-100)
- Joy (Psalm 63:5-6)
- Victory (Psalm 119:9-11)
- Love for God (John 14:21-23)
- Assurance of Answered Prayer (James 4; 1 John 3:22)

Meditating in Scripture is Following the Law of Sowing and Reaping

There are Four Parts to this law:

- The Seed – (the Word) Matthew 13
- The Soil – (our hearts) Matthew 13
- The Water – (the Holy Spirit) John 7:37-39; Ephesians 5:26
- The Harvest – (the fruit) Matthew 13:23

Meditation

How to Meditate in Scripture:

- Daily Receive God's Word
- Select One Key Passage
- Memorize the Passage
- Study the Passage

Meditate on the Passage:

Personalize the Passage ("Lord, you are my Shepherd"). Carefully go over each word and phrase.

- Turn the Passage into a Prayer
- Do What the Passage Teaches

Evangelism:

Sharing your faith with others as a daily pattern of life.

Stewardship:

Surrendering my possessions to the Lord and using them for His Kingdom. Serving: Intentionally serving others.

Journaling:

Keeping a written record of prayers, thoughts, events, and words from the Lord. Living by Faith: Being in harmony with God and with His purposes.

Living by Faith:

Walking in the Spirit "Now faith is the assurance of things hoped for, the conviction of things not seen... And without faith it is impossible to please Him, for he who comes to God must believe that He is and that He is a rewarder of those who seek Him" (Hebrews 11:1, 6).

Disciplines of Abstinence

1. Fasting - deliberately choosing to abstain from food.
2. Silence - not speaking for periods of time.
3. Simplicity - doing the same things with fewer resources.
4. Solitude - deliberately being alone with God.
5. Submission - choosing to yield your rights to another; humility.
6. Secrecy - doing acts of kindness secretly.
7. Watching - spending extended times in prayer.
8. Frugality - abstaining from using money to gratify our desires.
9. Sacrifice - abstaining from the enjoyment of necessary things.
10. Chastity - purposefully abstaining from sexual intercourse.

Corporate Disciplines

1. Corporate Prayer - prayer with others.
2. Confession - telling our faults and sins to another.
3. Celebration - honoring a person or event with others.
4. Worship - expressing praise and adoration for God with others.
5. Guidance - seeking the wisdom and counsel of others.

23.
Assisting The Sheep in Hearing the Voice of The Lord

As we have mentioned before, the Roles and functions on the prophetic have changed a lot within the New Testament context, we have also discussed these very roles but the one that we need to focus on in this teaching is the one of helping the sheep to hear the Voice of the Lord.

The Bible clearly says that the sheep hears God's voice. There are no questions or even private interpretations for this scripture. The true sheep will be able to hear God's voice.

My sheep listen to my voice; I know them, and they follow me (John 10:27).

John 10:14: "I am the good shepherd; I know my sheep and my sheep know me.

The sheep do not just wake up one morning and begin to hear the voice of God. Back in Jesus' day shepherds would bring their sheep into pens in the evening for protection. They would have flocks from several different shepherds in one large corral.

In the morning, the shepherd would come and call his sheep and the ones that recognized his voice would follow him out of the corral and into the surrounding fields to eat. Each shepherd had a different voice or mechanism to call the sheep and his flock would follow that sound.

They knew from experience that this was a sound they could trust and that it meant good things were ahead. All the other sheep in the corral would just ignore the sound because it meant nothing to them.

They did not recognize the voice of another shepherd. They only followed their own shepherd. The shepherd will spend a lot of time with the sheep. He will care for them, protect them and even go through trials and perils with them, he will rescue them when they are in trouble and weak, and he will protect and carry the helpless sheep. He will guide and lead them to the streams of water. He will lead them to green pastures. Because of this type of relationship and time spent together the sheep develops a closer relationship with him and then finally they can distinctly hear and know his voice.

Once they know his voice, they only follow him and not another.

As Prophets we must develop that intimate relationship with God if we expect to be able to help others hear for themselves. We must be experienced hearers. We must know intimately the way our great shepherd speaks and discern his voice.

Without that relationship we cannot hear him, and we cannot help others hear him.

John 10:4: when he has brought out all his own, he goes on ahead of them, and his sheep follow him because they know his voice.

One of the Roles of the Prophet in the New Testament Church is to help the sheep or to help the Church, the body of Christ, to hear God and discern his voice.

Many church people think that when you receive a prophet's reward, it will be blessings, houses, cars and money. They wrongly interpret this scripture to suit their greed and selfish desires.

Anyone who receives a prophet, because he is a prophet, will receive a prophet's reward, and anyone who receives a righteous man because he is a righteous man will receive a righteous man's reward (Matthew 10:41).

To "receive" a prophet is to embrace his doctrine, entertain him in a kind, generous manner; to practice hospitality to him. Those who regard such a prophet, and show him respect, by a hospitable entertainment of him; not because of manipulations or trying to bribe the prophet to prophesy wrongly from his soul.

If your motives are pure while doing this, then you shall receive a prophet's reward: either a reward from the prophet himself which means the prophet by the authority of God bestowing a blessing upon you.

The prophet will be able to interpret what is needed and declare a blessing from God according to God's will in that area.

Let's see an example in the Bible (2 Kings 4:10) Let's make a small room on the roof and put in it a bed and a table, a chair and a lamp for him. Then he can stay there whenever he comes to us.

Whenever the Prophet Came to Town this family made a small room available in their home. They made a bed and a table and a lamp for him. They gave him a room to stay in whenever he came to Town. They received a prophet and the Prophet's Reward was that the Prophets asked them what they needed. The prophet identified the need and used his authority to prophesy life into their situation, home and God heard it and gave them a child.

2 Kings 4:11: One day when Elisha came, he went up to his room and lay down there.

He said to his servant Gehazi, "Call the Shunammite." So, he called her, and she stood before him (2 Kings 4:12, 2 Kings 4:13) Elisha said to him "Tell her, 'You have gone to all this trouble for us. Now what can be done for you? (a prophet's reward) Can we speak on your behalf to the king or the commander of the army?'" She replied, "I have a home among my own people." (2 Kings 4:14) "What can be done for her?" Elisha asked. Gehazi said, "Well, she has no son, and her husband is old."

Then Elisha said, "Call her." So, he called her, and she stood in the doorway. 2 Kings 4:15 "About this time next year," Elisha said, "you will hold a son in your arms." "No, my lord," she objected. "Don't mislead your servant, O man of God" (2 Kings 4:16)!

2 Kings 4:17: But the woman became pregnant, and the next year about that same time she gave birth to a son, just as Elisha had told her.

This woman received a prophet and took care of him, housed and fed him. The prophet exercised his authority and brought forth comfort through a child. The reward was a child. That was a need that they had. But sometimes hosting a prophet in your church can also open the atmosphere for prophetic grace.

The greatest reward from a prophet is the ability to see and hear in the spirit. Prophets are seers. They have the gift of seeing what others can't see. They have insights into spiritual realms. The voice of God is very real to them. This reward can be graced to Churches or people who receive the prophet.

The benefits always lead us closer to God and not the prophet. Prophet's reward will lead to hunger for righteousness,

And Elisha prayed, "O LORD, open his eyes so he may see." Then the LORD opened the servant's eyes, and he looked and saw the hills full of horses and chariots of fire all around Elisha. 2 Kings 6:17 Prophets will be able in the New Testament to pray like Elisha for the eyes of the church to open so that they can see things in the spirit.

If you feel that God is speaking a message to you, but you are not really sure if it is from God, here are some good questions to ask yourself about the message.

- Does it line up with the Holy Bible, the written scriptures?
- Does it lead you into a closer relationship with God, a greater unity with Him?
- Does it lead you into expressing love, which is putting God's benefit and the benefit of others before your own benefit?
- Does it lead to a dying of yourself and a greater manifestation of Christ life in you?
- Does it cause greater humility in you, and a greater dependence upon God?
- Does it cause greater love, joy, and peace from God in you?

How to Hear God

HEBREW: *shamea* means to hear, *Shema* means to hear, *gashab* means to give attention, be attentive, *azan* means to give ear

- GREEK: *akouo* means to give ear, hearken, hear,
- *Diakouo* means to hear thoroughly.
- *Eisakouo* means to give ear to, hearken to
- *Epakroaomai* means to hearken unto

WAYS ONE CAN HEAR GOD:

- Through the Scripture
- Through the Holy Spirit
- Through prayer
- Through other believers in the Body of Christ: prophecy, teaching, exhortation, tongues & interpretation

- Through other gifts of the Holy Spirit: wisdom, knowledge & discernment
- Through visions
- Through dreams
- Through revelations
- Through angels
- Through the witness within your spirit
- Through being silent
- Through waiting upon the Lord
- Through "still, small voice"
- Through an inner voice
- Through strong impressions
- Through premonition
- Through fleeting thoughts
- Through circumstances and events
- Through "open" and "closed" doors
- Through creation (donkey, rocks, etc.)

Note: A safeguard to distinguish God's voice, our thoughts & Satan's? If it goes against the flesh, it's probably God's voice and if it pleases the flesh, it's probably our thoughts or Satan's.

Learning to clearly distinguish and discern God's voice is indispensable. Instead of going through life blindly, we can have the wisdom of God guide and protect us.

The Lord constantly speaks to us and gives us His direction. It's never the Lord who is not speaking, but it's us who are not hearing.

Jesus said in John 10:3-5.

To him the porter openeth, and the sheep hear his voice; and he calleth his own sheep by name, and leadeth them out. And when he putteth forth his own sheep, he goeth before them, and the sheep follow him: for they know his voice. And a stranger will they not follow but will flee from him: for they know not the voice of strangers."

In verse 3, His sheep hear His voice. He didn't say His sheep may hear, struggle to hear, should hear His voice. He told us his sheep do hear His voice.

Most believers would question this limpid statement since their experiences don't align. But it's not what Jesus said that is wrong; all true believers can and do hear the voice of God; they just don't recognize what they are hearing as being God's voice.

Radio signals are always transmitting twenty-four hours a day, seven days a week; but we only hear them when we turn the receiver on and tune it in. Failure to hear the transmitting signal doesn't mean the station isn't transmitting.

God is constantly transmitting His voice to His sheep, but only few are tuned in. Most Christians are busy begging God in prayer to transmit the signal when the problem is with their receivers.

The first thing we need to do is fix our receivers, fix our hearings. God is already speaking. We need to start listening. It takes time, effort, and discipline. All of us seem to be busier than ever, and that's one of the big reasons we don't hear the voice of the Lord better. Our soul is crowded with issues of life.

Psalm 46:10 says, "Be still, and know that I am God.

It's in stillness, not busyness, that we tune our spiritual ears to hear the voice of God. The Lord always speaks to us in that "still, small voice" (1 Kings 19:12), but often it's drowned out amid all the turmoil of our daily lives.

Second, which is very important, we often mistake the Lord's voice for our thoughts. That's right. I said the voice of the Lord comes to us in our own thoughts.

John 4:24 says, "God is a Spirit: and they that worship him must worship him in spirit and in truth."

This is saying that communication with God is Spirit to spirit, not brain to brain or mouth to ear, the way we communicate in the physical realm. The Lord speaks to our spirits, not in words, but in thoughts and impressions.

Our Heavenly Father speaks to every one of His children constantly, giving us all the information and guidance we need to be total overcomers. There isn't a problem with His transmitter; it's our receiver that needs help.

God speaks to us through the glory of His creation. He speaks to us through His Holy Spirit, through dreams, visions, and sanctified imagination. God will use events and circumstances to speak with us. More often God uses people He has placed in our lives to speak to us. He speaks through his written word, the Bible. The question is: Are humans listening?

"Today, if you hear his voice, do not harden your hearts (Hebrews 3:15).

Jesus rebukes and chides the seven churches mentioned in Revelation, "He who has an ear, let him hear what the Spirit says to the churches." The Holy Spirit is speaking to God's people. For those who listen and obey, they are about to move forward into the greatest outpouring of God's Spirit that the world has ever known. But this is what I commanded them, saying, 'Obey My voice, and I will be your God, and you shall be my people. And walk in all the ways that I have commanded you that it may be well with you. "Yet they did not obey or incline their ear but followed the counsels and the dictates of their evil hearts and went backward and not forward (Jeremiah 7:23-24).

God spoke to his people in the Old Testament through his chosen prophets. Whenever the King wanted to know something, he would request that the prophet consult God. Some kings even had their own sycophantic prophets of convenience. In the New Testament, God has spoken to us through Jesus Christ (Hebrews 1:2). Afterward, he continued to speak through the apostles.

This was recognized by the early believers who continued in the apostle's doctrine (Acts 2:14). Jesus had promised his apostles that there were things he could not reveal to them at the time he was on earth but would do so later through the Holy Spirit (John 16:12-15).

So, the prophets help the church in this dispensation by teaching the Church how to hear or discern the voice of God through cultivating a closer relationship with Jesus through the Holy Spirit. This will launch the church into an intimacy that will release the voice of God.

A prophet is a watchman standing on a watchtower. When He sees trouble coming and says to the shepherds to get the sheep into the safety of the fold, the shepherd must listen.

Good relationships between pastors and the watchman are essential. The watchman should communicate what they see to the pastors. The pastors can then prepare the sheep for what is going to happen.

The sheep know their shepherds and they will respond to them. If they do not know the voice of the watchmen, they will not respond to them.

A prophet is way ahead of the flock of sheep. He sees beyond ahead of the sheep. He is on the lookout. There he hears God's voice and sees visions,

The watchman is not just the gatekeeper, nor does he have the authority to open or close the gates of a city. His job was to communicate what he sees on the horizon to those who did have the authority to do something about it.

Hoisted on the city walls is a position of elevation in the spirit, to see realms both a distance outside and inside of the city. The watchmen were trained to spot both the enemies; however, they had no authority to confront either.

They gave their information to the elders who sat at the gates. Only the elders had the authority to either command the gates be opened or sound the alarm.

Receiving The Word

There is only one way to receive a word from the Lord. Wait on the Lord. Wait on the Lord. Wait on the Lord. Seek the Holy Spirit. Seek the Holy Spirit. Seek the Holy Spirit. Read the Word. Read the Word. Read the Word. Pray. Pray. Pray.

To recognize a person's voice, you must know him well. Prophets must develop a strong relationship with God before hearing his voice. The key is sitting in the presence of the Lord and walking in the Spirit. We cannot tell the Lord when he should speak. We must wait for him. Sometimes, he may talk to a person two or three times in quick succession; then he may go for several years without speaking.

He is sovereign. We must wait on him to come (Jeremiah 42:7). The angel said the following words to John seven times. He who has an ear, let him hear what the Spirit says to the churches (Revelation 2:7).

Jesus said something similar at least four times. He who has ears, let him hear (Matthew 13:9). These words must be really important. The first thing to note is that the Spirit speaks. He speaks clearly in a language that we can know. Secondly, we must listen to his voice.

The Holy Spirit loves to speak and longs for his people to listen. The most important ability needed for serving God is to be able to hear the Spirit speak. If we cannot hear him, it is unlikely that he has stopped speaking.

Different people and personalities hear God in different ways. Each prophet must find the way that is best for them. The Lord speaks to prophets through visions and dreams and sometimes face-to-face.

When the prophet of the Lord is among you, I reveal myself to him in visions. I speak to him in dreams. But this is not true of my servant Moses; he is faithful in all my house with him I speak face to face; clearly and not in riddles; he sees the form of the Lord (Numbers 12-8).

The most important skill is to learn to hear the Holy Spirit speaking. "I have much more to say to you than you can now bear. But when he, the Spirit of truth, comes, he will guide you into all truth. He will not speak on his own; he will speak only what he hears, and he will tell you what is yet to come. He will bring glory to me by taking from what is mine and making it known to you. All that belongs to the father is mine. That is why I said the Spirit will take from what is mine and make it known to you (John 16:12-15).

A prophet can choose not to receive a word. Elisha did not want to seek a word of guidance for a wicked King. But Jehoshaphat asked, "Is there no prophet of the Lord here that we may inquire of the Lord through him?" An officer of the king of Israel answered, "Elisha son of Shaphat is here. He used to pour water on the hands of Elijah." Jehoshaphat said, "The word of the Lord is with him." So the king of Israel and Jehoshaphat and the king of Edom went down to him. Elisha said to the king of Israel, "What do we have to do with each other? Go to the prophets of your father and the prophets of your mother." "No," the king of Israel answered, "because it was the Lord who called us three kings together to hand us over to Moab." Elisha said, "As surely as the Lord Almighty lives, whom I serve, if I did not have respect for the presence of Jehoshaphat king of Judah, I would not look at you or even notice you. But now bring me a harpist." While the harpist was playing, the hand of the Lord came upon Elisha (2 Kings 3:11-15).

Sometimes worship or song may help the prophet to hear the Lord speak. This is why Elisha wanted the harp to play.

Impressions:

Often, I get the sense that the Spirit is impressing upon me in a certain way. This is a form of discernment. The still small voice really is under this category. We are all in that category regarding what we can receive through inspiration.

- (A). knowing or witness Romans 9:1 says, "I tell the truth in Christ, I am not lying, my conscience also bearing me witness in the Holy Spirit." We all have an inner witness. It is called Christ in you. The mind of Christ tells us what we ought to do or should not do.
- (B). We can feel things. We can receive things in the emotions of our soul and in our bodies. The word does not come through your flesh but can affect the flesh. Often, I have had the sense that the Spirit is touching a part of my body to communicate a message to me.

Visions:

The first and most common manifestation of visions are visions of the spirit in the heart. The eyes can be open or closed. Seeing a vision and interpreting what is being seen are not one and the same.

- Supernatural senses. In this level, the five senses are amplified in sensitivity and ability. One can experience 'x-ray vision,' which gives the ability to see through something or a heightened sense of smell or hearing.
- One may hear a sound of conversation across a distance,
- The next level is dreams. They are seen all through the Bible. Jacob at Bethel saw the angels go up and down a ladder. Joseph saw the vision or dream of the moon and the stars. God will often use dreams to communicate.

Open visions:

This is where the eyes are open, and one sees spiritual things as if they appeared normal to the natural eyes. The open vision can be so real to our eyes that it is only later understood that it was an open vision at all.

It is likewise possible to actually be involved in the physical sense in a spiritual phenomenon only to realize later that it was not a vision. This happened to Peter in Acts 12:11; 8.

Trances.

This manifestation is distinct from visions because in a vision one is still aware of one's surroundings. In a trance, one's surroundings are blotted out temporarily, unless God wants them to be observed. This also occurred to Peter in Acts 10:9.

Audible voices.

Acts 9 accounts for Paul's encounter with the Lord while travelling to Damascus. He was knocked to the ground and a conversation occurred between him and the Lord. Verse 7 says the other men stood by and heard a voice, but they did not see anyone.

To Paul it was an audible voice. In my experience, the audible voice of God will always be life-changing, no matter the length or brevity of the conversation.

Visitations from angels.

Angels can bring us information. An angel came to Daniel to bring him understanding. Angels came to Abraham because there was something important that needed to happen that he needed to be informed about.

Mary spoke with the angel Gabriel, the same archangel who communicated with Daniel. Joseph was ministered by an angel through a dream, as was Jacob.

Visitations from the Lord.

Sometimes there may be a commissioning that the Lord Jesus Himself will administer. It is often difficult for the person to communicate what happened in human words. It may not be something they want people to know about, especially since many people would not believe it.

Translation in place or time.

Both Paul and John were caught up in the realm of the third heaven. They were used to bring the Word of God so that the Body would prosper,

When we have received a word from the Lord, the first thing we should do is ask what he wants us to do with it. We should not assume that he wants us to speak it out. He may want us to sit on it and wait and pray.

We should also ask for interpretation and guidance on how to deliver it. Many valid words are spoiled because they are incorrectly handled.

Dreams And Dream Interpretation

Defining Dream and Vision:

Dream - "A sequence of images, etc., passing through a sleeping person's mind" (Webster's Dictionary)

https://webstersdictionary1828.com/Dictionary/dream

Vision - "A mental image" (Webster's Dictionary)

https://webstersdictionary1828.com/Dictionary/vision

"In a dream, a vision of the night..." (Job 33:15)

The words dream and vision. The words are used almost interchangeably in Hebrew.

Dreams and visions involve viewing images on the screen within one's mind. Often, we would think of a dream as the flow of these images while sleeping and a vision as the flow of these images while awake. Daydreaming is carnal and should not be viewed as visions or visionary processes.

Why we should listen to Our Dreams?

God declared that He would speak through dreams and visions in the Old Testament.

And He said, "Hear now my words: If there be a prophet among you, I the LORD will make myself known unto him in a vision and will speak unto him in a dream" (Numbers. 12:6).

God declared that He speaks through dreams and visions in the Old Testament.

I have also spoken by the prophets, multiplied visions, and used similitudes, by the ministry of the prophets" (Hosea. 12:10).

God declares that He will communicate through dreams and visions in the New Testament.

And it shall come to pass in the last days," saith God, "I will pour out of My Spirit upon all flesh: and your sons and your daughters shall prophesy, and your young men shall see visions, and your old men shall dream dreams" (Acts 2:17).

God declares that He will counsel us at night through our dreams.

I will bless the Lord who has counseled me; indeed, my mind (inner man) instructs me in the night (Psalm 16:7).

Rather than our dreams being fatalistic, dreams are calling us to change. They serve as a warning to us.

For God speaketh once, yea twice, yet man perceiveth it not. In a dream, in a vision of the night, when deep sleep falleth upon men, in slumberings upon the bed; Then He openeth the ears of men, and sealeth their instruction, That He may withdraw man from his purpose, and hide pride from man. He keepeth back his soul from the pit, and his life from perishing by the sword (Job 33:14-18).

Dreams are very significant. For example, God established the Abrahamic Covenant in a dream.

And when the sun was going down, a deep sleep fell upon Abram; and, lo, a horror of great darkness fell upon him.... And God said to Abram....In the same day the LORD made a covenant with Abram, saying... (Genesis 15:12,13,18, emphasis mine).

Supernatural gifts given through dreams.

In Gibeon, the LORD appeared to Solomon in a dream by night, and God said, "Ask what I shall give thee...."

Give therefore thy servant an understanding heart to judge Thy people, that I may discern between good and bad: for who is able to judge this Thy so great a people?"

Behold, I have done according to thy words: lo, I have given thee a wise and an understanding heart; so that there was none like thee before thee, neither after thee shall any arise like unto thee...." And Solomon awoke; and behold, it was a dream (1 Kings 3:5,9,12,15).

Why does God give us dreams?

- To help us solve our problems.
- To reveal things, we didn't know (such as self-conditioning). To show His love to us. To give us Direction. To give us Correction.
- To give clues on how to pray about a situation, or person.

Why would God allow you to see what the enemy is doing (in a dream)? To reveal the enemy's plan so you can pray accordingly.

To show generational issues (legal ground the enemy may be using). To show sin issues that opened up wrong spiritual doors.

Behold, I have done according to thy words: lo, I have given thee a wise and an understanding heart; so that there was none like thee before thee, neither after thee shall any arise like unto thee...." And Solomon awoke; and behold, it was a dream (1 Kings 3:5,9,12,15).

Discerning the dreams

Dreams from God is what we should all want. How can you tell if it's from God? One very good indicator is Peace and Love from God that leads to intimacy with him.

Soul dreams can be deceptive, they are from your soul. Soul dreams are not bad, but we must filter them through prayer, they just need to be submitted to God and prayed through. A busy life or stress can cause one to have many soul dreams.

Black, scary, fearful midnight-type dreams are from the enemy (devil). Or to put it this way, God allows you to see the enemy's plans, so you can pray more specifically. Even some dark dreams are showing what the enemy is doing. One way to change this is to speak scripture over them, pray through it, give God the dream, and put it in His hands.

Sources Of Dreams

- Holy Spirit
- Soul: Life experiences, wants and desires
- Enemy: Satan / demonic

Holy Spirit

You may think: What does the Holy Spirit (or God) have to do with dreams? Everything.

God is spirit, you are composed of a spirit, and the enemy is also spiritual. Interpretation of dreams should come from the Holy Spirit.

The enemy can try to give you a wrong interpretation cloaked with nice words. Perhaps even with scripture but mixed with twisted meanings. This will result in deception and wrong interpretation, therefore more discouragement.

He (the devil) has come to steal, kill, and destroy you and your dreams. As Jesus said, he has sent us the Holy Spirit to counsel and guide us, to give us wisdom and reveal Himself to us. For example, God could highlight an issue at work and give you good counsel on how best to handle it and prepare you for the future.

Interpreting dreams and visions is an important aspect of prophetic ministry. Prophets are sometimes skilled in interpreting dreams.

If a prophet or a dreamer of dreams arises among you... (Deuteronomy 13:1)," makes it unequivocal that the Lord regards prophets and dreamers as one and the same. Unfortunately, the Body of Christ, for the most part, has not yet grasped that. It is imperative that at least His prophets, and hopefully the entire Body, comprehend how important this aspect of prophets' equipment is!

Daniel was a prophet who was skilled in interpreting dreams (Daniel 2:1-28). During the night, the mystery was revealed to Daniel in a vision. Then Daniel praised the God of heaven and said: "Praise be to the name of God for ever and ever; wisdom and power are his. He changes times and seasons; he sets up kings and deposes them. He gives wisdom to the wise and knowledge to the discerning. He reveals deep and hidden things; he knows what lies in darkness, and light dwells with him. I thank and praise you, O God of my fathers: you have given me wisdom and power, you have made known to me what we asked of you, and you have made known to us the dream of the king" (Daniel 2:19-23).

Dreams often include people and objects we are familiar with and use symbolically. We must not assume that they will be fulfilled literally.

For example, Joseph saw the sun, moon and eleven stars bowing before him. This was not literally fulfilled, but he eventually saw his father and eleven brothers bowing before him. (Genesis 37:5-12; 40:5-22; 44:11-32).

Dreams should be interpreted like parables. Kings and rulers will often hear God through dreams. Prophets can help them to understand what God is saying. It is the glory of God to conceal a matter; to search out a matter is the glory of Kings (Proverbs 25:2).

What is the best way to interpret a dream? Where do you start? Then where do you go next?

Discerning Dreams

Which aspect of the dream should be analyzed first? Can the way you feel upon waking provide clues? What if your heart is pounding in fear? What if you were confused, frustrated, angry, rejected, or threatened?

What do the people in your dreams often represent? You can determine their significance in each dream by asking yourself this simple question!

Could the name of the person that appears in your dream be significant? If so, how?

To Recall Your Dreams, ask God to speak to you through dreams as you fall asleep.

God does answer prayers, especially when prayed in accordance with His will! Put your journal beside your bed and immediately record your dreams upon awakening.

You will forget most of your dreams by the morning, so get up and write them down when you wake up.

Element:

Not everything in a dream is a key element. With the Holy Spirit's help, you can identify what elements will be important for a final interpretation.

If there is any bright or strong colors, that's a key element. Usually, the action taking place, or the emotions you feel, will play a part. Joseph interpreted a cow to be provision in the king's dream.

It depends on the context of your dream. It's important to look at other possible "cow" meanings, such as provision, milk, and meat.

You can place each meaning in your elements and see if it fits. Once you have a good meaning for each element, pray over each one and see if the Holy Spirit quickens you.

Once you fully interpret, say to God - What do you say? This is an important part, not to jump to conclusions without the guidance of the one who created you and all things.

God's dream language uses symbols. It's important to have some bible knowledge so that God will have something to work with.

The Holy Spirit will guide and prompt you into the meaning so that you can work on the next element. Take note of actions, feelings and whatever the spirit highlights you.

Your journal can be full of dreams and yet only a few resonate with your spirit. Remember that the Holy Spirit is a counselor, guide, teacher, and comforter.

A vision is usually while someone is awake but can happen in a dream. Visions are seeing images on the screen of your mind. They are usually literal and come to pass. (The vision definition does not include what we think of as imagination.)

You may be given a vision to pray for God's mercy, justice, wisdom, understanding, comfort, etc.

It can be given to be more aware of what God is doing. "I the LORD will make myself known unto him in a vision and will speak unto him in a dream" (Numbers 12:6).

Dreams are symbolic beginning with what the bible says about a certain word or situation. Remember all those parables? Dreams can be a foreshadowing or a warning of something that is occurring or can occur.

Dangers Of Pietism

Dreams or visions from the enemy can be deceptive and mixed with truth - which are given to mislead, confuse, and give doubt.

"I will bless the Lord who has counseled me; Indeed, my mind (inner man) instructs me in the night" (Psalm 16:7).

Today, there are those who communicate with the dead and with demons. What does the Bible say of Spiritism?

The Bible plainly teaches that supernatural powers control and operate this world.

Paul was inspired to write that human beings must struggle "against powers, against the rulers of the darkness of this world, against wicked spirits in high places" (Ephesians 6:12).

Jesus Christ never contested Satan's claim that all the nations of the world were his. Said Satan: "All this power" — the control of the nations — "will I give thee, and the glory of them: for that is delivered unto me; and to whomsoever I will I give it. If thou therefore wilt worship me, all shall be thine" (Luke 4:6-7).

2 Corinthians 11:14: And no marvel; for Satan himself is transformed into an angel of light.

The Dead Cannot Talk with the Living!

"Marvel not at this: for the hour is coming, in the which all that are in the graves shall hear his voice, and shall come forth... unto the resurrection" (John 5:28-29).

Ecclesiastes 9:5: "For the living know that they will die, but the dead know nothing; they have no further reward, and even their name is forgotten."

This verse does not validate annihilationism. This verse cannot mean the dead in Christ have no knowledge. For example, Matthew 25:46 speaks of everlasting consciousness:

"Then they will go away to eternal punishment, but the righteous to eternal life." Every person will spend eternity with God in heaven or apart from Him in hell. Each person will have feelings, thoughts, and abilities.

Luke 16:19–31 Lazarus is in paradise in eternal joy, while the rich man is in torment in hell (called "Hades"). The rich man has feelings, can talk, and can remember, think, and reason.

The statement "the dead know nothing" means that when a person dies "under the sun," the earthly people without God, it's over. There is no more knowledge to give or be given, just a grave to mark his remains. Those who have died have "no further reward" in this life; they no longer can enjoy life like those who are living. Eventually, "even their name is forgotten" (Ecclesiastes 9:5).

But the devil must perpetuate his lie! He wants it to appear like the dead can communicate with the living. That is why the manifestations of Spiritism perpetuate a lie!

Spiritism is a work of darkness:

"Have no fellowship with the unfruitful works of darkness, but rather reprove them" (Ephesians 5:11). Many people who have lost loved ones and who have sought to contact them in the darkness of seances have contacted demons impersonating them. god's blessings come "without money and without price." But it costs money to fellowship with darkness!

Acts 16:16-20: "And it came to pass, as we went to prayer, a certain young woman possessed with a spirit of divination met us, which brought her masters much gain by soothsaying; The same followed Paul and us, and cried, saying, These men are the servants of the most high God, which shew unto us the way of salvation.

Extorting money from innocent victims on behalf of the dead is a racket controlled by Satan, the devil. This type of swindling even manifests itself in powerful denominations like the catholic churches. Indulgences. Indulgences are a Roman Catholic teaching that the Church can remit the temporal punishment for sin. Sorrowing relatives are asked to pay to relieve their loved ones from suffering supposedly occurring on the other side of death!

https://www.britannica.com/topic/indulgence

Remember Satan is called the prince of this world in three distinct Scriptures — (John 12:31, 14:30 and 16:11). He is the god of this age whom the world worships in ignorance! Paul said, "… the god of this world (or "age") hath blinded the minds of them that believe not, lest the light of the glorious gospel of Christ, who is the image of God, should shine unto them" (2 Corinthians 4:4).

The Bible reveals that there are only two classes of spirit beings created by God. Man is not spirit. He is composed of spirits. He is mortal flesh. Paul wrote of man: "For this corruptible must put on incorruption, and this mortal must put on immortality" (1 Corinthians 15:53).

Here are the two classes of spirits:

1) Holy angels of God:

"But to which of the angels did He say at any time: Sit on my right hand, until I make thine enemies thy footstool? Are they not all ministering spirits, sent forth to minister for them who shall be heirs of salvation?" (Hebrews 1:13-14). Obedient angels are spirits sent to minister to mortal, fleshly human beings who are heirs to salvation — heirs to immortality!

2) Demons or fallen angels.

Satan is the "prince of demons" (Mark 3:22). We read of Satan and his angels in Revelation 12:9: "And the great dragon was cast out, that old serpent, called the Devil, and Satan, which deceiveth the whole world: he was cast out into the earth, and his angels were cast out with him." The apostle Peter wrote of them: "For if God spared not the angels that sinned, but cast them down to hell, and delivered them into chains of darkness, to be reserved unto judgment" (2 Peter 2:4).

The two classes of created spirit beings are both angels. The only difference is that one class is obedient, the other class disobedient.

The spirits manifesting themselves through Spiritism are wicked spirits. The demons manifest their powers in various ways — sometimes in the darkness of Spiritist seances, sometimes through possessing human beings' mental and physical attributes. This latter form is often termed "demon possession." Spirit of divination is the fake simulation of prophecy.

Acts 16:16-18: "And it came to pass, as we went to prayer, a certain damsel possessed with a spirit of divination met us, which brought her masters much gain by soothsaying: The same followed Paul and us, and cried, saying, These men are the servants of the most high God, which show unto us the way of salvation. And this did she many days. But Paul, being grieved, turned and said to the spirit, I command thee in the name of Jesus Christ to come out of her. And he came out the same hour."

Notice that evil spirits can possess the mental and vocal faculties of human beings. They impersonate or pretend that they are human beings. They often manifest their powers in connection with religion to deceive innocent victims — or to bring reproach upon the name of God by their misconduct,

In other instances, they utilize human faculties to violently express their evil nature. Example in Matthew 8:28-33: 28 And when he was come to the other side into the country of the Gergesenes, there met him two possessed with devils, coming out of the tombs, exceeding fierce, so that no man might pass by that way.

And behold, they cried out, saying, what have we to do with thee, Jesus, thou Son of God? art thou come hither to torment us before the time? And there was a good way off from them a herd of many swine feeding. So, the demons besought him, saying, if thou cast us out, suffer us to go away into the herd of swine. And he said unto them, Go. And when they were come out, they went into the herd of swine: and behold — the whole herd of swine ran violently down a steep place into the sea and perished in the waters."

Spiritism is Condemned in Bible. God condemned Spiritism centuries ago. His words are: "Regard not them that have familiar spirits, neither seek after wizards, to be defiled by them: I am the Lord your God" (Leviticus. 19:31).

A familiar spirit is a particular spirit who associates itself with a medium, usually a woman. A familiar spirit is often called a "guide" because it guides or controls the seance for the medium. A wizard is a male human being who acts as an instrument of wicked spirits.

God's condemnation of Spiritism in Deuteronomy 18:9-12: "When thou art come into the land which the Eternal thy God giveth thee, thou shalt not learn to do after the abominations of those nations. There shall not be found among you anyone that maketh his son or his daughter to pass through the fire, or that useth divination, or an observer of times, or an enchanter, or a witch, or a charmer, or a consulter of familiar spirits, or a wizard or a necromancer. for all that do these things are an abomination unto the eternal: and because of these abominations the eternal thy god doth drive them [the gentiles) out from before thee."

Spiritism is an abomination to God. He drove out the Gentiles in the days of Joshua for permitting Spiritism. And the same punishment is coming upon our nations for encouraging Spiritism to flourish!

God condemns the witch — a woman who pretends to contact the "spirit" of a beloved one who has recently died — and a consulter of familiar spirits — usually a woman who contacts a particular spirit for information — and wizard and a necromancer — one who professes to predict the future by the art of communicating with the dead.

Spiritism is the products of human carnality, a fruit of the flesh. "Now the works of the flesh are manifest, which are these; Adultery, fornication, uncleanness, lasciviousness, idolatry, witchcraft, hatred, variance, emulations, wrath, strife, seditions, heresies, envyings, murders, drunkenness, revellings, and such like: of the which I tell you before, as I have also told you in time past, that they which do such things shall not inherit the kingdom of god" (Galatians 5:19-21).

Saul's Experience with a Witch

One of the most noted portions of scripture — yet one of the least understood — is the case of Saul and the witch at Endor. This story is found in 1 Samuel 28. Notice verse 3 of this chapter: "Now Samuel was dead, and all Israel had lamented him, and buried him in Ramah, even in his own city."

Notice that Samuel was dead and buried. He was not alive "And Saul had put away those that had familiar spirits, and the wizards, out of the land. And the Philistines gathered themselves together... and when Saul saw the host of the Philistines, he was afraid, and his heart greatly trembled. And when Saul inquired of the Eternal, the Eternal answered him not, neither by dreams, nor by Urim [through the high priest], nor by prophets" (Verse 6).

God would not listen to Saul. Saul had been disobedient. Samuel had been inspired to tell Saul: "For rebellion is as the sin of witchcraft" (1 Samuel 15:23).

What did Saul do? "Then said Saul unto his servants, seek me a woman that hath a familiar spirit, that I may go to her, and inquire of her. And his servants said to him, Behold, there is a woman that hath a familiar spirit at Endor" (Verse 7).

Remember that Samuel was buried in Ramah, located in the territory belonging to the tribe of Ephraim (1 Samuel 1:1, 19). But the Philistines and Saul were now near Lake Galilee, in Mount Gilboa, near Endor — about 50 miles from the place in which Samuel was buried. The night before the battle "Saul disguised himself, and put on other raiment, and he went, and two men with him, and they came to the woman by night: and he said, I pray thee, divine unto me by the familiar spirit, and bring me him up, whom I shall name unto thee" (Verse 8).

Saul sinned by seeking a witch. If God would not answer Saul by a prophet because of Saul's disobedience in government administration, how much more would God refuse to answer Saul by a prophet when Saul seeks to a witch! Remember that Samuel was a prophet (Acts 13:20) and a judge (1 Samuel 7:6, 15-17). And God would not use a prophet to answer Saul! In other words, God would not use Samuel the prophet to answer Saul; neither would God use any other means, for that matter. God absolutely refused to listen to Saul because of his rebellious attitude.

The Spirit Masquerades as Samuel

But notice what happened: "Then said the woman, whom shall I bring up unto thee?" Notice that the woman spirit medium claimed to contact the dead by supernaturally bringing them up from the grave through the familiar spirit.

This form was practiced when the people believed that the dead were in their graves. In the Old Testament you still had Abraham's bosom.

Today spirit mediums have the familiar spirit produce a voice from the air — because it is commonly believed today that the dead are not in their graves but somewhere else!

Saul replied to the woman: "Bring me up Samuel."

Instead of the familiar spirit appearing first, and then the visionary form of a dead person, the woman saw first a form that looked exactly like Samuel! "And when the woman saw Samuel, she cried with a loud voice: and the woman spake to Saul, saying, why hast thou deceived me? For thou art Saul And the king said unto her, Be not afraid: for what sawest thou?" (1 Samuel 28:12-13).

Notice that the familiar spirit did not manifest itself first at Saul's I. Instead, the familiar spirit produced the form of Samuel which only the woman saw! Saul did not see it! He asked the woman what she saw!

"And the woman said unto Saul, I saw gods ascending out of the earth" (Verse 13, last part). This is an incorrect translation. The word translated" "gods" is Elohim in the Hebrew. It can mean either the true God, pagan gods or judges.

In Exodus 22:8, 9, the Hebrew word Elohim is translated judges. In 1 Samuel 28:13, the verse should have been translated: "I saw a judge ascending out of the "rth." This is proved by what follows:

"And he said unto her, What form is he of! And she said, An old man cometh up; and he is covered with a mantle. And Saul perceived that it was Samuel, and he stooped with his face to the ground, and bowed himself" (Verse 14).

Deception

Notice that Saul still did not see anyone! He only perceived by reasoning that the form which the woman saw was that of Samuel! Here we have a perfect illustration of evil spirits' impersonation of human beings. The familiar spirit produced an illusion which only the woman saw. To her, the illusion was that of a judge rising from the earth. Remember that Samuel was actually buried about 50 miles away, not: In Endor where the seance was occurring! Samuel was not resurrected. The whole thing was chicanery.

While impersonating Samuel, the spirit spoke to king Saul thus: "And Samuel said to Saul, Why hast thou disquieted me, to bring me up?" — notice the Lying spirit. Satan similarly lied to Eve! "and Saul answered, I am sore distressed; for the philistines make war against me, and god is departed from me, and answereth me no more, neither by prophets, nor by dreams: therefore I have called thee, that thou mayest make known unto me what I shall do" (verse 15).

The spirit continues impersonating Samuel by reprimanding Saul for all his evil deeds. Finally, the spirit concluded: "Tomorrow shalt thou and thy sons be with me: and the Lord also shall deliver the host of Israel into the hands of the Philistines" (verse 19).

How did the spirit know what was to happen? Because God often makes His plans known to evil spirits! Notice 1 Kings 22:22-23 and 2 Chronicles 18:21-22. God permitted "lying spirits" to know His plans. God rules over all. But He has allowed Satan and his demons to control and influence this entire world. The familiar spirit of the witch at Endor must have known that God would deliver Saul that next day. So, it told Saul what would happen so that its impersonation of Saul might seem real!

Saul's Punishment

"So, Saul died for his transgression which he committed against the Eternal, even against the word of the Eternal, which he kept not, and also for asking counsel of one that had a familiar spirit, to inquire of it; and inquired not of the eternal: therefore he slew him, and turned the kingdom unto David the son of Jesse" (1 Chronicles 10:13-14).

God took the life of Saul for seeking information at a seance! In His Revelation to the apostle John, Jesus warns us of the growing influence of wicked spirits. They will become so influential in world affairs that the rulers of nations will act upon their deceptive, lying words. The control of these wicked spirits, described in Revelation 16:13-16, will lead to Armageddon!

Today we are warned: "believe not every spirit but try the spirits whether they are of god (1 John 4:1). We need to prove whether spirits are good or evil.

"And when they shall say unto you, seek unto them that have familiar spirits, and unto wizards that peep, and that mutter: should not a people seek unto their God? for the living to the dead? To the law and to the testimony: if they speak not according to this word, it is because there is no light in them" (Isaiah 8:19-20).

Evil Spirits Pretend to Bring Light

The spirits who masquerade as human beings at Spiritist seances pretend to bring light and knowledge. "For such [ministers who pretend to serve Jesus Christ] are false apostles, deceitful workers, transforming themselves into the apostles of Christ. and no marvel; for Satan himself is transformed into an angel of light. Therefore, it is no great thing if his ministers also be transformed as the ministers of righteousness; whose end shall be according to their works" (2 Corinthians. 11:13-14).

James tells us what to do when the influence of wicked spirits is present: "submit yourselves therefore to god. Resist the devil, and he will flee from you" (James 4:7). You must not obey the devil by yielding to his temptations. Instead, ask God for help. Refuse to yield to satanic influence. Submit to God's correction. Let him guide you!

24.
Circumcised Ears

Genesis 17:1-2, 9-10: When Abram was ninety-nine, the Lord appeared to him and said, "I am God Almighty; walk before me faithfully and be blameless. Then I will make my covenant between me and you and will greatly increase your numbers."

Then God said to Abraham, "As for you, you must keep my covenant, you and your descendants after you for the generations to come. This is my covenant with you and your descendants after you, the covenant you are to keep: Every male among you shall be circumcised…"

Whatever circumcision symbolized at the start, at the very least, it was a physically distinctive mark that set the tribes of Israel apart from the surrounding and neighboring tribes. Circumcision meant that these people were set apart for God--distinctive, holy, consecrated.

But it wasn't too long before the notion of circumcision began to drift to another body part. In the giving of the Law to Israel after the Exodus, we see circumcision shift from the genitalia to the heart. The idea of being "set apart" and "consecrated" shifted from a physical mark to behavioral distinctiveness.

Deuteronomy 10:16; 30:6

Circumcise your hearts, therefore, and do not be stiff-necked any longer.

The Lord your God will circumcise your hearts and the hearts of your descendants and live.

Circumcision becomes less about ethnic identification than an issue of obedience and love of God.

In the New Testament, Paul echoes this behavioral shift, arguing that "true circumcision" is a matter of obedience to the Law and not simply the physical mark. Circumcision is a matter of the heart.

Romans 2:25-29

Circumcision has value if you observe the law, but if you break the law, you have become as though you had not been circumcised. So then, if those who are not circumcised keep the law's requirements, will they not be regarded as though they were circumcised? The one who is not circumcised physically and yet obeys the law will condemn you who, even though you have the written code and circumcision, are a lawbreaker.

A person is not a Jew who is one only outwardly, nor is circumcision merely outward and physical. No, a person is a Jew who is one inwardly; and circumcision is circumcision of the heart, by the Spirit, not by the written code. Such a person's praise is not from other people but God.

In this we see a spiritualization of the concept of circumcision. Circumcision is less a matter of the flesh than it is obedience to God. And beyond the genitalia and the heart we see circumcision also applied to a third body part.

The ears.

In the Old Testament prophets, there is a growing concern with ears: the ability to hear the Word of God and be open and receptive to God. In the prophets there is a lot of discussion about ears that are "closed," "deaf," or "stopped up" to the Word of God.

Ezekiel 12:2

"Son of man, you are living among a rebellious people. They have eyes to see but do not see and ears to hear but do not hear, for they are rebellious people."

Jeremiah 5:21

"Hear this, you foolish and senseless people, who have eyes but do not see, who have ears but do not hear…"

This culminates in using circumcision to designate ears closed to the Word of God:

Jeremiah 6:10: To whom shall I speak and give warning, that they may hear? Behold, their ears are uncircumcised, they cannot listen; behold, the word of the Lord is to them an object of scorn; they take no pleasure in it.

In the gospels, particularly in his parables, Jesus also draws attention to the ears: "He who has ears to hear let him hear."

In the New Testament, it is Stephen,- in his sermon before the Sanhedrin, who makes the explicit connection between spiritual deafness and uncircumcision:

Acts 7:51: "You stiff-necked people! Your hearts and ears are still uncircumcised. You are just like your ancestors: You always resist the Holy Spirit!"

What I find of interest here is how circumcision is a deliberate act of setting something apart, an act of consecration. Which is interesting given the anatomical relationship between ears and heart. A relationship that I think the prophets were getting at.

The ears function as gatekeepers. If the ears are "closed" then nothing gets to the heart. Thus, the shift to the ears.

Zechariah 7:11: But they refused to pay attention; stubbornly they turned their backs and covered their ears.

I find the connection between circumcision and ears interesting. Circumcision is a deliberate act of "setting apart." So, what might it mean to "circumcise your ears?" To have holy, consecrated ears? Ears to cultivate to "hear" God in the babel of the world?

Guard What Comes Through Your Eye- and Ear-Gates

My son, give attention to my words; incline your ear to my sayings. Do not let them depart from your eyes; keep them in the midst of your heart; for they are life to those who find them, and health to all their flesh (Proverbs 4:20–22).

The Book of Proverbs "My son, give attention to my words; incline your ear to my sayings. Do not let them depart from your eyes; keep them in the midst of your heart; for they are life to those who find them, and health to all their flesh."

God tells us to guard what we hear, see, and what is in our hearts. He wants us to have our ears full of the gracious words of Jesus, our eyes full of the presence of Jesus and our hearts meditating on what we have heard and seen in Jesus. That's what "give attention to my words" means today in the new covenant, for Jesus is God's Word made flesh.

John 1:14 says, "And the Word became flesh and dwelt among us, and we beheld His glory, the glory as of the only begotten of the Father, full of grace [unmerited favor] and truth."

It is all about beholding Jesus, and as we behold Him, we are transformed more and more into His likeness, full of unmerited favor and truth! Don't miss this powerful promise, my friend. Turning our ear- and eye-gates to Jesus means that He will be life and health to us.

The Bible shows us that there is a direct correlation between hearing and seeing Jesus, and the health of our physical bodies. The more we hear and see Jesus, the healthier and stronger we become! Our mortal bodies become infused with His resurrection life and power!

But blessed are your eyes because they see, and your ears because they hear" (Matthew 13:16).

25.
How To Minister Prophetically

Practical Applications

- Know when God is speaking within your spirit. Your spirit is the secret place. Don't prophesy from your soul.
- Discern within your spirit if it is a word for you personally or other people.
- Determine through the leading of the Holy Spirit if God wants the prophecy to be shared with others or to be prayed about. Not every prophecy is to be shared.
- Using words of wisdom and words of knowledge, decide with whom to share the word!
- Know when to share the word. Allow God to prompt you before releasing the word.
- Discern if the prophetic word is to be shared publicly or privately. Sometimes God will lead you to speak privately to people just like Nathan went to David privately.
- Be willing to submit the prophecy to other prophets to see if there is witnessing before giving the word publicly if you are unsure of the authenticity of that word.
- Be willing to wait. Trust God and wait on Him to release the word in a timely way. If God does not lead you, don't speak.
- Determine to keep the word without ever sharing it with others if God leads you that way!
- Be willing to risk humiliation, to share the word even if you are being scorned and mocked.
- Say only what God says and don't add anything to it.
- Don't summarize the prophetic word of God. That can allow for additional soulish mixture.

- Do not try to "play god" in the lives of others! Be careful with the words you speak. They can alter and even destroy lives. If God doesn't speak to you, don't try to make up words. This can lead to divination.
- Allow God to take the word given and confirm it to the hearer!
- Do not "interpret" the word that is spoken unless the Holy Spirit gives you the leading.

My Response to The Message of The Lord

Possible Reactions

Humility: Test the message, then decide from there. Write it down. Pray/intercede. Wait. Teach and Role model. Allow the prophecy to manifest.

Humility

Remember the source, the Author and Finisher of our faith.

Hebrews 12:2: looking unto Jesus the author and finisher of our faith, who for the joy that was set before him endured the cross, despising the shame, and is set down at the right hand of the throne of God.

Keep the cross and the message of Christ's resurrection ever before you Stay acquainted and regularly fellowshipping with the personhood of the Holy Spirit. Be humbled that he, the Lord, would count you worthy to speak for him.

Test the Message

The Possible Voices

Voice of God, Voice of Self/Flesh, Voice of Others (Opinions), Voice of the Devil, (Romans 8:12-14 and Galatians 5:16-25) regarding discerning the voice of God versus other voices.

The Voice of God

Called (2 Corinthians 1:22) "inner man" (Romans 7:22) Must be consistent with Scripture will always take us back to Jesus as our first love (Revelation 2:4). We allow ourselves to be wooed by the Holy Spirit and are eager to get to know the Lord better.

We don't just want to grow in knowing about Him but knowing Him- intimacy surface level religious experience is not enough and does not satisfy.

Voice of Self

Your thoughts, your feelings, your will. Romans 8:7-8- the mind of the flesh [with its carnal thoughts and purposes] is hostile to God, for it cannot submit itself to God's Law; indeed, it cannot. So then those who are living the life of the flesh [catering to the appetites and impulses of their carnal nature] cannot please or satisfy God or be acceptable to Him.

1 Corinthians 3:20: The Lord knows the thoughts and reasoning's of the [humanly] wise and recognizes how futile they are.

Galatians 5:16-17: walk and live [habitually] in the [Holy] Spirit [responsive to and controlled and guided by the Spirit]; then you will certainly not gratify the cravings and desires of the flesh [of human nature without God]. For the desires of the flesh are opposed to the [Holy] Spirit, and the [desires of the] Spirit are opposed to the flesh (godless human nature); for these are antagonistic to each other [continually withstanding and in conflict with each other].

The Voice of People's Opinions

1 John 5:19: The whole world is under the influence of the evil one. Our home is in heaven (Philippians 3:20) and this place is only temporary (John 15:19, 17:15-17, James 4:4, 1 Peter 1:1, 17, 2:11; 2 Corinthians 5:20). Guard our hearts and minds from being contaminated by the world (Acts 20:30-31, 1 Corinthians 16:13, Philippians 4:7, 1 Timothy 6:20, 2 Timothy 1:14, 4:14-15, 2 Peter 3:16-17). We live in the world, but we are not of the world (1 Corinthians 2:12, 7:31), (James 4:4, 1 John 4:4-5).

Example: Paul going to Jerusalem debate (Pauls' opinion in Acts 20:22-24- compelled by the Holy Spirit-versus the people's opinions). In Acts 21:10-15 a prophet told Paul that he would suffer in Jerusalem, and Paul's traveling companions pleaded with him not to go there. Paul knew the Spirit was compelling him to go to Jerusalem, yet all the Christians around him kept trying to talk him out of it.

The apostle Peter (In Galatians 2:11-14) The apostle Paul said that the opinions of others swayed Peter into separating from Gentile Christians, and in turn Peter swayed other Jewish Christians to do the same. In this case, an apostle was led astray by the "voice" of other Christians, and an apostle led other Christians astray!

When Jesus told the apostles that He would suffer and die, Peter took Him aside and tried to talk Him out of letting this happen. Do you remember Jesus' reply? He said, "Get behind me, Satan! You are a stumbling block to me; you do not have in mind the things of God, but the things of men." (Matthew 16:21-23). The devil was speaking through an apostle! Of course, Peter was not possessed by the devil, but he was still choosing to follow his thoughts, reasoning, opinions and emotions.

Sometimes, people tell you that they believe they have a word from the Lord for you. Set it aside rather than being so eager to quickly accept or reject it. Allow time to pass. What you do in response to the words of people is important. Get away with the Lord. Not all counsel and talking to everyone is helpful unless it is righteous, biblically backed counsel. Recall Jesus' example. He was not big on seeking people's opinions because He "knew what was in man." The Father's truth was always the most important.

The Voice of the Devil

James 4:7 says: "Submit yourselves, then, to God. Resist the devil, and he will flee from you." When your life is lived in daily submission to God, you have power over the devil. However, submitting to God means that you have to give up your "self," because the more that you are dead to "self" the less there is in you for the devil to grab hold of.

Try repeating Scripture out of your mouth several times a day, such as these, for example: "I have been crucified with Christ and I no longer live, but Christ lives in me. The life I live in the body, I live by faith in the Son of God, who loved me and gave himself for me." (Galatians 2:20) "Submit yourselves, then, to God. Resist the devil, and he will flee from you. Come near to God and he will come near to you" (James 4:7-8).

Speaking Scripture will overcome the enemy's deception and lies (Luke 4:1-13). Scripture cannot be spoken unless we know it and make it a regular part of our lifestyle and unless it is illuminated to us.

The Holy Spirit

May come in the form of a feeling, a warning in your Spirit man or a hesitancy to go ahead with something- a conviction. Obedience is key: What He says, how he gives the instruction, the timing or what is warned against.

Small is the gate and narrow the road that leads to life, and only a few find it" (Matthew 7:14). Be in love with pleasing God more than anything or anyone.

Romans 9:1: I speak the truth in Christ--I am not lying; my conscience confirms it in the Holy Spirit. 2 Corinthians 1:12: Now this is our boast: Our conscience testifies that we have conducted ourselves in the world, and especially in our relations with you, in the holiness and sincerity that are from God. Our consciences "bear witness" to the truth (Romans 2:15) The truth is "plain to your conscience" (2 Corinthians 5:11) Romans 8:16: The Spirit himself testifies with our spirit to confirm the truth.

Writing Down the Message

Habakkuk 2:3 KJV

For the vision is yet for an appointed time, but at the end it shall speak, and not lie; though it tarries, wait for it; because it will surely come, it will not tarry.

When the message is not heeded

Nehemiah 9:17: "They refused to listen and did not remember Your wondrous deeds which You had performed among them; So, they became stubborn and appointed a leader to return to their slavery in Egypt. But You are a God of forgiveness, Gracious and compassionate, Slow to anger and abounding in lovingkindness; And You did not forsake them."

Our job is to have the heart of Christ. Let Him deal with the reactions and responses of people- good or bad, righteous or unrighteous. We Don't Own the Outcomes.

Speak, Even When No One Wants to Listen

Those who unflinchingly and relentlessly proclaim the truth are becoming endangered. Truth itself is under attack, and those who speak it are increasingly treated as bigots. People want to be told what they want to hear than what they need to hear.

This is not just true of non-believers, but increasingly of Christians. They prefer to hear the pleasant, fluffy stuff that tickles their ears and makes them feel good.

The Prophets were rejected, Jesus was crucified, and the disciples persecuted and killed, all because truth-telling was far more important to them than men-pleasing.

Jeremiah 5:30-31: A horrible and shocking thing has happened in the land: The prophets prophesy lies, the priest's rule by their own authority, and my people love it this way. But what will you do in the end?

Jesus himself pointed out: "Jerusalem, Jerusalem, you who kill the prophets and stone those sent to you, how often I have longed to gather your children together, as a hen gathers her chicks under her wings, and you were not willing" (Matthew 23:37).

Stephen confronted the religious leaders of his day just before his death: "Was there ever a prophet your ancestors did not persecute? They even killed those who predicted the coming of the Righteous One. And now you have betrayed and murdered him" (Acts 7:52).

God calls a prophet to speak to the people, to warn the people, to plead with the people, and he tells them ahead of time that the people will not receive them. Yet these brave prophets do what they have been called to do, even knowing their words will fall on deaf ears. And often they do it for many decades on end.

Isaiah 6:8 puts it this way: "Then I heard the voice of the Lord saying, 'Whom shall I send? And who will go for us?'

And I said, 'Here am I. Send me!'" Consider the verses immediately following this (verse 9-13): He said, "Go and tell this people:" 'Be ever hearing, but never understanding; be ever seeing, but never perceiving. 'Make the heart of this people calloused; make their ears dull and close their eyes. Otherwise, they might see with their eyes, hear with their ears, understand with their hearts, and turn and be healed. "Then I said, "For how long, Lord?"

And he answered: "Until the cities lie ruined and without inhabitant, until the houses are left deserted, and the fields ruined and ravaged, until the Lord has sent everyone far away and the land is utterly forsaken. And though a tenth remains in the land, it will again be laid waste. But as the terebinth and oak leave stumps when they are cut down, so the holy seed will be the stump in the land." Later on, we read more of the same.

As we find in Isaiah 30:9-11: For these are rebellious people, deceitful children, children unwilling to listen to the LORD's instruction. They say to the seers, "See no more visions! "And to the prophets, "Give us no more visions of what is right! Tell us pleasant things, prophesy illusions. Leave this way, get off this path, and stop confronting us with the Holy One of Israel!"

Things are the same for the prophet Jeremiah. In Jeremiah 7:21-29 we read this: This is what the Lord Almighty, the God of Israel, says: Go ahead, add your burnt offerings to your other sacrifices and eat the meat yourselves! For when I brought your ancestors out of Egypt and spoke to them, I did not just give them commands about burnt offerings and sacrifices, but I gave them this command: Obey me, and I will be your God and you will be my people. Walk in obedience to all I command you, that it may go well with you. But they did not listen or pay attention; instead, they followed the stubborn inclinations of their evil hearts. They went backward and not forward. From the time your ancestors left Egypt until now, day after day, again and again I sent you my servants the prophets. But they did not listen to me or pay attention. They were stiff-necked and did evil than their ancestors.'

"When you tell them all this, they will not listen to you; when you call to them, they will not answer. Therefore, say to them, 'This is the nation that has not obeyed the Lord its God or responded to correction. Truth has perished; it has vanished from their lips."

"'Cut off your hair and throw it away; take up a lament on the barren heights, for the Lord has rejected and abandoned this generation that is under his wrath'."

Things are so bad that God actually says this in Jeremiah 7:16: "So do not pray for this people nor offer any plea or petition for them; do not plead with me, for I will not listen to you." That is not the only time in Scripture we read about God actually saying that prayers should not be offered or will not be heard. That is scary stuff indeed.

And we find the same thing with the prophet Ezekiel. He too is warned about the hardness of heart that he will encounter. In Ezekiel 2:3-8 we read these words:

He said: "Son of man, I am sending you to the Israelites, to a rebellious nation that has rebelled against me; they and their ancestors have been in revolt against me to this very day. The people to whom I am sending you are obstinate and stubborn. Say to them, 'This is what the Sovereign Lord says.' And whether they listen or fail to listen—for they are a rebellious people—they will know that a prophet has been among them. And you, son of man, do not be afraid of them or their words. Do not be afraid, though briers and thorns are all around you and you live among scorpions. Do not be afraid of what they say or be terrified by them, though they are rebellious people. You must speak my words to them, whether they listen or fail to listen, for they are rebellious. But you, son of man, listen to what I say to you. Do not rebel like that rebellious people; open your mouth and eat what I give you."

And in Ezekiel 3:4-9 we get similar warnings from God:

He then said to me: "Son of man, go now to the people of Israel and speak my words to them. You are not being sent to a people of obscure speech and strange language, but to the people of Israel— not too many peoples of obscure speech and strange language, whose words you cannot understand. Surely if I had sent you to them, they would have listened to you. But the people of Israel are not willing to listen to you because they are not willing to listen to me, for all the Israelites are hardened and obstinate. But I will make you as unyielding and hardened as they are. I will make your forehead like the hardest stone, harder than flint. Do not be afraid of them or terrified by them, though they are a rebellious people."

These are just three of the various Old Testament prophets. It was pretty much the same for all of them. They were given a word to tell the people, but that word was not what they wanted to hear. Often it was a word of coming judgment and a call for repentance. Sometimes it also contains rays of hope if they respond correctly.

But more often than not the word was rejected, along with the carrier of the word. I share all this with you for a reason. It is not to discourage you, but to encourage you. With the prophets we have examples to follow. We have models we can emulate. The prophetic task is never a picnic. The ministry of the watchman on the wall is never a pleasant one. It will always be costly and unpleasant.

You plead, warn, beg, pray, call out and it seems your words are falling on concrete. No response. No appreciation. Just anger, rejection, hostility and opposition. It is easy to give up under those conditions. But we dare not. The prophets did not give up. The disciples did not give up.

And most importantly, Jesus did not give up. All of them proclaimed God's truth even though the normal reaction was for the people to fully reject what was being said, and to reject the messengers as well. But every Christian must share truth, regardless of the response.

Truth matters, and the eternal destiny of our listeners depend on what they hear and how they respond to it. So, if it seems like you are just knocking your head against the wall, remember that this is just how the prophets would have felt.

But they kept at it regardless. They did not give up.

26.
Financial Support for Ministry

Ministers are worthy of financial support: 1 Corinthians 9:7-18, the military pays its soldiers, the farmer eats of his crops, and the shepherd drinks the milk of the sheep. Also, even the ox pulling the threshing sled was allowed to eat some of the crops to keep working.

Why?

Receiving cheerful love offerings, given out of love and not with compulsion and manipulation is right, because God is providing for the life of the pastor and any family he may have. Not providing for one's family, even for God's service, is a denial of the faith, making a Christian worker worse than an unbeliever, who may not know better (1 Timothy 5:8).

Sometimes the Apostle, prophet, Pastor, evangelist, or teacher may pay an opportunity cost, giving up the opportunity to earn financial support through other employments. And they spend time preparing sermons, visiting the sick, providing oversight, comforting the grieving, and counseling the confused.

"Scripture says anyone who receives instruction in the word must share all good things with his instructor." Galatians 6:6.

The "worker deserves his wages" (1 Timothy 5:18).

Worthy pastors, "who direct the affairs of the church well are worthy of double honor, especially those whose work is preaching and teaching." (1 Timothy 5:17).

Who Funded Jesus's Ministry?

Did you ever wonder how Jesus funded his ministry? The disciples left tax collecting jobs and fishing businesses to follow him. They were not working a side job during this time. Who paid their expenses?

The question for those called into ministry is always how will I sustain myself? What will happen to me without an income? How will I pay my bills? I need to care for my family; how will I do that?

The disciples of Jesus left their boats and jobs to follow Jesus without a promise of a paycheck.

Luke tells us. "After this, Jesus traveled about from one town and village to another, proclaiming the good news of the kingdom of God. The Twelve were with him, and some women who had been cured of evil spirits and diseases: Mary (called Magdalene) from whom seven demons had come out; Joanna the wife of Chuza, the manager of Herod's household; Susanna; and many others. These women were helping to support them out of their own means." (Luke 8:1–3)

Three women who his ministry had helped funded it so others could be helped too. Their names were Mary, Joanna, and Susanna. There were many others as well. But these three women played such an important role that we know their names today.

Jesus had no need for money (Mark 6:8; Luke 9:3), except to pay taxes (Matthew 17:24–27; 22:17–21). For nourishment, He and His disciples ate in people's homes (Matthew 9:11; Mark 2:16; Luke 5:30; 7:36; 9:2–10; 11:37; 14:1; John 12:2). He ate from the trees (Matthew 21:19; Mark11:13*) and fields (Matthew 12:1; Mark 2:23; Luke 6:1). He also ate after the miracle of the bread and fish (Matthew 14:15–21; 15:32–38; Mark 6:34–44; 8:1–9; Luke 9:12–17; John 6:2–13).

The Bible clearly teaches that he had financial support from his close followers. Luke 8:3 clearly tells us that even the people in Herod's household helped him financially. This is true even today. Most of all the Gospel workers are financed by the people who believe in the God they represent.

The Way God Does Things

Why did God choose to make his son's ministry dependent on a few generous women? He could have had Peter catch more fish with gold coins in their mouths more often and build a treasury of gold like The United States Bullion Depository, often known as Fort Knox. Jesus could have started a business making wine out of water. But God chose to expand his ministry through the generosity of those blessed by it.

God funds ministry through the people who have been helped by it. Jesus and the disciples preached the gospel and did miracles. God funded them through people.

Mary was a woman with seven demons. Jesus set her free and she wanted to extend that freedom to others. Joanna's husband Chuza was a high-ranking government official who managed the king's money. All her connections and wealth couldn't buy her the healing that she found with Jesus. She wanted others to experience the same. Susanna is unknown to us except for this verse. But she is not unknown to Jesus. She was a disciple who contributed in a significant way to his ministry!

A church should provide for the financial needs of its pastor(s), ministers, and any other full-time ministers.

1 Corinthians 9:14 gives the church clear instruction: "The Lord has commanded that those who preach the gospel should receive their living from the gospel." 1 Timothy 5:17–18 says, "The elders who direct the affairs of the church well are worthy of double honor, especially those whose work is preaching and teaching.

For the Scripture says, 'Do not muzzle the ox while it is treading out the grain,' and 'The worker deserves his wages.'" There are several points made in this passage. Church elders should be honored, and this honor includes wages.

Those elders who serve the church well—especially teachers and preachers—should receive double honor. They have earned it. It would be cruel to work an ox while denying it grain, and we should take care not to treat our pastors or ministers cruelly. Again, funds should not be given to lazy pastors who are not busy serving the Lord. Those who are not committed to feeding the flocks should not be supported. But faithful ministers who are serving God faithfully let them share in the material blessings of the congregation they serve. Our pastors are worth more than many oxen.

There is nothing spiritual about making a pastor "suffer for the Lord." Yes, a pastor has been divinely called to his ministry, but it does not follow that a congregation should say, "Let God take care of him." God says the local church is responsible to take care of him and his family if he is faithful and committed to serving Christ.

Caring for the spiritual needs of a congregation is an important work—probably more important than other things we normally spend money on, such as meeting our physical needs, maintaining our vehicles, and entertaining ourselves (1 Corinthians 9:7).

The apostle Paul indeed supported himself as he ministered in Corinth (1 Corinthians 9:12). And many in the prophetic ministry will be required to start their own side business or what we call tent business. This does not mean that this is the only source of God's blessings. As we have seen, Jesus was funded by women but also by gold from a fish's mouth and sympathizers of his ministry. Do not limit God to only your tent business. Also allow those that your ministry has blessed to be a blessing to you.

Paul drew no salary from the Corinthians. But he made it clear that he did this as a voluntary sacrifice on their behalf, "that in preaching the gospel I may offer it free of charge, and so not make full use of my rights as a preacher of the gospel" (verse 18). Paul did take wages from other churches (2 Corinthians 11:8). His arrangement in Corinth was the exception, not the rule.

Sometimes a church cannot provide sufficient finances for a pastor or the ministers. The pastor or minister in such cases is forced to be bi-vocational, having no choice but to work outside the church to support his family.

This is a regrettable and distracting situation but sometimes necessary. It is usually better for a pastor to be paid full-time so he can fully dedicate himself to the Lord's work of ministering to and shepherding the congregation God has entrusted to him.

God still works through people. He doesn't drop food out of the sky to feed starving prophets or preachers. It doesn't mean that he cannot do it. He fed Elijah with ravens but later sent him to a widow. Maybe he could have just sent more ravens. Nope! He sent him to a person with a need. The widow had a need. Elijah also had a need. They fulfilled each other's needs and God provided.

Ministries don't expand without people leading them and people funding them. Buildings for churches to meet in don't build themselves. God works through people whose lives have been changed by his grace. You are God's plan!

The ministry continued because of the support of those who the ministry had blessed. Not that these women and men were trying to pay back a debt, but instead, they wanted to see this good thing continue. They wanted others to be reached with the same message that had changed them. Today, giving carries that act of thankfulness and gratitude. If your life has been changed by the message of Jesus, specifically at your church, and you want to see the message of Jesus continue, then give generously.

In the Old Testament, Elijah and Elisha marked the transition to a new image of the Prophet. Just like the Apostle Paul, they were not demanding pay through manipulations. But those blessed by their ministry or those compelled by the Holy Spirit to support them, supported them willingly and cheerfully.

These two prophets would refuse payments (2 Kings 5). But even when payment was being made in previous times, it was simply for the upkeep of the 'man of God' and not for him to get rich.

For example, the wife of Jeroboam gave only food to the prophet Ahijah (1 Kings 14:3). Because some prophets were now asking for payment for their ministry and hence compromising the word of God, we hear the rebuke of the prophet Micah: "Yahweh says this against the prophets who lead my people astray: So long as they have something to eat, they cry 'Peace'. But on anyone who puts nothing into their mouths they declare war." "You Kings make decisions based on bribes; you Priests teach God's laws only for a price; you Prophets won't prophesy unless you are paid. Yet all of you claim to depend on the LORD. "No harm can come to us," you say, "for the LORD is here among us" (Micah 3:5, 11).

There is no blessing of God related to paying a prophet. Any preacher who wants to be paid before ministering is a diviner and a manipulator. He wants to take advantage of people's ignorance.

False teachers are interested in exploiting you and are characterized by greed (2 Peter 2:2-3, 15), by pride (2 Peter 2:9-10; Jude 10) and by immorality (2 Peter 2:13-14; Jude 4). They devour the flock, rather than taking only what is needed for their needs and ministry.

We should not attempt to force people to give or extort money from people. Giving should not be "under compulsion" but cheerful (2 Corinthians 9:7).

We shouldn't keep passing the offering plate until we get what we think we should have.

We shouldn't make tithing a public matter, exalting the tither with special boxes located in front of the church. Giving should be done in secret so that even our right hand would not know what the left was giving (Matthew 6:2-4).

As you use your gift faithfully, the gift will make a way for you. Proverbs 18:16 is a powerful statement that reveals the answer: "A man's gift makes room for him" (NKJV). ... God has put a gift or talent in every person that the world will make room for. It is this gift that will enable you to fulfill your vision. It will make a way for you in life. As you use your gifts God will begin to change people's lives. And those people will be used by God to be a blessing in your life.

Trust God with provision. Make sure that you are released by God. Never release yourself. Those who release themselves will fund themselves. Those released by God will be funded by God.

What are some of the godly-inspired ideas that God has given you that he can bless to sustain you?

What are the natural gifts and talents that you feel strongly that God has given you and can be used by God to bless others and to open doors for you?

Do you plan to have a tent business like Paul?

27.
What does the Bible say about ordination?

DO you feel you have been called to ministry? Like preparing for any job, there is knowledge to gain and skills to acquire to become successful in the field. As you respond to God's calling and pursue a ministry, here are some things to keep in mind.

Upon entering a position in ministry, it is important to have a strong biblical foundation so you can represent Christ and defend what you believe. Having a hunger for His Word will allow you to continue to study it in-depth and, as a result, gain a deeper understanding of who God is. There is always something more to learn, so continue to be a student of God's Word

Having a strong prayer life will allow you to grow in your personal relationship with Christ. Everything you do in ministry must flow from what God has put on your heart to do. It can be detrimental to your ministry if you are not dedicated in your prayer life, because you may become distracted and feel the need to take matters into your own hands. However, remaining in Christ will allow you to hear His voice and fulfill the plan He has for you. Remember that no matter what the circumstance may be, God is there to comfort you when you come to Him through prayer.

Passages such as 1 Corinthians 12 and Romans 12 discuss spiritual gifts and what their purposes are. As followers of Christ, we are all given different gifts by the Spirit to glorify Him. We are each unique in our purpose, and together, we make up the body of Christ.

Therefore, especially before entering ministry, it is important to understand who God created you to be.

Wonderful things often come from humble beginnings. Jesus came into this world in unusual circumstances for a king. He was born unto Mary, a young girl, in a manger in Bethlehem because there was no room for them at the inn. Throughout His life, Jesus demonstrated what it means to live in humility and to love others. He came to serve rather than to be served. We are called to live as Jesus did, serving others in all we do. It can be dangerous when we lose sight of His glory and begin living for ourselves. However, when we keep Christ at the center of all we do, He will bless us.

Being involved in a Christian church family that loves and supports you as you serve Christ and grow to your full potential is important. For example, having an accountability partner in your local church leadership can help you to stay committed and disciplined in your walk with Christ.

A mentor can pray for you, disciple you and provide support in challenging times. In addition, they can provide guidance when it comes to making big decisions.

Oftentimes, ministry jobs can take you places you never imagined. While you may start with a certain plan, God might surprise you in how He uses your life to be a testament to Him. For this reason, it is important to trust in His plan. Listen to Him and remember that He is at work in all situations, even when you feel discouraged or confused. Romans 8:28 says, "And we know that for those who love God all things work together for good, for those who are called according to his purpose."

Do not go before God releases you in a time of prayer and fasting like he did with Acts 13:2 (Paul and Barnabas).

It took 30 years for preparation for both John the Baptist and Jesus. It took only three years for Jesus to accomplish his ministry. Preparation is more important than ministering. Paul prepared for 3 years in Arabia after God appeared to him. It took Moses 40 years in the wilderness before God appeared and commissioned him. We are not saying that you will wait for 40 years like Moses. What we are saying is that there is wisdom in waiting for God's timing.

Preparing for Ordained Ministry

An Ordained ministry is an exciting and big commitment. It requires thought and prayer as you prepare.

The modern definition of ordination is "the investiture of clergy" or "the act of granting pastoral authority or sacerdotal power." Usually, we think of an ordination service as a ceremony in which someone is commissioned or appointed to a position within the church. Often, the ceremony involves the laying on of hands. However, the biblical definition is a little different. The word ordain in the Bible refers to a setting in place or designation; for example, Joseph was "ordained" as a ruler in Egypt (Acts 7:10); the steward in Jesus' parable was "ordained" to oversee a household (Matthew 24:45); deacons were "ordained" to serve the Jerusalem church (Acts 6:1-6); and pastors were "ordained" in each city in Crete (Titus 1:5). In none of these cases is the mode of ordination specified, nor is any ceremony detailed; the "ordinations" are simply appointments. The word can even be used negatively as an appointment to punishment (Luke 12:46).

Acts thirteen includes a good example of a ministerial appointment: "While they were worshiping the Lord and fasting, the Holy Spirit said, 'Set apart for me Barnabas and Saul for the work to which I have called them.' So, after they had fasted and prayed, they placed their hands on them and sent them off. The two of them, sent on their way by the Holy Spirit, went down to Seleucia" (vv. 2-4). In this passage, we note some key facts: (1.) It is God Himself who calls the men to the ministry and qualifies them with gifts (Acts 20:28; Ephesians 4:11). (2.) The members of the church recognize God is clear leading and embrace it. (3.) With prayer and fasting, the church lays hands on Paul and Barnabas to demonstrate their commissioning (cf. Acts 6:6; 1 Timothy 5:22). (4) God works through the church, as both the church and the Spirit are said to "send" the missionaries.

Paul regularly ordained pastors for the churches he planted. He and Barnabas directed the appointment or ordination of elders "in each church" in Galatia (Acts 14:23). He instructed Titus to "appoint elders in every town" on Crete (Titus 1:5). Titus himself had been ordained earlier, when "he was chosen by the churches" (2 Corinthians 8:19). In the above passages, the ordination of elders involves the whole congregation, not just the apostles. The Greek word used in 2 Corinthians 8:19 for Titus's appointment and in Acts 14:23 for the choosing of the Galatian elders means "to stretch forth the hands." It was a word normally used for the act of voting in the Athenian legislature. Thus, the ordination of church leaders involved a consensus in the church, if not an official vote. The apostles and the congregations knew whom the Spirit had chosen, and they responded by placing those men in leadership.

When God calls and qualifies a man for the ministry, it will be apparent both to that man and to the rest of the church. The would-be minister will meet the qualifications set forth in 1 Timothy 3:1-16 and Titus 1:5-9, and he will possess a consuming desire to preach (1 Corinthians 9:16). It is the duty of the church elders, together with the congregation, to recognize and accept the calling. After that, a formal commissioning ceremony—an ordination service—is appropriate, though by no means mandatory. The ordination ceremony itself does not confer any special power; it simply gives public recognition to God's choice of leadership.

Paul and Barnabas were both fasting and praying before they ordained the elders of every church by only focusing on the Lord.

And when they had appointed elders for them in every church, with prayer and fasting they committed them to the Lord in whom they had believed (Acts 14:23).

You will need 5 days to fast and pray. Why five? Five is the number of the fivefold ministry or God's governing leadership authority. At the conclusion of the fast God will lead and direct the leaders on the timetable of your ordination, graduation, or commissioning.

Ministry Planning

Let us face it. None of us has extra time. If you want to have more impact with less time, planning is necessary. Planning makes it easier to involve other people, strengthens your credibility as a leader, and minimizes stress.

Planning your ministry area within your church family and the outside community in mind, you will be riding a giant wave of momentum instead of struggling to swim upstream.

Strategic Thinking

What Is Strategic Thinking?

Many leaders have an exciting vision for ministry but lack a workable plan to bring their vision to pass. This can lead to frustration among the members and hinder growth in the church or ministry.

What is needed is strategic thinking. Strategic thinking is planning according to the vision God has given to us. A vision is just the beginning. Strategic thinking puts "legs" on the vision. Remember:

A vision without a plan is just a dream.

Every vision needs to have a step-by-step plan that is flexible enough to be changed when needed but structured enough to keep the church focused on and moving towards the fulfillment of the vision. Vision is the target we are hoping to hit. Strategy is aiming at the target, so we do hit it. Strategic thinking requires:

Doing the right things and Doing things right.

We must do both. We must do the right things, and we must do them in the right (or correct) manner.

Doing the right things comes from the vision. We will know what to do when we discover God's purpose in the vision He gave us. Everything the church does must be measured by the vision it has. The most important question every church must ask about each of its activities and decisions is:

How is this helping us fulfill the vision God has given to us?

Often, churches or ministries struggle because they are doing the wrong things. What are the right things? The right things are those things that allow us to fulfill God's purpose. We may be doing good things, but good things can be wrong if they do not fulfill God's purpose. Our vision will help us determine the right things and keep us from wasting our time and resources on the wrong things.

Godly leadership creates opportunities for God's people to do the right things in the right way, fulfilling God's purpose. Doing the right things comes from the vision. Doing things right comes from leadership.

Christian leaders must learn to think strategically about the future. Strategic thinking includes the following elements (Luke 14:28-33).

Strategic thinking begins with the specific promise. God has given to us relative to our vision ("Come after Me, and I will make you fishers of men"). Visions have two parts: the command and the promise.

Its foundation is a specific intention or goal; ("For which one of you, when he wants to build a tower...").

It involves an assessment of our available spiritual and material resources, which have been given to us by God and are therefore definitive in nature ("...does not first sit down and calculate the cost to see if he has enough to complete it?").

Strategic planning is best accomplished in a group or corporate setting ("... and consults whether he is able..." KJV). Visionary leaders are not always the best methodical thinkers.

It finishes the task God gave us ("...This man began to build and was unable to finish"). Jesus said in John 4:34, "My food is to do the will of My father, and to finish His work." One of the first questions we must ask is, "How will we know when this vision has been completed?"

Strategic thinking will help us clarify many issues and steps needed to fulfill God's will. The process of working through these critical issues will strengthen our character, reveal our values, and help us more effectively impact the lives of those around us positively. Some leaders fear that strategic planning is "unspiritual" and will hinder the fulfillment of their visions. Just the opposite is true. "If you aim at nothing, you're sure to hit it!" That is also true if you are aiming at too many targets. In either case, we will be ineffective until we have a specific target to hit.

Allow the Holy Spirit to lead you as you carefully apply the vision to your situation through the process of strategic thinking.

Many leaders begin well and finish poorly. A lack of strategic planning is one of the reasons a leader may not finish well. A leader will often begin with a powerful vision and go to great lengths to communicate it excitingly and relevant to his followers, bringing them to a place where they are ready and willing to sacrifice whatever is necessary to accomplish it. But it will remain a dream if he does not have a workable plan to execute that vision. No vision is complete without a workable plan. Visions without plans are simply dreams.

Some leaders leap without thinking. This is a lack of planning. Some leaders think without leaping. This is a lack of proper implementation. Both can be equally devastating. Planning is not the same as planting, but one without the other will certainly be fruitless.

The process of strategic planning can do five important things:

- Strategic thinking makes the plan clear.
- Strategic thinking increases ownership in the plan.
- Strategic thinking builds confidence.
- Strategic thinking ensures productivity.
- Strategic thinking maximizes results.

Start by clearly identifying your prophetic mission or purpose.

Why do you exist? What is the purpose? Why are you part of a family (church)? Why is your ministry important to this family or the body of Christ? And what does God want you to accomplish in the local body and without the walls? Sit down and write a clear, concise, biblical, measurable mission statement. What do you think of our mission as CTHIM? How can you adapt these core ideas of CTHIM to the specific area you seek to plan?

Write out what you believe are your strengths and weaknesses. What are the greatest threats to the accomplishment of your mission? What are the most significant opportunities that lie ahead? Invite others to give you honest input and evaluation. What do they think you are doing right? How do they believe you need to improve?

Begin writing down all the things you could do in the coming year to best accomplish your prophetic mission. Ask God to give you unusual creativity vision. Do not be afraid to dream. Remember, because we are the children of God, we have significant resources at our disposal if our goal is to truly glorify Him.

The Lord Himself will bless plans that have a godly mission and focus. Proverbs 16:3: Commit your works to the Lord and your plans will be established. That is a promise, from God Himself.

Vision, Mission, and Core Values

There is a clear relationship between growth and vision ministries where clearly communicated visions grow; ministries without an unclouded vision do not grow.

Seeing and Understanding Your Ministry

The tree represents your ministry. Fruit is the natural result of a healthy tree. Just as a healthy tree has many parts that are necessary to produce fruit, your ministry also has many parts designed by God to enable you to produce spiritual fruit. When each part is developed and working properly, the harvest of fruit will be great. The harvest of fruit will be less than it could be if one or more parts of the tree is not developed or working properly. One of your most important leadership responsibilities is ensuring each part is developed and working properly.

The Basic Parts of Your Ministry

- Soil: Your Vision
- Roots: Your Core Values
- Trunk: Your Mission Statement
- Branches: Your Strategy and Activities
- Leaves: Your Goals and Objectives
- Fruit: Reproducing Disciples and Churches
- The following is a list of some terms we will use throughout this Seminar training.

Your Vision

Vision is seeing what God has called you to accomplish. It is important to put your vision into a vision statement, a simple and clear declaration of what God is calling you to do. Your vision statement should be short, easy to remember, specific, and unique about what you are doing in ministry. It should also be built around the Great Commission.

Your Core Values

Core values are the things we believe deeply enough that they "determine our priorities, influence our decisions, drive our ministry, and are always demonstrated by our behavior."

Your Mission Statement

A mission statement briefly describes those you seek to reach and how you will reach them.

Your Strategy and Activities

Your ministry strategy is the step-by-step plan you develop to accomplish your vision. It is a detailed mission statement that includes the structures and activities you will use to reach your target group.

Your Target Group

Your target group is the people you are reaching. Knowing those you are reaching will help you to develop a specific strategy to reach them.

Your Goals and Objectives

Your goals and objectives are the things you must accomplish to fulfill your vision and conduct your mission.

Your Fruit

Your fruit is the result and true measure of your ministry.

The Law of Reproduction

The Law of Reproduction reveals that God's purposes in creating man are most fully realized and expressed through reproduction.

- Vision creates Passion.
- Passion gives birth to Relationships.
- Relationships release Church Life.
- Church Life multiplies the Vision.

Communication of the vision must bring about ownership of the vision. The members must own the vision as much as the leaders.

Vision is seeing and understanding God's will and purpose.

- Four priorities for every local church vision (in order):
- Purpose
- People
- Programs
- Property

A Vision is:

- Birthed in Revelation
- Nothing can be born without intimacy.

- That which is birthed must be carried to full term.
- Multiplied in an environment of faith.
- Perfected by the needs it meets.
- Every vision is God's response to an existing or future need.

People Are Willing to Sacrifice for What They Deeply Believe.

The Vision of Your ministry must Be Something worth the Sacrifice of Your Members' Time, Resources, and Even Lives! If Not, You Are Wasting Their Time, Resources, and Lives.

Some Truths about the Modern Western Church System

One of the major weaknesses in the modern church system is that it forces you to build the church on the desires and needs of uncommitted people.

There are three levels of church affiliation for the average person:

- Attendees - attend church services.
- Members - join the church through regular attendance.
- Ministry Partners - have bought into the vision.
- Every church will have all three levels of affiliation.

What is a Vision Statement?

A vision statement is a brief, memorable expression of what God has called you to do.

It should be centered on the fulfillment of the Great Commission.

It should complete the thought, "We exist to _____."

It should be action - not being - oriented. It is primarily concerned with what you are doing rather than who you are, though it may briefly state your identity if your identity helps to communicate your assignment.

It should state who you are, what you are called to do, and your target group or area.

Make it simple, catchy - "Cape to Cairo" - and easy to say.

What is a Mission Statement?

A mission statement is a description of how you will accomplish your vision.

It should clearly state the main means by which the church or ministry functions in its vision.

- Discipleship?
- Evangelism?
- Worship services?
- Events?

It should include your target group or area.

It should feature your strengths and values.

Core Values

Core values are the things we believe so deeply that they touch every area of our lives and ministries. When a church has discovered and established its core values it is more likely to have "agenda harmony" – agreement on the purposes and direction of the church and its ministries. Churches that have not discovered and established their core values are less likely to grow and more likely to split.

Core values are consistent, enthusiastic, biblical, distinctive convictions that determine our priorities, influence our decisions, drive our ministry, and are demonstrated by our behavior.

- Core values are consistent – they rarely change.
- Core values are enthusiastic - they generate emotion and energy.
- Core values are Biblical – they are rooted in Scripture.
- Core values are distinctive – they reflect God's unique assignment.
- Core values are convictions – they influence everything we do.
- Core values determine our priorities.
- Core values influence our decisions.
- Core values are demonstrated by our behavior.
- Core values are measured by our diaries and our checkbooks.
- Core values drive our ministry.

- Core values are not our statement of faith, belief, or theology.
- Core values are not a biblical purpose statement that could describe any or every congregation.
- Core values are not a list of our favorite programs.

Why Values Are Important

Values provide the foundation for goals and setting the direction of the church's ministry.

Strategic planning will fail if values are not made clear at the beginning of the process.

Conflict in the body often arises from differing values.

If your ministry were really a functioning organism within the community, what would it be doing?

- What do you get enthusiastic about?
- How do you invest your time and money?
- For what do you want your ministry to be known for?

28.
APPENDIX A

OTHERS CAN...YOU CANNOT

Author Unknown

If God has called you to be really like Jesus, He will draw you into a life of crucifixion and humility, and put upon you such demands of obedience, that you will not be able to follow other people. Or measure yourself by other Christians, and in many ways, He will seem to let other people do things He will not let you do. Other Christians and ministers, who seem very Religious and useful, may push themselves, pull wires, and work schemes to carry out their plans, but you cannot do it, and if you attempt it, you will be met with such failure and rebuke from the Lord as to make you sorely penitent. Others may boast of themselves, of their work, of their successes. But the Holy Spirit will not allow you to do any such thing and if you begin it, He will lead you into some deep mortification that will make you despise yourself and all your good works. Others may be allowed to succeed in making money or have a legacy left to them, but it is like God will keep you poor because He wants you to have something better than gold, namely a helpless dependence upon Him, that He may have the privilege of supplying your needs day by day out of an unseen treasury. The Lord may let others be great but keep you small. He may let others do a work for Him and get credit for it, but He will make you work and toil on without knowing how much you are doing; And then to make your work still more precious, He may let others get credit for the work which you have done, and thus make your reward ten times greater when Jesus comes. The Lord may let others be honored, put forward and keep you hidden in obscurity because He wants to produce some choice fragrant fruit for His coming glory, which can only be produced in the shade. The Holy Spirit will put a strict watch over you, with a jealous love, and will rebuke you for little words and feelings or for wasting your time, which other Christians never feel distressed over. So, make up your mind that God is infinitely Sovereign and has a right to do as He pleases with His own. He may not explain to you a thousand things which puzzle your reason in His dealings with you, but if you absolutely sell yourself as His love slave, He will wrap you up in a jealous love, and bestow upon you many blessings. That comes only to those who are in the inner circle. Settle it forever, that you are to deal directly with the Holy Spirit, and He is to have the privilege of tying your tongue or closing your eyes, or chaining your hands in ways that He does not seem to use with others. Now when you are so possessed with the living God that you are in your secret heart, pleased and delighted over this peculiar, personal, private, jealous guardianship and management of the Holy Spirit over your life, you will have found the vestibule of Heaven!

29.
Inaugural Fast

The Secret Place

He that dwelleth in a secret place of the Highest shall abide under the shadow of the Almighty (Psalm 91:1).

Every Christian has a secret place. Whether he's aware of it or not. There's a room in your (imagination) (Spirit) Imaginations:

The act or power of forming a mental image of something not present to the senses or never before wholly perceived in reality.

https://www.merriam-webster.com/dictionary/imagination

Jesus is the ultimate image-bearer of God. Jesús fully reflects God's image; he is the true representative of God in his creation.

Bearers of his Image

We are called to live daily in such a way that embodies more and more what that image looks like. Jesus is the model we follow as we try to live that way. For Christians participating in the image of God experience means following Christ in both his exaltation and humiliation.

Simply put, we bear the renewed image of God daily as our lives conform to Jesus'. Being part of the renewed image of God means being "Conformed to the image" of Jesus (Romans 8:29).

We become more and more like him in every way. That image was marred and eventually restored and transformed in Jesus the Son of Man, the exact representation of the image of God.

Those who are in Christ take part in this new humanity. So, you meet God in your spirit, your subconscious, you are using your imagination as a portrait canvasing the Lord. There is danger here if our imaginations are not pure.

Genesis 6:6: And GOD saw that the wickedness of man was great in the earth, and that every imagination of the thoughts of his heart was only evil continually.

Genesis 8:21: And the LORD smelled a sweet savor and the LORD said in his heart, I will not curse again. The ground any more for man's sake; for the imagination of man's heart is evil from his youth neither will I again smite any more everything? living, as I have done.

1 Chronicles 28:9: And thou, Solomon my son, know thou the God of thy father, and serve him with a perfect heart and with a willing mind: for the LORD searcheth all hearts, and understandeth all the imaginations of the thoughts: if thou seek him, he will be found of thee; but if thou forsake him, he will cast thee off forever.

1 Chronicles 29:18: O LORD God of Abraham, Isaac, and of Israel, our fathers, keep this forever in the imagination of the thoughts of the heart of thy people, and prepare their heart unto thee:

Proverbs 6:18: A heart that deviseth wicked imaginations, feet that be swift in running to mischief, 2Corinthians.10 [5] Casting down imaginations, and every high thing that exalteth itself against the knowledge of God and bringing into captivity every thought to the obedience of Christ.

1 Corinthians 2:9: But, as it is written, "What no eye has seen, nor ear heard, nor the heart of man imagined, what God has prepared for those who love him"— the Bible calls us to adopt a sanctified imagination that helps us look beyond our own experience.

As created beings, one of our greatest treasures, perhaps the dearest fingerprint of God in us, is our ability to imagine. In the Old Testament, King James uses the term "imagination" five times (Genesis 6:5; Deuteronomy 29:19; Jeremiah 3:17; Proverbs 6:18; Lamentations 3:60). In four of the five references, the Hebrew word heart (lav) is used Literally, the Old Testament speaks of the "conceptions" of the heart (Genesis 6:5) or the stubbornness of the heart (Deuteronomy 29:19; Jeremiah 3:17) or the evil plots of the heart (Proverbs 6:8).

In Lamentations 3 the same word for "plots" of the heart that is used in Proverbs 6 appears (mahashbet). In the Old Testament "plots and evil schemes" happen in the heart.

There is no singular word for "imagination." In Hebrews in the New Testament, the word "imagination" appears three times in King James (Luke 1:51; Romans 1:21; 2 Corinthians 10:5). In these references, two of the three also speak or refer to the heart. (kardia).

In the final New Testament reference in which King James uses the word "imagination" (2 Corinthians 10:5), another form of the word "reasonings" (logismos) from Romans 1:21 is used.

Again, though the word "heart" (kardia) does not appear In the New Testament, as in the Old, the place where "dark reasonings" occur are primarily in the heart.

The problem then, is not in the simple use of the word "Imagination." The problem is one of the hearts. The Word of God is seeking to recapture and redeem our hearts for God's glory.

So how does God want us to use our imagination?

1 — Imagine His promises being fulfilled in your life.

2 — Imagine what He's calling you to do.

David had to imagine himself defeating Goliath. He envisioned putting the stone in the slingshot and falling the giant.

3 — Imagine His splendor and majesty daily David knew the secret place. He was in a secret place of the Highest shall abiding under the shadow of the Almighty (Psalm 91:1).

Start thinking about this imagination room, the spiritual secret place. It's the most important place in your life.

When the priest entered into that place just outside the veil, he had blood in one hand and incense in the other in which he could not by any means let touch the ground.

The veil was a high curtain made of scarlet material (Exodus 36:35) and was 3 inches thick.

Standing before the veil presented a problem because the fabric was thick and heavy, and the priest could not just part it. There was no opening to the veil so he could not just walk in.

The priest had gone as far as he could go in killing his flesh. He had been justified (outer court). He had been sanctified in his soul (Holy place) and the rest was up to God. The spirit of the Lord had to supernaturally usher him behind the veil.

It has always been taught among the Jews to this very day that the spirit of God would then transfer the priest from one side of the veil to the other side.

Because on the side of the veil where Jesus lives, the holiest of holiest, all logic and reasoning ceased to exist and it's all about him. The veil and all that was behind it was God's world.

Jesus operated in the spirit, allowing the flesh to follow the spirit within him. He never let the flesh lead him at any time but always operated in that realm on the other side of the veil.

The priest would wait at the veil and God would transfer them from one side to the other using his spirit "only."

The word "veil" in Hebrew means a screen, divider or separator that hides. What was this curtain hiding? Essentially, it was shielding a Holy God from sinful man.

Whoever entered the Holy of Holies was entering the very presence of God. Anyone except the high priest who entered the Holy of Holies would die.

Even the high priest, God's chosen mediator with His people, could only pass through the veil and enter this sacred dwelling once a year, on a prescribed day called the Day of Atonement.

The picture of the veil was that of a barrier between man and God, showing man that the holiness of God could not be trifled with.

God's eyes are too pure to look on evil and He can tolerate no sin (Habakkuk 1:13). The veil was a barrier to make sure that man could not carelessly and irreverently enter God's awesome presence.

Even as the high priest entered the Holy of Holies on the Day of Atonement, he had to make some meticulous preparations: He had to wash himself, put on special clothing, bring burning incense to let the smoke cover his eyes from a direct view of God, and bring blood with him to make atonement for sins (Hebrews 9:7).

This is the room where you meet with Jesus. When we perceive Jesus on the screen of our mind, the imagination, or the veil, we are at once in the secret place. We are in his presence. We see ourselves with him on that screen.

2 Corinthians 4:18 While we look not at the things which are seen, but at the things which are not seen: for the things which are seen are temporal: but the things which are not seen are eternal.

2 Corinthians 5:7 (For we walk by faith, not by sight:) This is why we say faith can go where reason cannot follow.

The veil is the imagination screen. The perception (veil) it is like a divider that makes a duplex of our mind allowing the Lord to dwell on one side and we the other.

We put the picture on this screen through our daily experience or awareness, but God can put pictures from the other side in the form of dreams.

Job 33:15: In a dream, in a vision of the night, when deep sleep falleth upon men, in slumbering's upon the bed.

Matthew 2:12: And having been warned in a dream not to return to Herod, they withdrew to their country by another route.

Matthew 27:19: While Pilate was sitting on the judgment seat, his wife sent him this message: "Have nothing to do with that innocent man, for I have suffered terribly in a dream today because of Him."

Genesis 46:2: And that night God spoke to Israel in a vision: "Jacob, Jacob!" He said. "Here I am," replied Jacob. No matter how the pictures originate. We see them on this Veil.

"Therefore, the LORD God expelled the man from the Garden of Eden so he would work the ground from which he had been taken. After he had expelled the man, the LORD God placed winged angels at the eastern end of the Garden of Eden, along with a fiery whirling sword, to prevent access to the tree of life." – Genesis 3: 23-24

God placed Cherubim at the gate of Eden to ensure the two (and by extension, mankind as a whole) would not find entrance again.

Exodus 26:31: And thou shalt make a vail of blue, and purple and scarlet, and fine twined linen of cunning work: with cherubim's shall it be made:

In the Garden of Eden, they were guarding the way to the tree of life, The LORD God placed winged angels at the eastern end of the Garden of Eden, along with a fiery whirling sword, to prevent access to the tree of life" (Genesis 3: 23-24).

The tree of life, mentioned in the books of Genesis and Revelation, is a life-giving tree created to enhance and perpetually sustain the physical life of humanity.

More details concerning the tree of life come after Adam and Eve's sin: "The LORD God said, 'The man has now become like one of us, knowing good and evil. He must not be allowed to reach out his hand and take also from the tree of life and eat and live forever'" (Genesis 3:22).

In his disobedience, Adam lost his eternal life. The tree of life in Eden must have had some role to play in maintaining the life of Adam and Eve (and possibly the animals). Adam would "live forever," even in his fallen condition, if he had eaten the tree of life after his sin.

God placed a sword-wielding cherub at the entrance to the garden specifically "to guard the way to the tree of life," (verse 24). It seems access to the tree of life would have prolonged Adam's physical life indefinitely, dooming him to an eternity in a cursed world.

Christ is indeed the Tree of Life from the Garden (of Eden). They would have lived forever if Adam and Eve had reached out and eaten from the Tree of Life in the Garden. Yes? Well, Christ tells us that we must eat from him to have eternal life and so, to live forever (see John 6:32–58) ... and He also tells us that He is the Life (see John 14:6; 11:25).

"I am the Way, the Truth, and the Life." "I am the Resurrection and the Life."

John 6:35: I am the bread of life.

He told them that their ancestors ate the manna in the wilderness, yet they died. But was the bread that came down from heaven, which anyone may eat and not die.

The bread was his flesh, which he would give for the life of the world. And "unless you eat the flesh of the Son of Man and drink his blood, you have no life in you. Whoever eats his flesh and drinks his blood has eternal life, and he will raise them up at the last day.

For his flesh is real food and his blood is real drink. Whoever eats his flesh and drinks his blood remains in him, and he in them.

Christ is the truth, the way, and the Life (and so also the Tree of Life). "I am the true vine, and My Father is the keeper of the vineyard. He cuts off every branch in me that bears no fruit, and every branch that does bear fruit, He prunes it to make it even more fruitful."

This tree is an entry point, it is a portal, the veil. Hebrews 10:20: "By a new and living way, which he hath consecrated for us, through the veil, that is to say, his flesh."

"It's called imagination screen because we do all our self-examination and perception on it. Even though we have no direct contact with the Lord, via our imaginations, we can bring him to our side and enjoy him."

1 Corinthians 11:28: But let a man examine himself, and so let him eat of that bread, and drink of that cup.

1 Corinthians 11:29: For anyone who eats and drinks without recognizing the body eats and drinks judgment on himself.

2 Corinthians 13:5: Examine yourselves to see whether you are in the faith; test yourselves. Can't you see for yourselves that Jesus Christ is in you--unless you actually fail the test?

Matthew 5:23,24: Therefore, if thou bring thy gift to the altar, and there rememberest that thy brother hath ought against thee; the process looks something like this.

The Lord continues to remain on the unconscious side of the screen, cool of the day Genesis (3:8). the spirit, wind or breathe of God came every day, afternoon. They heard the sound of God coming during the time of the Spirit, implying that there were specific times God's Spirit would meet them in the Garden. We can bring God by faith over to our side by removing the dividing line, (flesh) Jesus' flesh was the veil that was torn to reveal God (Hebrews 10:20).

Going past the flesh is equal to removing our carnal nature out of the way to be able to bring him to us. When we do this, our side becomes the secret place.

This ability sets us apart from the animals and makes us unique. The ability to imagine by means of our imagination, we can see things that do not exist.

The noblest glorious purpose for the imagination is giving reality to the unseen Lord. Yet we can't see him, touch him or contact him. Yet we believe (John 20:29). Jesus saith unto him, Thomas, because thou hast seen me, thou hast believed: blessed are they that have not seen and yet have believed.

1 Peter 1:8: Though you have not seen Him, you love Him; and though you do not see Him now, you believe in Him and rejoice with an inexpressible and glorious joy, we know by faith he lives within us, our faith allows us to accept what we can't see.

Imagination allows us to picture what we cannot see. Therefore, imagining our Lord is the most thrilling and exciting use of our imagination.

Proverbs 4:21: Let them not depart from thine eyes; keep them in the midst of thine heart.

Psalm 16:8: I keep my eyes always on the LORD. With him at my right hand, I will not be shaken. The dual purpose of our imagination can be used in two ways to please God or the devil.

Satan loves to have us create scenes that don't exist in our minds. By imagining wrong things, we have to work at keeping the Lord before us in our imagination. For this is the best way to frustrate the work of the devil.

God Guards His Privacy.

Isaiah 45:15: Verily thou art a God that hidest thyself, O God of Israel, the Saviour.

The secret place is the most private for you to commune with God. Only two people belong there. You and Jesus in this very private place. You and the Lord share your innermost thoughts, hopes and desires. Here, you worship him in the spirit, making it the holiest place in your life.

The more time you spend here with him, the more you become to like him. You enter the secret place, shut the door, and leave the world outside. All it takes is a little bit of practice. You can commune with the Lord everywhere, even in crowded places. You can slip into the secret place for a chat with the Lord. You can transport yourself in the spirit into that secret room.

1 Corinthians 13:12

Now we see but a dim reflection as in a mirror; then we shall see face to face. Now I know in part; then I shall know fully even as I am fully known.

Fasting

There are five phases a person goes through on an extended fast. Extended means 20, 30 or 40 days. You may not go through all these phases, but you should know about them.

Phase one (Hunger)-- For the first day or so, you will feel hunger. But it will not be because your body needs food. Your body can go for days and days without food. When your stomach is used to receiving food regularly, it will protest when you deny it. The body will act just like a spoiled child begging and nagging for what it wants. But you must ignore those cries. Those are the voices of the habit. The voice of the appetites.

Find a glass of water. It will take care of the hunger pangs. The hunger pangs will only last for 15 minutes anyway. The hardest part of your fast will be going through withdrawal symptoms.

Withdrawal is the combination of physical and mental effects a person experiences after they stop eating or reduce their intake.

If you have been overeating, have a dependency upon food and you suddenly or abruptly cut down your intake drastically, you can experience a variety of withdrawal symptoms. The intensity and duration of these withdrawal symptoms can vary widely, depending on your biological make-up.

Satan has turned many people into foodaholics. So, when we quit eating, we go into withdrawal symptoms. Symptoms will vary with each person. But usually, a headache, dizziness, feelings of weakness, pain in your body, it is a normal part of fasting.

Phase Two (Hunger Leaves)

Hunger leaves. This may vary with every individual. The fact that hunger leaves in 48 hours is a natural phenomenon confirmed by medical doctors and fasting supervisors alike. A hunger pang is a stomach contraction that occurs when it has nothing in it. In a non-fasted state, by the time you reach the point where you feel hunger pains, then yes, your ghrelin levels have increased, and the brain and stomach are telling you it's time to eat. What if you can't eat though because you're fasting? The reasonable expectation is that the hunger pains are only going to get worse the longer you go without food. Yet that's not what happens. In a 2005 study published in The Journal of Clinical Endocrinology and Metabolism, the researchers found that ghrelin will increase 24 to 48 hours into your fast and then drop consistently from there.

https://academic.oup.com/jcem/article/84/3/883/2864116?login=false

So yes, the first day or two of your fast may be difficult and even a little painful, and you may be able to think of nothing else except when your next meal will be. Just know if you can hold on for one or two more days. You'll feel better in the end. The body can draw on stored carbohydrates for about 48 hours and when that is gone, a chemical signal is sent from the pituitary gland into the bloodstream by a chemical magic known as ketosis. Your body shifts from burning food as fuel and starts living off the stored fat.

The body begins to feed on itself. Digesting its own fat. The body always needs fuel. Yet it is so designed that if it cannot get it from food, it will draw on the reserves stored in your body.

During the fast, you live off your own fat. There's no hunger because the body satisfies its hunger by burning its fat as fuel. Food may still look good to you, but you will have no craving for it.

Phase Three (Deficiency)

After hunger leaves you will experience weakness. For many people, this is the most difficult part of the fast. This could last as long as four days. Once it passes fasting becomes effortless. During the weakness interval, you may want to rest a lot. Your body is throwing off its waste and poisons so stay around restrooms or be conscious of your limitations without them.

When this phase is over, you're going to end up with much healthier organs and cleaner skin. If the 10 days are gone before your weakness is gone, don't worry.

Phase Four (Increasing Strength)

This is the unexacting phase; the weakness passes, and your strength returns. Fasting becomes routine from here on. You can return to your usual work. You will have plenty of strength to rely on. You may still have bouts of weaknesses now and then.

But don't let that disturb you. Any such episode will pass very quickly. God has designed the body to live off its own stored resources for days with no ill effects.

This is why the body stores excess food. The same God who designed the camel to store water in its hump, He also designed us to store food for the body to shift from burning food to burning stored fat.

Phase Five (Hunger Returns)

Suppose you went on an extended fast for 21 or 40 days. How would you know when it was time to break the fast? The body has a way of letting you know when the cleansing process is over. And all the fats, the waste and the bad cells have been eliminated. The body will then start feeding on healthy tissue. When that starts to happen, the body will sound an alarm. (Hunger) Fasting has now ended and starvation is beginning to occur. The body sounds a warning bell. When you come to the end of the fasting period, hunger returns and you know it's time to break the fast.

That's why in Matthew 4, Jesus became hungry as it reads in Matthew 4:2. During the 40 days, the Lord experienced no hunger and was not tempted. Then came the warning signal of hunger.

There are hindrances to fasting.

One of the greatest hindrances to fasting is not the hesitancy to try it. But the warnings of well-meaning friends and doctors.

They will not only try to keep you from fasting, but they will also tell you you're damaging your body, you are crazy, or you are committing suicide and starving to death.

The devil will reinforce their words. It will take willpower to resist them. Doctors refuse to face the fact that God has built a fantastic intelligence into the human body. It is far wiser for believers to take God's word over the theories of doctors.

We still recommend going to the doctor for a physical examination before beginning the fast if you are not used to fasting. You should ask for a glucose tolerance test; discuss any medication you are taking to see if you should discontinue it or find a substitute.

People with certain chronic liver and kidney diseases should not fast, neither should those with diabetes or tuberculosis or any with a blood disease or cerebral disease Also, fasting is not for pregnant women either. But for a normal healthy person, there shouldn't be any problem whatsoever.

People are starving themselves to death. But that is not fasting. Fasting and starvation are two separate things. Starvation feeds on good tissue while fasting feeds on fat.

Fasting is one of the finest healings and corrective methods available to men. So don't let fears instilled by friends and physicians rob you of one of the greatest experiences God has for you.

Breaking The Fast

When it is time to break your fast some caution is needed. How you come off a fast is more critical than how you begin. It must be done gradually. Why? Because of the colon and stomach, both have been shut down for 10 to 21 days. It will need to be eased back into action. If you broke your fast with a large solid food, it might pass solidly into the intestinal tract. It might have to be removed by surgery. Your organs are not ready for solid food. They need to be started up again.

Psalms 69:10: I have broken my (soul) with fasting.

Animals also fast. A female bear, for example, takes no food at all during her hibernation. She gives birth to cubs and has plenty of milk for cubs long before she can start eating again. This milk comes from a store of nutritive materials inside her body which adequately serves her for four months.

Where do animals get that wisdom? God has already deposited knowledge into their brains. No animal thinks to himself. God programs animals for fasting and he also programs them for breaking the fast.

When you watch them break their fast you see how slowly they return to normal eating as the Lord designed; we automatically do what our bodies tell us, but we are not creatures of instinct. Our bodies are not supposed to tell us what to do; it is the other way around. God wants us to be in charge of our bodies. He has designed us after his image as creatures who think that way; we decide what is best for us, not our bodies deciding for us.

Why is care needed?

- The stomach shrinks far below its normal size and the gastric juices cease to flow.
- The organs involved in digesting food and intestines go into hibernation.
- All new energy processes are activated as the body converts from food to fat burning machines.

This rejuvenated stomach will be just like that of a new baby when you are done with the fast. The organs will enjoy a deep rest. Care is needed to bring the digestive system out of hibernation and get it back into full operation.

The stomach may not digest at all; it could bring a lot of distress. Your organs will appreciate it if you give them a few days of special care rather than abuse. Every authority in the field of fasting agrees the safest way to break the fast is with juices, either fruit or vegetables. Juices that are easily digested by the linings of the stomach and intestines.

These linings become extremely sensitive during the fast and are almost sure to react to anything abrasive. The best way is to start with un-strained juices. Most supervisors prefer unstrained orange juice, which seems to get the bowel action started easily. If you do not have access to fresh orange juice, then apple juice, tomato juice, or grape juice will do.

- Milk is harder to digest, so it is not preferable.

One of the best vegetable juices is carrot juice. Before breaking your fast, start laying out the juices and items you will be using to awaken your digestive system. Use freshly extracted juice.

If melons are in season, get some of them too. If you must get carrot juice at the food store, do so only for a few days. Do not use canned or bottled juices. The fast can be broken anytime, day or night. The body now needs wholesome food, though not much of it.

Congratulations on your robustness and fortitude. You have endured and completed your CTHIM Prophetic school training.

Your dedication and determination have led you to a successful completion. We thank you for your participation in the CTHIM School of Prophets. We treasure your contributions and time with us, and we hope you have come away with transformative and impactful insights that will lead your life and ministry to greater prominence in Jesus.

UPON COMPLETION OF THE CTHIM PROPHETIC SCHOOL, YOU WILL RECEIVE:

- An invitation to a graduation seminar
- Certification
- Ministerial Credentials through ordination if you decide to serve with CTHIM.
- The laying on of hands ordination by Prophet Theodore and Esther Aluoch and CTHIM apostolic presbytery.
- (If eligible through qualification) an invitation to continue with us as a Prophetic Trainer or Lecturer Intern in one of our schools.
- 30-minute Teaching Slot every month on the CTHIM YouTube Channel

School Of Prophets

THEODORE S. ALUOCH

30. About The Author

Theodore S. Aluoch, a revered prophet, revivalist, and preacher, is the visionary founder of the CTHIM ministry. His passion lies in guiding the church toward a deep-rooted lifestyle of holiness, as he believes in waiting earnestly for the blessed hope. Author of the inspiring book "Recover Thyself," Theodore possesses a unique spiritual grace that includes the gift of healing, the ability to work miracles and prophecy. More than just a preacher, he is a profound teacher of the word, fulfilling his role as a prophet with unwavering commitment. Alongside his wife, Esther Aluoch, Theodore leads the congregation at CTHIM Church in Grove City, Ohio. Together, they are dedicated to spreading their spiritual insights and leading their community toward a fulfilling journey of faith and holiness.